D0843040

Whitehead's Metaphysics of Creativity

Whitehead's Metaphysics of Creativity

EDITED BY

Friedrich Rapp
and
Reiner Wiehl

State University of New York Press

Published by
State University of New York Press, Albany

© 1990   State University of New York

For information, address State University of New York
Press, State University Plaza, Albany, N.Y., 12246

Library of Congress Cataloging-in-Publication Data

Whitehead's metaphysics of creativity / edited by Friedrich Rapp and
    Reiner Wiehl.
        p.   cm.
    Includes indexes.
    ISBN 0-7914-0202-9 — ISBN 0-7914-0203-7 (pbk.)
    1. Whitehead, Alfred North, 1861-1947. I. Rapp, Friedrich.
II. Wiehl, Reiner.
    B1674.W354W53   1990
    192 — dc20   89-4479
                                                                               CIP

10 9 8 7 6 5 4 3 2 1

Contents

IV. CREATIVITY AND CREATION

Preface

At present a significantly increasing amount of attention is being paid to Whitehead's philosophy in the German-speaking world. This increased interest, which manifests itself in a somewhat different approach from the English-speaking world, is documented by the present volume. The editors hope that this book will be welcomed by the English public even the more because it may serve as an introduction to German Whitehead scholarship. The contributions it contains were first presented at the International Whitehead Symposium held on October 3-5, 1983, in Bad Homburg, where we enjoyed the hospitality of the Werner-Reimers-Stiftung.

Contemporary Whitehead scholarship has been stimulated by the fact that Alfred North Whitehead relates to the tradition of metaphysical thought while simultaneously giving serious consideration to the methods and results of the modern positive sciences. A metaphysical synthesis such as the one Whitehead aimed at in the various phases of his philosophic development forms the essential counterpart to the subtle investigation of details, practiced in analytic philosophy, where by the mere agglomeration of these details it is impossible to conceive of a complete whole. Inclusion of both the experiences of everyday life and the experiences that figure in the sciences is essential, then, if philosophy is to accomplish this task and not be empty speculation far removed from reality. His education and his professional formation equipped Whitehead particularly well to formulate such a synthesis.

The principle of creativity, along with the principle of reason, is at the center of Whitehead's metaphysical cosmology. This is, of course, not radically new, but it certainly opens up a new perspective. Creative advance into novelty is also decisive for Hegel, Bergson, and the conception of Emergent Evolution—of course for each of them with different emphasis. Yet none of these doctrines falls into irrationality. Whitehead chooses frontally to approach the concept of creativity by making it the fundamental concept in a novel system of categories in which becoming is accorded priority over being. The papers that constitute the present volume are devoted to exploring the solutions Whitehead achieved and the problems raised by his organic philosophy of nature.

The first section of the book is concerned with Whitehead's place in the history of philosophy. In a broad historical survey *Ivor Leclerc* investigates the ontological premises that led Whitehead to the conception of his actual entities; by regarding these actual entities as the real beings proper and as the bearers of all activity, simultaneously ascribing a physical as well as a mental pole to them, Whitehead succeeded in avoiding both neoplatonic panpsychism and rationalist *apriorism*. *Ernest Wolf-Gazo* examines Berkeley's importance for the beginning of Whitehead's philosophical development. He shows that Whitehead's confrontation with Berkeley's subjectivist epistemological analysis of sense perception led him to his objectivist ontological theory of prehension as a universal phenomenon of interaction. In contrast to these two investigations, which are directed toward assessment of the systematic gains, Whitehead was able to draw from the history of philosophy. *Rainer Specht* undertakes a detailed scrutiny of Whitehead's claims that his *opus magnum*, *Process and Reality*, draws on Locke. As a comparison of the precise wording shows, Whitehead's philosophy of organism does not adopt Locke in a way that is at all accurate philologically. This is another example of the independence and sovereignty of a great thinker in dealing with his predecessors.

The second section of the book is devoted to the examination of the general connections between the results achieved in empirical research and their metaphysical interpretation. *Dorothy Emmet* recalls the conception of the passage of nature, which in Whitehead's early work is developed in analogy to the flow of energy , and she compares this with the later concept of creativity central to *Process and Reality*. In this way, a less spectacular explanation of the creative advance into novelty is achieved, which, in turn, can lead to a generalized concept of organism. *Friedrich Rapp* compares the way in which the phenomenon of creativity is dealt with by Whitehead and in the natural sciences. It is apparent that in the theoretical framework of the sciences, creative novelty is conceptually underrated, yet not even Whitehead can avoid measuring the new against what is already known. *Hans Poser* investigates the implications of a metaphysics that is dependent upon the state of the empirical sciences. By contrasting the empirical with the rationalist position, he develops the concept of a hypothetical, revisable metaphysics that represents a creative achievement of speculative reason.

The theme of the third part of the book is the cosmological and the anthropological dimension in Whitehead's philosophy. *Wolfgang*

Künne discusses a topic of recent analytic philosophy of mind. His starting point is Whitehead's observation that propositional feelings can be distinguished according to the subjective form they have and to the propositions they represent. He shows that further distinctions are needed, because Whitehead tends to blur the difference between the intentional object and the meaning-content of propositional acts or states. *Reiner Wiehl* argues that a philosophical theory of the principles of the life of feeling demands the surmounting of modern metaphysical dualism. With a view to these principles as well as to the priority of life over understanding, he investigates the dualism of the concrete and the abstract in Whitehead's cosmology. This amounts to a consequential position that is opposed to Hegel's idealistic metaphysics of spirit. As *Robert Spaemann* shows, Whitehead's ontology, oriented on the biological concept of organism, is able to counteract the reduction of actuality to a subjectivity, which constitutes its own object. Simultaneously, however, Spaemann criticises Whitehead for adhering to the cosmological model of sensible experience and, accordingly, for conceiving of reason and the identity of the person merely as a function of organic creativity.

The fourth and final part of the book discusses the relation between the philosophical and the theological interpretation of creativity. *Wolfhart Pannenberg* demonstrates *aporiai* emerging from Whitehead's thesis of the ontological priority of atomistic actual entities. The interrelation of these entities, founded by reciprocal prehensions, cannot explain the nature of the living entity as in continuous process and at the same time as substantial. Moreover, the radical self-construction of the actual entities is incompatible with the biblical notion of creation. Following Whitehead's interpretation, *Jan Van der Veken* advocates a definition of creativity as substantial or universal activity. God, then, would be a category of meaning, a religious qualification, by which the believer interprets the universal process on the basis of his own particular experiences. *Reto Luzius Fetz* understands Whitehead's concept of creativity as a transcendental in the scholastic sense and as a successor to the theological concept of *creatio*. In the theological sense, however, this is a *creatio ex nihilo*, while, contrary to Whitehead, the nonevolutionary Aristotelian and Thomistic philosophy of nature does not recognize anything essentially novel as far as the inner-worldly process of reproduction is concerned.

We should like to thank Gordon Treash for having undertaken the difficult task of translating most of the essays. His work is even more appreciated in view of the complexity of the German language. Dorothy Emmet and Ivor Leclerc have presented their contributions at the conference in English. The English version of Wolfhart Pannenberg's essay is reprinted here from *Process Studies* 14 (1984) in the translation by John C. Robertson, Jr., and Gérard Vallée; Jan Van der Veken's paper was provided by George R. Lucas, Jr.

An extensive undertaking of this kind would not have been possible without the generous support that we received in various forms from the following institutions: The Deutsche Forschungsgemeinschaft, Inter Nationes, the Werner-Reimers-Stiftung, and the Stifterverband für die Deutsche Wissenschaft. To all of them, we are most grateful for their assistance.

F. Rapp   R. Wiehl

Part I

The Philosophical Tradition

1.

Whitehead and the Dichotomy of Rationalism and Empiricism

Ivor Leclerc

I.

The issue of how Whitehead's philosophy stands with regard to the dichotomy of rationalism and empiricism, which has been so profound a feature of modern philosophy since the seventeenth century, is clearly one very worthwhile examining. Has the outcome of Whitehead's thought been to affirm one side or the other of that dichotomy, or has his scheme genuinely and effectively superseded that dichotomy? This topic is more complex than it might seem. First, although that dichotomy most evidently concerns a difference in epistemology, it is not only that, for at its base are profound metaphysical issues. Then there is the question of the interpretation of Whitehead's position. For example, if his philosophy be taken to be a panpsychism—as it is by many[1] —would this not in effect decisively point to his being on the rationalist side of the dichotomy, analogously to Leibniz? The interpretation of Whitehead's philosophy is evidently crucial here.

It seems to me that neither the question of the interpretation of Whitehead's philosophy, nor that of its relation to rationalism and empiricism, can effectively be dealt with unless both are seen in the historical context, and in addition, unless full acount be taken of the *ontological foundations* of the entire modern development from the seventeenth century. I shall particularly emphasize the latter, both because it has been so much neglected, and because ontological concepts, being the most fundamental, readily become accepted as presuppositions which decisively determine thought without their being recognized as doing so. Ontological issues need to be explicitly taken into account

for an accurate understanding and assessment of the various philosophical positions. In particular, as we shall see, these issues are crucial
to the question whether Whitehead's philosophy is a panpsychism.

II.

Modern science and modern philosophy arose, in rejection of the natural science and the philosophy of Aristotelian scholasticism, upon a
new basis, which was the neoplatonism that had been resuscitated in
the fifteenth century, this steadily affecting scientific thought, and coming into full effect in the early decades of the seventeenth century.

Fundamentally and especially relevant in this is the neoplatonic
ontology,[2] the basic doctrine of which is that that which 'is' in the primary sense, must be immutable. The neoplatonic inheritance which
had been particularly influential on Descartes, and also other thinkers
of the time, was the Augustinian, and according to this the primary
'being', the being which is immutable in the strictest sense, is God.
However, since the forms also are changeless in themselves, they too
are 'beings'. Further, according to Plotinus, the forms, in enaction, constitute soul,[3] which entails that souls also are beings, the embodied souls
being the principles of agency — the *rationales seminales* of Augustine — of
the physical. Further, in the neoplatonic doctrine all change, *motus*,
including becoming, pertains strictly to the physical, to the realm of
nature. Plotinus had made a very clear distinction between, on the one
hand, the agency, the acting, of soul and, on the other, the *kinesis*,
motus, of the physical. That is, the acting of soul, which is thinking, is
not a species of change (*motus*) or becoming, but stands in contrast to
the *motus*, change, and becoming of the physical. This doctrine, a central tenet of neoplatonism, was carried over into the modern period.[4]

But a very considerable and crucial modification of the neoplatonic
scheme came to be introduced in the seventeenth century. This was in
respect of the status of matter. In classical neoplatonism, matter pertained to the physical as the recipient of form, and was conceived as
having an ontological status the very contrary of that of form, namely
that of 'not-being' — for Augustine a *prope nihil*. But in the late middle
ages certain developments gradually led to a change in the conception
of matter,[5] culminating, in the first two decades of the seventeenth
century, in the introduction, through Descartes' elder compatriot,
Sebastian Basso,[6] of the conception of the physical as constituted by
matter alone — in contrast and opposition to the antecedent conception of the physical as composite of form and matter.

Descartes was the first to appreciate fully the philosophical implications of this new theory of nature. In this view matter was an ulti-

mate; it was simply matter, being everywhere the same, and thereby incapable of changing into anything else. What Descartes recognized was that since matter is in itself changeless, this implies that matter accords fully with the neoplatonic criterion of 'being', namely immutability, which entailed that, ontologically considered, matter is indeed 'being'—and not 'not-being' or a *prope nihil*. Therefore, in the new theory, matter alone is physical being, i.e. matter per se is substance, a *res*, thus having its own essence whereby it is a *res*.

Now in traditional neoplatonism 'essence', viz. that whereby a being is what it is, was conceived as necessarily determined and constituted by forms. Further, these forms determining the essence were held to be necessarily qualitative. The reason is that in classical neoplatonism *anima* (soul) is the paradigmatic being, and when soul is considered in terms of the categories, it is only the category of quality which is relevant—soul is not, for example, quantitative nor in any place, etc.; that is, the only categoreal question relevant in determining 'what' a soul is, is *qualis*, "of what kind or sort."

But Descartes saw that since matter does not admit of any differences of kind, this entailed that the qualitative does not pertain to matter at all. On the other hand, the most completely general feature of matter is that it is extensive, which meant that the category of quantity alone pertained to matter. Accordingly, Descartes concluded, it is extensiveness and that only which constitutes the essence of matter. Thus matter as the physical, ontologically considered, is a *res extensa*. It was further clear to Descartes, that the neoplatonic ontology, applied to the new conception of the physical as matter, ineluctably entailed a metaphysical duality of two separate and mutually exclusive *res*: in addition to the physical or nature as a *res extensa*, there is also a separate realm constituted by souls, the realm of *res cogitantes*.

It is highly pertinent to our concern in this paper to be clear that this metaphysical dualism, which has so profoundly affected subsequent philosophy, involved not only a new conception of nature, of the physical; it also involved a significantly different conception of soul. In the antecedent philosophy—both traditional neoplatonism and also scholastic Aristotelianism—which this new metaphysical dualism replaced, *anima*, soul, was included in the physical in the fundamental role of the principle of life, of emotion and feeling, and thus of the agency of the physical. But in the new doctrine, since matter is without any change in itself, and thus devoid of agency, there was no room in the physical per se for any principle of agency. This meant that soul, as thus extruded from the physical, had thereby also lost that part of its nature whereby it had previously functioned as a principle of agency, of life, etc., of the physical. Descartes drew the evident conclusion, that soul is left with only the activity of 'thinking', whence it had to be a *res cogitans*. The logic of this carried over into subsequent philosophy; as a consequence of the metaphysical dualism, 'soul' had become *mens*, 'mind', i.e. 'intellect'.

For the proper understanding of modern philosophy it is important to appreciate not only that it involved a rejection of the Aristotelian conception of soul, but also that the conception which replaced it was essentially the neoplatonic one, which differed from the Aristotelian in a singularly fundamental respect. In the Aristotelian doctrine soul is not an ontologically separate entity, but is integral to the physical as the *eidos*, form, of physical beings. A physical or natural being, for Aristotle, was one which has the capacity and power of action (*energeia*), and it is *psyche*, soul, which is the *arche*, source, of that power in a natural being. Aristotle distinguished natural beings into nonliving and living, and in the case of the living its *kinesis*, motion, includes nutrition, sensation, as well as locomotion.[7] Man, as a living being, shares these powers of the soul with other living beings, but man's soul, *in addition*, has another power, namely that of *nous*, mind or intellect, i.e. the power or faculty of "thinking." The fundamental difference from this of the neoplatonic doctrine of soul is that, what in the Aristotelian theory was an *additional* factor in the soul of man, in the neoplatonic conception was the very essence of soul. The ontological basis of this is that in Plotinian neoplatonism 'being' is primarily *nous*, intelligence, and *psyche*, soul, derives from *nous* its essential character, namely 'intelligence'. In Augustinian neoplatonism, the doctrine historically most influential, it is God which is 'being' and God is 'intelligence', whence the essence of *anima*, soul, too is 'intelligence'. This conception of soul carried through into the modern period. It was this neoplatonic conception of soul as 'intelligence', i.e. as 'mind', which replaced the Aristotelian conception, not only in Descartes and other thinkers such as Locke, who accepted the new conception of the physical as matter, but also by others such as Leibniz and Berkeley, who rejected the conception of the physical as matter. This neoplatonic conception of the soul also carried over into the eighteenth century with Hume and with Kant, and consequently into the empiricism and rationalism of the nineteenth century and later.

III.

It was this modern form of neoplatonic tradition introduced in the seventeenth century which Whitehead came to reject in its entirety. However, because the neoplatonic ontology and the new metaphysics of nature erected on it as its basis had by the nineteenth century come to be accepted as tacit presuppositions which thus determined the climate of thinking of Whitehead's time, the development of his thought represented a rather gradual process of extrication from that inherit-ance. This extrication was indeed not a complete one, for some of his thought remained affected by it, as we shall see.

When Whitehead, in his earlier period, in developing a philosophy of nature adequate to the twentieth-century developments in physical science, inveighed against the 'bifurcation of nature' and its concomi-tant theory of 'psychic additions'[8] to nature — i.e. the theory of the sub-jectivity of the 'secondary qualities' — it was basically the metaphysical dualism which he was rejecting. He insisted at that time on explicitly placing not only man, but also the colors and other sensuous qualities, within nature. But this necessitated, as he soon came to see, a new metaphysical basis in terms of which this was possible. This new meta-physics was first fully revealed in his Gifford Lectures at Edinburgh University in June 1928, and published in a somewhat expanded form in his book *Process and Reality* in 1929.

In this he propounded a theory of an indefinite plurality of ultimate beings, which he termed 'actual entities'.[9] This theory, as he had himself noted, is analogous to that of Leibniz in that Whitehead's actual enti-ties, like Leibniz's monads, are the ultimate metaphysical beings out of which all composite entities are constituted. But the analogy does not go much further than that, for Whitehead's theory differs fundamen-tally from that of Leibniz, in a number of respects, but basically in that whereas Leibniz's monads were conceived as neoplatonic souls, in Whitehead's doctrine actual entities are *not* souls — the interpretation of Whitehead's position as panpsychist,[10] I shall argue, is consequently a grave error. Whitehead held that actual entities are 'dipolar', physical and mental. To comprehend this doctrine it is essential that both these terms, physical and mental, be properly understood as Whitehead used them.

The meaning of the adjective *physical* underwent a significant change in connotation with the new seventeenth-century conception of nature as matter. In terms of that conception the word *physical*, i.e. 'natural', came to mean 'material', and since matter is 'bodily', *physical* also came to mean 'bodily' — but 'body' in a sense quite excluding 'soul'. This meaning of *physical* stands in contrast to the antecendent scho-lastic Aristotelianism, in which the *physical* was certainly 'bodily,' but not to the exclusion of soul. Whitehead's rejection of the modern doc-trine of the physical as matter entailed also his rejection of the modern connotation of *physical* as 'material', and also of it as 'bodily,' as well as of it as essentially 'extensive' — Descartes' doctrine.

In opposition to the modern doctrine of the physical as immutable matter, Whitehead maintained that the physical must be conceived as essentially "in a process of becoming." This entailed, Whitehead saw, that fundamental in the physical must be 'acting', this acting, in his theory, being that of 'prehending'. The notion of 'acting', however, requires clarification, for it can be, and has been, differently conceived. Historically first there is the position of Aristotle, he having maintained that 'acting' (*energeia*) is fundamental to the physical. And there is the position which has historically been dominant, that of classical neoplatonism, according to which 'acting' is essentially and primarily attributable to soul, and to the physical bodies only derivatively through the acting of indwelling souls. This is the conception which Leibniz had taken over in his doctrine of monads. The modern metaphysical dualism, from Descartes, also maintained the neoplatonic conception of acting as pertaining only to souls. It is important to appreciate that it was this neoplatonic conception of 'acting' as fundamentally and primarily pertaining to soul which Whitehead rejected. The position at which he had arrived is close to the Aristotelian one.

Whitehead in his doctrine made a distinction between two kinds of acting, physical acting and mental or conceptual acting—this distinction is there in Aristotle too, although terminologically less distinct. Whitehead explicitly conceived physical acting to be the acting of an actual entity in which that acting is in reference to or involves another actual entity or other actual entities. In contrast to this there is mental or conceptual acting, which is the acting of an actual entity in reference to 'eternal objects' (what in the philosophical tradition had been termed 'forms').

There has, however, been a not inconsiderable amount of confusion respecting Whitehead's conception of 'acting', which is the result of the terminology in respect of this 'acting' which he had developed in *Science and the Modern World* in the context of his consideration of the interrelatedness of physical beings. He began this with a quotation from Francis Bacon,[11] and drew the reader's attention to "the careful way in which Bacon discriminates between *perception*, or *taking account of*, on the one hand, and *sense*, or *cognitive experience*, on the other hand," agreeing with Bacon on the primacy of the former. But because the word *perception* in our contemporary customary usage has the connotation of conscious cognitive experience, Whitehead chose the word *prehension* for unconscious "taking account of."[12] Then, in *Process and Reality*, he used the word *prehension* as the general term for "concrete facts of relatedness."[13] But thereby he became entangled in the presuppositions of neoplatonism.

To appreciate this it must be borne in mind that, in terms of neoplatonic ontology, 'acting' is that of soul: it is soul, as 'being', which 'acts', and it is *only* soul which is, in the primary sense, active. Moreover— and this is a most important feature of the neoplatonic doctrine—soul is *purely* active, in the sense that it is not able to be 'acted upon'. A clear illustration of this is provided by Leibniz's monads, which are neoplatonic souls whose acting is that of 'perception',[14] which, as he stresses, is a completely 'internal principle',[15] this meaning that a monad is wholly active, in no respect being 'acted on' by any other monad. Because of this there can be no causal relatedness between monads, even in respect of perception. Thus perceptions of other monads can arise in the perceiving monad only by its own internal and autonomous activity of perceiving, a consequence of which is that perceptions of other monads are purely subjective to the perceiver, and thus necessarily phenomenal.

We can readily appreciate the extent to which Whitehead, with his use of the term *prehension*, became enmeshed in the neoplatonic position by noting the similarity of his doctrine in this respect to that of Leibniz. For Whitehead the acting of an actual entity is that of 'prehending', analogously to that of Leibniz's monad being 'perceiving'. Furthermore, Whitehead did explicitly maintain that this notion of *prehension* is a "generalization from Descartes' mental 'cogitations', and from Locke's 'ideas' "[16] — both of which are the product of wholly subjective actings, in accordance with the neoplatonic doctrine which they accepted — Whitehead emphasizing there that his philosophy "starts with a generalization of Locke's mental operations." Moreover, in *Process and Reality* Whitehead also used the word *feeling* as a synonym for *prehension*, the word *feeling* having, in recent times, come to acquire a very largely subjective connotation.[17] The implication is readily drawn that the 'prehending' of a Whiteheadian actual entity is to be conceived as a wholly subjective acting, with the actual entity, like the Leibnizian monad, not being capable of being 'acted on' — this being so since an actual entity can prehend only other actual entities which are in its past, i.e. ones whose acting is over, and which are thereby unable to act on the present prehending actual entity. The outcome thus is the conception of 'prehension' as an essentially 'mental' act. This is indeed the basis of the interpretation of Whitehead's position as 'panpsychist'.

But as against that, Whitehead did insist, contrary to Leibniz and others in the neoplatonic tradition, that the 'prehensions' cannot be wholly subjective, originating entirely in the experiencing or prehending subject. The subjectivism of the modern tradition had necessitated, for the veridicality of experience and knowledge, having to have recourse either to God (explicitly in Descartes and Leibniz, implicitly in very many others), or to transcendental categories (Kant), or to mere pragmatism or 'animal faith' (Santayana). Whitehead, on the contrary, maintained a necessary objectivism as to the 'data' of prehension. Of special concern to Whitehead in his insistence on the necessity for the objectivity of the data was that unless that objectivity were able to be validly maintained, there would be no foundation for any claim to 'scientific knowledge'.

The question is whether this insistence by Whitehead on objectivity constitutes a fatal incoherence in his system, as would be the case if his conception of 'prehensive acting' were indeed essentially that of the neoplatonic tradition. The issue is how, in terms of his conception of the acting of an actual entity, that objectivity of the data is to be secured. Whitehead was well aware of this issue, and of the problem it constituted for him, and he clarified his position in his chapters on "Objects and Subjects" and "Past, Present, Future" in *Adventures of Ideas*. He pointed out there that for an actual entity to be an 'object' for a prehending actual entity necessitates the former being 'given', which means that it is antecedent to the latter, and experienced as such,[18] affirming that "thus an object must be a thing received, and must not be either a *mode* of reception or a thing *generated* in that occasion."[19] The emphasis is on the object as 'received', and this is crucial.

Two pages later he observed that the "objects are the factors in experience which function so as to express that that occasion originates by including a transcendent universe of other things."[20] This is essentially the Aristotelian position — to be seen as standing in contrast to the neoplatonic one. The issue, for Whitehead, is how precisely this 'receiving' is to be understood. Whitehead argued here against the supposition "that an occasion of experiencing arises out of a passive situation which is a mere welter of many data,"[21] which entails that for him the things as data must themselves be 'active'. This again is the Aristotelian position. The issue then is what exactly is the relation between those active things, which constitute what Whitehead terms the 'actual world' of the perceiver, and the 'receiving' by that perceiving subject. Whitehead's analysis is as follows:[22]

> The initial situation includes a factor of activity which is the reason for the origin of that occasion of experience. This factor of activity is what I have called 'Creativity'. The initial situation with its creativity can be termed the initial phase of the new occasion. It can equally well be termed the actual world relative to that occasion. It has a certain unity of its own, expressive of its capacity for providing the objects requisite for a new occasion, and also expressive of its conjoint activity whereby it is essentially the primary phase of a new occasion.

It is clear from this that Whitehead did not conceive of that 'receiving' as being a quasi-mental 'grasping' of the antecedent data — as he would have done had he proceeded on a neoplatonic conception of 'acting'. It is to be emphasized that Whitehead was explicitly concerned here with *physical* acting. He maintained that the initial situation in the prehending actual entity includes a factor of *physical* activity, which is 'conjoint', i.e. it is the activity not only of the prehender but also that of the prehended; and it is a 'physical' acting, i.e. one of each actual entity in reference to the other. In other words, at that juncture the physical activity of the antecedent and of the consequent actual entity is 'common'. This means that what we have here is a *continuity* of physical activity constituted by a 'contiguity' of the two entities at a crucial juncture, at which, as Aristotle argued,[23] it is necessary that they have their 'point of contact' in common. This common activity, for Aristotle, is to be analysed as constituted by the antecedent thing 'acting on' the perceiver, and the latter 'being acted on'. This 'being acted on', however, is not to be construed as mere and sheer 'inertness', but as indeed an 'activity', the activity of 'receiving' — the contrary presupposition derives from the neoplatonic conception of 'acting'. My point is that Whitehead's position in this argument is essentially that of Aristotle, which means that the 'initial situation' of the prehending actual entity is a 'being acted on' — which entails an 'acting on' by the object actual entity — and this means that the 'inital situation' is an 'interaction', a 'giving' and a 'receiving', in that 'receiving' the given actual entity being 'objectified'.

Thus, despite his confusing term *prehension*, Whitehead has in fact avoided being trapped in a neoplatonic position. Nevertheless it seems to me that that term (and its synonym *feeling*) is further unfortunate in that it is a hindrance to the conception of *physical actings* as an 'interacting' of actual entities — for this 'interacting' is essentially what for Whitehead 'physical prehension' is. I would suggest that this is much more effectively conceived in terms of the generic term *act*: 'interacting, is both an 'acting on' *and* a 'being acted on'. This is the Aristotelian conception of physical acting,[24] and Whitehead's position is in fundamental agreement with this.

This conception and analysis of physical acting, in Whitehead's theory, becomes further intelligible in contrast to his conception of 'mental prehension'. Whitehead defined *mental* or *conceptual* prehension as that in which data are 'eternal objects', i.e. 'forms'.[25] For Whitehead, as for Aristotle, eternal objects or forms are the determinants of the definiteness of physical beings. As such these forms are 'particular'; i.e., each is 'this' definiteness to the exclusion of 'that' or any other definiteness. These are the forms (*eide*) which for Aristotle are the forms of sensible things (*ta aistheta*). In contrast to these are the eternal objects or forms which, for Aristotle, are 'universal' (*katholou*)[26] — Whitehead's preferred term is 'pure potentiality'.[27] Aristotle held that the latter forms are, "in a manner, in the soul itself,"[28] in that intellect (*nous*) is not dependent for these upon sensible perception. It is by virtue of this that Aristotle held that *nous* is a distinct activity of *psyche* which alone is capable of 'separation' (*chorizesthai*);[29] in contrast, that activity of *psyche* which is sensible perception (*aisthesis*) is not independent of body. This means that forms as universals are not derived by *nous* by its being 'acted on' by body.[30] On the contrary, these forms are 'conceived'—in the etymological sense of 'grasped','held'—by its own autonomous acting; this is the point of Aristotle's doctrine that "it is this *nous* which is separable, and impassive, and unmixed, being in its essential nature (*ousia*) an activity (*energeia*)."[31]

Whitehead's position is similar to Aristotle's in that for him *pure* mental or conceptual prehension is the prehension, i.e. the 'conceiving', 'grasping' of forms in their sheer generality and pure potentiality. This pure mental or conceptual prehension is an *autonomous* 'act', it is not a 'being acted on'. Whitehead did indeed hold that in pure conceptual prehension the forms or eternal objects are 'derived' from the eternal object or form determinant of the defininteness of an actual entity or nexus of actual entities physically prehended,[32] but this 'derivation' does not consist in a 'receiving' of those forms in the sense of mental activity being initially a 'being acted on' as in physical prehension; mental prehension per se is an autonomous 'grasping', 'conceiving', of the forms in abstraction from their physical determination of actual entities. This is the essence of *mental*, i.e. *conceptual*, acting in Whitehead's doctrine, which is clearly very close in this respect to that of Aristotle. But Whitehead proceeded to a distinction which is only implicit in Aristotle. Whitehead termed this mental 'deriving' of a form or eternal object, in the way just indicated, a "conceptual valuation,"[33] distinguishing it from the further autonomous mental act of 'conceptual reversion', i.e. conceiving a form which is 'reverse', viz. opposite or contrary to that in conceptual valuation.[34] It is by virtue of this latter mental power that possibilities divergent from those deriving from the data become conceptually accessible. This mental power is, in Whitehead's theory, the basis of 'imagination'.

In Whitehead's philosophy, therefore, although mental acting is analysed as being distinct and different in kind from physical acting, Whitehead does not ascribe to mental acting an independent ontological status, as does neoplatonism. He maintains that that which is ontologically independent, an actual entity, requires *both* kinds of acting, since both are necessary for the philosophical understanding of 'what is', and neither of them is derivable from, or reducible to, the other. Thus in Whitehead's doctrine an actual entity is 'dipolar', physical and mental, which means that it is *one* actual entity which is the subject of both physical and conceptual acting. To characterize this position as 'panpsychist' is entirely incorrect: the mental 'pole' is not a *psyche*, and it is not a 'being', nor is physical 'prehending' accurately to be understood as a quasi-mental 'grasping'. For Whitehead the actings of these 'poles' of an actual entity are both intrinsically different, but they are also interconnected and complexly interdependent. A full systematic analysis of this interrelationship will not be possible within the scope of this paper; I shall concentrate on only one pertinent aspect of it.

IV.

On the basis of this metaphysical position of two poles of acting involved in every actual being, Whitehead developed an epistemology in terms of which he was able to evade the kinds of difficulties involved in the epistemologies of empiricism and rationalism. For Whitehead a major consideration in this—and on which I shall particularly concentrate—was the problem of the knowledge of nature.

This had indeed been a primary concern for historical empiricism; it had been this which had led Locke to carry over the scholastic Aristotelian position that *nihil est in intellectu quod non prius fuerit in sensu*. Locke, however, did not appreciate the fundamental incompatibility of this Aristotelian position with the neoplatonic subjectivism involved in his acceptance of the metaphysical dualism, and this inevitably landed empiricism in a fatal epistemological difficulty.

In Whitehead's view, what is crucially necessary to examine in this empiricist position is its conception and analysis of sensuous perception. As we have seen, on the basis of the neoplatonic ontology sensuous perception is a purely *mental* act, i.e. an autonomous act of the mind (it not 'being acted on' by matter, as Locke was very clear), giving rise to 'ideas' of sensation, these being 'qualities' inhering in the mind alone, and not in material things. Further, these sensuous 'ideas', Whitehead emphasized,[35] are essentially 'universals'. This entails that on that position, contrary to Aristotle, sensuous perception (*aisthesis*) cannot be of particulars which are, in Whitehead's words, "other things which are in the world in the same sense as we are."[36] In this empiricist theory, therefore, there is no basis for any knowledge of physical things other than by inference. Locke recognized this, and indeed maintained that a valid inference can be made from the occurrence of sensuous ideas in the mind to "*the particular existence of finite beings* without us."[37] Whitehead has insisted that there can be no such valid inference—as had indeed been clear to Hume. For Hume, consequently, there could be no genuine 'knowledge' of nature, but only a 'probability'.

This empiricist doctrine, Kant saw, in effect left natural science without a foundation, and it was a primary concern of his critical philosophy to provide such a foundation to secure genuine scientific 'knowledge', which he did by grounding it in the mind. For Whitehead, however, this version of the rationalist position was subject to the same fundamental objections as had to be directed against that of Descartes. Descartes, with much greater perspicacity than the empiricists respecting the implications of the neoplatonic ontological foundations which they shared, saw that on that basis knowledge of nature had to be grounded, not on *sensuous* ideas, but on *intellectual* ideas. But these are necessarily 'universal', and the difficulty is that from universality there can be no inference to any 'particular' entity—this is why Descartes' pure mathematics cannot be knowledge of particular physical things. Kant, being clear that the universal categories of the understanding cannot give knowledge of particular things, held that for knowledge there is also required sensibility, by means of which there is 'intuition' (*Anschauung*) of objects. But he accepted the modern neoplatonic conception of sensibility as strictly subjective,[38] which entails that 'things-in-themselves' cannot directly be objects; they can be objects only by inference. We shall return below to the issue whether this does indeed enable Kant validly to have 'knowledge' of particular things.

Adequately to appreciate Whitehead's criticism of both the rationalist and empiricist positions, it is necessary at this point to pay particular attention to two features of the conception of 'knowledge' as carried over by Descartes from medieval thought, and which were crucial not only to Descartes' philosophy but also to that of subsequent thinkers, rationalist and empiricist, including Kant. Whitehead found it necessary to question and reject both these features as traditionally maintained. One of these is that of genuine knowledge as necessarily 'intuitive'. The other feature of this conception of knowledge is that it be 'certain'.

The former conception, that knowledge is necessarily 'intuitive', derives from Plato's *noesis* of the forms.[39] This accorded fully with the neoplatonic doctrine of the soul as mind or intellect, and thus was accepted by Descartes. Consistent with this, Descartes held that knowledge is essentially 'mathematical'—for it is mathematics which is the exemplification *par excellence* of knowledge as intuitive—and he accordingly developed the conception of knowledge as a 'general mathematics', this encompassing metaphysics. On this basis he was then able consistently to hold that physics, i.e. the knowledge of nature, is no other than "geometry or abstract mathematics."[40]

The second feature of this conception of knowledge, viz. that it is 'certain', also derived from Plato, but it underwent a significant change effected by the neoplatonic subjectivist position. Plato had spoken of knowledge (*episteme*) as per se 'true' and thus as 'infallible' or 'not false'.[41] This 'infallibility', however, is significantly different from 'certainty', for the concept of 'infallibility' is a logical entailment of 'truth', whereas 'certainty' has an essential reference to the thinking subject: it is the thinker which has the subjective feeling or conviction of 'certainty'. Descartes, with his neoplatonic subjectivism, required this feeling of 'certainty' as the warrent of authentic 'knowledge' (as had Augustine). He maintained further that it was this 'certainty' that attested mathematics as being genuine 'knowledge', and this was accepted by the subsequent thinkers in the neoplatonic tradition, including the empiricists. Kant carried this to its logical conclusion: taking the term *scientia* strictly as the Latin rendering of *episteme*, he held that "only that can be called true science whose certainty is apodictic,"[42] and consequently maintained, like Descartes, that science in this strict sense had necessarily to be mathematical.[43]

We can now return to the issue raised above, whether Kant, with his doctrine of sensibility, is indeed able to have genuine knowledge of particular things. He believed himself able validly to maintain this because of his conception of 'knowledge' as 'apodictic certainty', such knowledge being mathematical. Against this Whitehead argued that, on the basis of Kant's neoplatonic subjectivism the objects are universals, both in mathematical thought and in sensibility. But, as Whitehead retorted in a characteristic epigrammatism: "You cannot know what [thing] is red by merely thinking of redness;"[44] and, we can add, that you cannot know what thing is of a certain particular mathematical quantity by merely thinking of mathematical pattern or equations. On the contrary, Whitehead insists, "You can only find red things by adventuring amid physical experiences in *this* actual world. This doctrine is the ultimate ground of empiricsm."

V.

Whitehead has concluded that, in order validly to have knowledge of the physical or nature, it is necessary to have a conception and analysis of 'knowledge' different from that of the traditional modern one.

Having rejected the neoplatonic subjectivism, Whitehead was not in need of 'certainty' as the criterion of knowledge. As to the conception of knowledge as 'intuitive' (i.e. a direct, non-discursive 'seeing'), Whitehead held that 'intuition' pertains primarily to *pure* mental or conceptual prehension.[45] Thus this 'intuitive' grasping of the forms would hold only in respect of the realm of pure possibility—which for him is the concern, for example, of pure mathematics.[46]

This, however, as a kind of 'knowledge', is to be distinguished from the knowledge of nature, of the physical—and not confused with it, as had occurred, for example, in the systems of Descartes and Kant—and also from that knowledge which is 'metaphysical',—'metaphysics', for

Whitehead being the science which seeks to understand all 'that which is' in terms of its most general features.[47]

Now Whitehead maintained that genuine knowledge of nature, of the physical, as well as of the metaphysical features of things, cannot be attained by reason alone; to be possible, this knowledge necessitates the 'perception' of physical entities, and moreover, necessitates that this knowledge be grounded in such perception. In this respect he is in accord with Aristotle and with the empiricist tradition. But, for Whitehead, this indispensably requires an analysis of 'perception' which is very different from that of traditional philosophy. First, Whitehead maintained, it is necessary to bring into question and reject the virtually universally held presupposition according to which vivid conscious sensuous perception has a status of ultimacy. He held that this conscious sensuous perception is analysable as derivative from the primary actings, physical and mental, of actual entities, and thus is not ultimate.

His argument is that if there is to be valid and genuine knowledge of nature, then the first requirement is to admit—what the neoplatonic ontology precludes—a physical acting of the perceived actualities on the perceiver. This physical interacting, however, is insufficient per se to constitute 'perception' since, Whitehead insisted as did Plato, *any* 'perception' requires not only physical acting but also mental acting. There is required an 'interrelation' between pure mental prehension and physical interacting. Whitehead spoke of this interrelation as the 'integration' or 'synthesizing' of the conceptual and the physical. The most primitive kind of such 'integration' constitutes what Whitehead termed a 'physical purpose'.[48] In this the form which determines the antecedent actual entity involved in physical interaction, is 'conceived' mentally, and is then 'integrated' or 'synthesized' with the form as in the physical 'reception', this occurring with a 'special appetition—adversion or aversion', thereby affirming the 'purpose' of the actual entity in becoming.[49] This integral acting rules throughout the realm of nature.

The next, and more complex, kind of integration of the physical and mental is that which is particularly pertinent from the point of view of the understanding of 'perception' and 'knowledge'.[50] This is the integration constituting a 'proposition'. This integration of the physical and mental is one in which 'mentality' becomes much more prominent than it is in a 'physical purpose', this coming about as follows. 'Pure mentality', as we have seen, is the 'conceiving' or 'grasping' of a form in its complete generality, i.e. as an abstract potentiality, the term *potentiality* meaning its having a completely general reference to "any among undetermined actual entities."[51] Now in a 'proposition' there is a loss of that complete generality, for in this the mentally conceived form is 'integrated' with a *particular* actual entity or nexus of actual entities physically received, not however as in 'physical purpose', but with the conceived form being 'proposed' as the 'hypothetical' definiteness of those particular actual entities. Remembering that the forms mentally conceived could be ones constituting either 'conceptual valuation' or 'conceptual reversion', it is clear that with respect to any particular set of actual entities, an indefinite plurality of 'proposals' is possible.

For our present concern it is not necessary to enter into further complexity of detail. The essential point is that in Whitehead's analysis this act of 'propositional' integration of the physical and the mental is the basis from which and upon which arise all species of 'perception', and all 'knowledge' of nature. That is to say, sensuous perception is not, as so frequently believed in the past, a direct 'intuition' of physical things; it is a 'proposition' about them.[52] And all 'thought', in so far as it has actual entities as its subject, must necessarily be 'propositional', since those actualities must be 'given' in physical prehension, and then 'integrated' with concepts, these constituting the 'predicate' of the proposition, with those particular actual entities as the 'logical subject'.

In the last hundred years the view has come to be increasingly accepted that scientific inquiry proceeds by the method of hypothesis, and also that hypothesis is basic to scientific observation, particularly to the *perception* involved: in the first place, the selection of data admitted as relevant 'evidence', is in terms of hypothesis; and secondly, the very 'perception' of the data is determined by hypothesis. The conclusion, that therefore scientific 'knowledge' per se is hypothetical, that it is a 'theory', has also been widely acceded to, however without its full implications having been appreciated, and without an adequate philosophical basis for that doctrine. It is this basis which Whitehead was concerned to provide.

In Whitehead's philosophy, this basis is constituted by all *perceptions* of things and all *thought about* things necessarily having to arise from the integration of physical acting and mental acting. Perception and knowledge unquestionably necessitate mental acting, but mental acting is vacuous without physical acting. Kant saw this in holding that "thoughts without content are empty,"[53] but as a 'content' he, on his subjectivist basis, could only have 'appearances', subjective 'representations', which are universals, not particular physical things-in-themselves. The prime requirement, Whitehead maintained, is that physical things-in-themselves be *received* and 'objectified' in the perceiving or knowing subject.

Therewith propositions can per se be 'true': and they *are* true when the proposed predicative pattern in fact conforms to or coheres with that of the actualities constituting the logical subjects of the proposition. This means, as Whitehead put it, that "the logical subjects of the proposition supply the element of givenness requisite for truth and falsehood"[54] – this element of 'givenness' will be lacking if the actual entities constituting the logical subjects be merely inferred, for example. Further, by this givenness of the logical subjects the necessary condition is met for valid 'judgment' respecting the truth or falsity of a proposition. Whitehead's doctrine is that propositions per se are either true or false; but that there then requires to be a 'judgment' on the proposition respecting its truth or falsity. This judgment is effected by an act of integration contrasting the proposition on the one hand, with its logical subjects as objectified in the physical prehension on the other. That is, by this contrast, an 'intuitive judgment' is then possible respecting the conformation of the predicate of the proposition with its logical subjects, in such a judgment this conformation being directly evident. Most judgments, however, are 'derivative,' this meaning that their predicate is derived from other actual entities than those constituting the logical subjects of that proposition – for example, one observed in the past – or from conceptual 'reversion'. Owing to lack of time we will, however, not be able to go further into a consideration of the kinds and complexity of judgment and the conditions for the elimination of error in judgment.

On the foregoing basis Whitehead was then able to analyse scientific inquiry as involving 'general' propositions or hypotheses, i.e., propositions with their logical subjects being, not particular sets of actual entities, but "any set [of actual entities] belonging to a certain sort of sets"[55] of actual entities, these depending upon what sets the particular branches of science are concerned with. However, the same fundamental principles as apply to judgment on singular propositions, pertain also respecting judgment with regard to the truth or falsity of the scientific propositions or theories – albeit that these theories and judgments involve a vastly greater complexity, the analysis of which requires consideration of the theories of induction, probability, statistics, etc., as well as the metaphysical analysis of 'scientific law'. Further, the same fundamental principles hold also respecting the judgment of 'universal' propositions, those of metaphysics, these pertaining to all actual entities.[56]

In conclusion I want to emphasize the difference between this conception of Whitehead's of metaphysics and metaphysical knowledge, and that of the rationalist philosophers, from Descartes to Hegel, according to which metaphysics is an a priori deductive scheme from premises assumed to be apodictically certain. In Whitehead's doctrine metaphysics is explicitly maintained to be a 'theory', i.e., a 'universal proposition' with all actual entities as its logical subject, its proposed 'predicate' purporting to hold for 'all that is'. As a theory, what it 'proposes' respecting the nature of actuality, cannot claim 'apodictic certainty' and unquestionable 'truth'. In the general conception of 'knowledge' which Whitehead's theory entails, metaphysical 'truth'—like scientific 'truth'—can only be asymptotically approached. One highly important consequence of this position is the difference it entails with regard to metaphysics as a 'discipline', especially respecting what constitutes its distinct and particular 'problematic', i.e. set of problems and the methodology for their resolution. Crucial to this methodology must be the 'testing' of metaphysical theories. Whitehead's position entails that this testing cannot only be in respect of their internal consistency and coherence, as in the rationalist position. There necessarily also has to be what in some respects is even more important, and definitely more difficult, the testing respecting the extent to which all experience can be successfully understood in terms of its categories. In the case of Whitehead's metaphysics, which is one of the great new systems in the history of philosophy, the testing of it is a task for generations of scholars. We are still much at the stage of gaining an adequate comprehension of it, and not a great deal has been done in regard to the testing of the scheme. In our time the most decisive test consists in displaying the scheme in question, Whitehead's or any other, as effectively and adequately providing a metaphysical basis for the understanding of the highly important scientific advances of recent decades, more particularly in theoretical physics, in chemistry, in biochemistry, in biology, and in neurology.

Notes

1. Cf. e.g. Charles Hartshorne: *Whitehead's Philosophy*, (Lincoln: University of Nebraska Press 1972); Victor Lowe: *Understanding Whitehead*, (Baltimore: The Johns Hopkins Press 1962); Nathaniel Lawrence: *Alfred North Whitehead*, (New York: Twayne Publishers Inc. 1974).

2. I have shown this in some detail in my paper "The Ontology of Descartes", in *The Review of Metaphysics* 34 (1980/1981) pp.297-323.

3. Cf. Plotin: *Enneads*, VI, 6,6.

4. Cf. e.g. Descartes: *Principles of Philosophy*, II,25.

5. See my *The Nature of Physical Existence*, (London: Allen & Unwin/New York: Humanities Press 1972), Part II, pp. 101-148, for this development.

6. Sebastian Basso: *Philosophiae naturalis adversus Aristotelem Libri XII. In quibus abstrusa veterum physiologia restauratur, et Aristotelis errores solidis rationibus refelluntur*, Geneva 1621.

7. Cf. e.g. Aristotle *De Anima*, 413 b 11-13.

8. CN Ch. II.

9. This theory had been first somewhat sketchily introduced in *Science and the Modern World*, as a development of his earlier theory of 'events', and in this work also referred to as 'primates'; and then adumbrated in *Religion in the Making*, where they were referred to as "a multiplicity of occasions of actualization" and as "epochal occasions" (RM 78).

10. The issue of 'panpsychism', as we shall see, is complex. A distinction can be made between an actual entity as 'being' a soul, and its 'having' a soul. But the crucial issue is whether the 'acting', i.e. 'prehension', of an actual entity is to be understood as essentially a 'mental' act.

11. SMW 52.

12. SMW 86.

13. PR 22 ("The Categories of Existence").

14. G.W. Leibniz: *Monadology*, para. 16.

15. Ibid. para. 11.

16. PR 19.

17. This is not the case in the earlier use of the word (cf. *Oxford English Dictionary*, "Feel," verb, Art. I) Whitehead's use is in fact in this original sense.

18. AI 229.

19. This is an obvious reference to the Kantian doctrine.

20. AI 231.

21. AI 230.

22. Ibid.

23. Aristotle: *Physics*, Book V, Ch. 3.

24. Aristotle: *De Anima*, 417 a 13-18.

25. PR 23 ("Categories of Explanation XI").

26. Aristotle: *De Anima*, 417 b 16-26.

27. PR 22, 23 ("Categories of Existence V" and "Categories of Explanation VII").

28. Aristotle: De *Anima*, 417 b 24-25: *"tauta d'en autei pos esti tei psychei"* (tr. R. D. Hicks: *Aristotle De Anima* [1907], Amsterdam: Adolf M. Hakkert 1965).

29. Ibid. 413 b 22-27.

30. Cf. ibid. 429 a 10-b 9.

31. Ibid., 430 a 17-18: *"kai houtos ho nous choristos kai apathes kai amiges tei ousiai on energeiai"* (tr. Hicks, op. cit.). Whitehead seems to have been unaware of the similarity of his position to that of Aristotle in this, as in so many other respects. He does not appear to have made a study in depth of Aristotle — as he did of Plato, especially the *Timaeus* — but to have relied considerably on the exposition and interpretation of Sir David Ross.

32. PR 26 ("Categoreal Obligation IV").

33. Ibid.

34. PR 26 ("Categoreal Obligation V")

35. Cf. PR 52, 146, 151-152, 158, 190.

36. PR 158.

37. Locke: *Essay*, IV, II, 14 (Italics in original).

38. Cf. Kant: *Critique of Pure Reason*, B 45: "For these [colors, taste, etc.] cannot rightly be regarded as properties of things, but only as changes in the subject, changes which may, indeed, be different in different men." (Tr. Kemp Smith)

39. E.g. as brought out in the simile of the divided line at the end of Book VI of the *Republic*, in which *noesis* is the direct apprehension of the forms per se.

40. Descartes: *Principles of Philosophy*, II, 64.

41. *apseudes*. Plato: *Republic*, 485 c; *Theaetetus*, 160 d. This means "infallible" in the sense of "not liable to be deceived or mistaken" (*Oxford English Dictionary*).

42. Kant: *Metaphysische Anfangsgründe der Naturwissenschaft*, Vorrede: "Eigentliche Wissenschaft kann nur diejenige genannt werden, deren Gewißheit apodiktisch ist." Engl. tr. by James Ellington in: *The Metaphysical Foundations of Natural Science*, (= The Library of Liberal Arts), Bobbs-Merrill 1970.

43. Unlike Descartes, for whom pure mathematics was identified with physics as a general conception of nature, for Kant there is a 'science' (in the strict sense) of nature only if the phenomena of nature be understood in terms of mathematics — cf. *Metaphysische Anfangsgründe*, Preface, and *Prolegomena zu einer jeden künftigen Metaphysik*, Part II, esp. Section 24. Engl. tr. by Lewis White Beck: *Proglegomena to Any Future Metaphysics* (= The Library of Liberal Arts 17), Bobbs-Merrill 1950.

44. PR 256.

45. Whitehead also admits 'intuition' in respect of one kind of 'impure' prehension, that constituting an 'intuitive judgment'—see below p. 6.

46. Cf. SMW 44.

47. PR 3.

48. PR 184, 266.

49. PR 184.

50. This word is used by Whitehead in its etymological sense and not in that now common in logical theory as an element in judgment; cf. PR 22 ("Categories of Existence VI"), 184-185, 256-257.

51. PR 256.

52. Conscious perception, in Whitehead's analysis, arises by a further integration, that of 'propositions' with the physical prehension, in what Whitehead terms an "affirmation—negation contrast"—i.e. the contrast is between the data of the physical prehension and the proposition about them—the proposition "which in its own nature *negates* the decision of its truth and falsehood" (PR 261).

53. Kant: *Critique of Pure Reason*, A 51.

54. PR 259.

55. PR 186.

56. Ibid.

2.

Whitehead and Berkeley:
On the True Nature of Sense Perception

Ernest Wolf-Gazo

James Boswell reports an encounter he had with Samuel Johnson on August 6, 1763:

> We stood talking for some time together of Bishop Berkeley's ingenious sophistry to prove the nonexistence of matter, and that every thing in the universe is merely ideal. I observed, that though we are satisfied his doctrine is not true, it is impossible to refute it. . . . Johnson answered, striking his foot with mighty force against a large stone, till he rebounded from it, "I refute it thus" . . . "To me it is not conceivable how Berkeley can be answered by pure reasoning."[1]

This reaction of Dr. Johnson's corresponds to the reaction of many philosophers still typical today. In our time, too, the understanding of Berkeley's thought leaves something to be desired. Whitehead, however, does not wish to avoid the issue. His intellectual confrontation with the bishop began in the early twenties. This was a crucial period for Whitehead during which he formulated his first *philosophic* thoughts, which appeared later as the 'philosophy of organism' in the extended philosophical cosmology of his major work, *Process and Reality*. The fact that George Berkeley is the philosopher whose influence was decisive for Whitehead's development towards formulation of a 'metaphysics of nature' has hitherto not been noted sufficiently, or has been ignored altogether in Whitehead scholarship. John Locke became important later for the "Gifford Lectures" published as *Process and Reality*, but Berkeley provided the most important impulses for the beginning of Whitehead's philosophical development until *Science and* the Modern World. We need to recall only the criticism Berkeley directed against Newton and Locke. Whitehead was well-acquainted with this criticism and in discussion of it developed his own criticism of scientific materialism. No one was as vital as Berkeley to the ways in which Whitehead presented himself as opposed to the dualism between rationalism and empiricism. For Whitehead found in the very *structures of cognition* highlighted by Berkeley a potential with which he could work out the *true* nature of sense perception. We intend to show how the discussion of this problem led Whitehead to his theory of prehension, and in this way hope to fill a gap in Whitehead scholarship.

A brief inventory of the citations of Berkeley in Whitehead's works will be helpful for the expert, as well as for anyone interested, in assessing the relation between Whitehead and Berkeley. Whitehead concerned himself *directly* with Berkeley in three books as well as in two papers presented to the Aristotelian Society, namely in *Principles of Natural Knowledge* sections 8-14, *Concept of Nature* page 28f, *Science and the Modern World* pages 65-69, in the "Philosophical Aspects of the Principle of Relativity,"[2] and in "The Problem of Simultaneity."[3] Whitehead was very familiar with Berkeley's works, especially with *A Treatise Concerning the Principles of Human Knowledge* 1710, *Three Dialogues between Hylas and Philonous* 1713 and *Alciphron, or The Minute Philosopher* 1732. He quoted from these works and enlisted them as examples in order to clarify the notions he derived from Berkeley's position.

In his book *Principles of Natural Knowledge*, which he begins with a passage from the first dialogue between Hylas and Philonous, Whitehead deals with Berkeley's concern to determine the axioms of human knowledge. Whitehead *translates* Berkeley's principles of *human* knowledge into principles of *natural* knowledge. This is significant inasmuch as Whitehead intends to treat human knowledge from the perspective of the *philosophy of nature*, and not, as apparently is the case with Berkeley, from the *epistemological* point of view. Whitehead wants to include Berkeley's epistemological approach in the wider context of a natural philosophy, thereby extending the '*explanatory context*' of Berkeley's statement of the problem.

In the preface to *Principles of Natural Knowledge* it is stated that: "We are concerned only with Nature, that is, with *the object of perceptual knowledge*, and not with the synthesis of the knower with the known. . . . Our theme is the *coherence of the known*." This statement is a first indication of Whitehead's attempt to distance himself from Berkeley. Expressed in Berkeley's language, Whitehead's interest is in the "objects of natural knowledge" and not in "the ideas actually imprinted on the senses."[4] Whitehead speaks of the 'Berkeleyan dilemma,' since "*Perceptions are in the mind and universal nature is out of the mind, and thus the conception of universal nature can have no relevance to our perceptual life.*"[5] The essential problem, which in Whitehead's judgement Berkeley was unable to resolve, consists in the *relation* between the knower, that is the perceiving subject, and his environment. Since Berkeley concentrated exclusively on the act of perception he seemed to overlook that the perception *and* the perceiving subject are a part of space-time. Whitehead hoped to be able to make a definite statement about the subject, that is about Berkeley's 'mind', once he had settled the question of *relatedness*. Yet, even Berkeley's 'mind' has a bulk, or rather a '*body*', and this body is likewise a part of space-time. Accordingly, this *status* of the body in space-time becomes a problem of *natural* knowledge and not only of *human* knowledge. Whitehead describes the situation as follows:

> Natural knowledge is exclusively concerned with *relatedness*. The relatedness which is the subject of natural knowledge cannot be understood without reference to the general characteristics of perception. Our perception of *natural events* and *natural objects* is a perception from *within* nature, and it is not an awareness contemplating all nature impartially from *without*.[6]

The problem of the body brings us back to the notion of nature as 'relatedness *within* nature'. The *true* nature of perception ought to reveal this relatedness to us. It is clear, then, that in his early writings it was a problem for Whitehead to free himself from Berkeley's snares. In order to do justice to the problem of perception, Whitehead transposes Berkeley's dilemma into the context of *philosophy of nature*. The act of perception is thus included within the network of relatedness and investigated as a part of the concept of nature. In *Principles of Natural Knowledge* and *Concept of Nature*, it becomes apparent that Whitehead attempts to save not only Berkeley but also his opponent Dr. Johnson, who was mentioned earlier. This remarkable feat is only accomplished in *Process and Reality*. Neither Berkeley nor Johnson would have been content with that solution; for the former, it would have contained rather too much realism, for the latter too much panpsychism. Incidentally, an analogous situation exists in contemporary Whitehead scholarship, where interpretations vary from extreme realism to exclusive panpsychism. Whitehead was convinced that Berkeley's dilemma could be resolved only with an adequate concept of nature in a 'natural philosophy'. His optimism proved to be premature, but a first attempt at a systematic elaboration of Berkeley's problems in the sense of a 'metaphysics of nature' was undertaken by Whitehead in *Science and the Modern World* and developed later in *Process and Reality*.

But to return to the concept of nature in Whitehead's early works. In *Principles of Natural Knowledge* he says:

> *Perceptual knowledge* is always a knowledge of the *relationship* of the *percipient event* to something else in nature. The conception of knowledge as *passive* contemplation is too inadequate to meet the facts. Nature is ever originating its own development, and the sense of action is the *direct* knowledge of the percipient event as having its very being in the *formation* of its *natural relations. Perception is always at the utmost point of creation.* We essentially perceive our relations *with* nature because they are *in the making.*[7]

The act of perception is thus understood as a constituent element of a natural process 'in the making'. There can no longer be any question of passive perception. In Whitehead's view, it becomes from now on a creative act, and creativity suddenly becomes a constituent element of 'perceptual knowledge'. Relatedness is creatively constituted through the act of perception. The idea of a passive perception is therewith dismissed. Whitehead has reinterpreted Berkeleyan epistemology — *epistemology becomes philosophy of nature.* However, he does not go beyond the threshold of metaphysics, and consciously so. He was not yet prepared to integrate *ontologically* the act of perception into his nascent philosophical cosmology. His intuition proved him right; for in *Science and the Modern World* he would find himself once again compelled to engage in a critical discussion of Berkeley, and this time on the *ontological level* with regard to the perceiving subject.

In *Principles of Natural Knowledge* and *Concept of Nature*, Whitehead could contend himself with the discussion of the problem of perception as a problem of 'natural philosophy', expressed, for example, in assertions like "we leave to *metaphysics* the *synthesis* of the knower to the known"[8] or in the dictum "Nature is closed to mind."[9] Whitehead's notion that the metaphysical treatment of Berkeley's perceiver must once more be subjected to an *ontological* examination is made clear in the later statement that "Nature is a process"[10] and in the important passage in note 2 to the second edition of August 1924 of *Principles of Natural Knowledge*: "But the true doctrine that '*process*' is the fundamental idea, was not in my mind with *sufficient emphasis*";[11] it also appears in the announcement in the preface to that same edition: "I hope in the *immediate future* to embody the standpoint of these volumes in a more complete *metaphysical study.*" This was accomplished in *Science and the Modern World*. In other words, in the early twenties Whitehead was by his discussion of Berkeley confirmed in his conviction that the problem of the 'bifurcation of nature' must be solved.

In his early efforts in *Principles of Natural Knowledge* and *Concept of Knowledge*, he attempted to deal with this problem within the framework of a philosophy of nature. But Berkeley's dilemma continued to remind him once again that the bifurcation can only adequately be resolved by an *ontological* investigation — as a problem, that is to say, of the *synthesis* between the knower and the known. This task was tackled for the first time in *Science and the Modern World*.

In the paper for the *Aristotelian Society* on the problem of simultaneity, Whitehead also said, "The whole controversy as to the character of time, and indeed the whole philosophy of nature, hinges upon the great question of the bifurcation of nature."[12] However, contrary to Whitehead's earlier assumption, the problem of the bifurcation of nature could not be confined to the philosophy of nature; rather, it had to be viewed *ontologically*. Whitehead was thus forced to pursue a 'third way', which led neither to Hume nor to Kant. Berkeley was obviously of decisive importance for the formulation of this third way, which Whitehead also called 'provisional realism', if only for the reason that Whitehead found in the intellectual confrontation with him an approach that was to lead to the *philosophy of organism*.

Let us now move on to consider *Science and the Modern World*. Whitehead appreciates Berkeley's contribution, which led to the extension and deepening of the *foundation* of our scientific thought. In particular, he values Berkeley's criticism of Newton and Locke. Furthermore, Whitehead presents the reader with an interesting alternative, that is to say his third way out of the Berkeleyan dilemma, which would otherwise lead either to a subjective idealism or to a crass realism. Obviously, Whitehead wishes to avoid both, but he is still confronted with certain difficulties. In *Science and the Modern World*, he comments on this issue:

> I do not propose to consider either the subjective idealism which has been derived from him, or the schools of development which trace their descent from Hume and Kant respectively. My point will be that . . . there is another line of development embedded in Berkeley, *pointing to the analysis which we are in search of.*[13]

The analysis Whitehead has in mind would not only extend our field of abstraction, but also include a concrete analysis of our intuitive experience. The difference between Whitehead and Berkeley concerning the question of how *objectivity* is rooted in the world ultimately lies in their different conceptions of God. But the question Whitehead approaches is: "What do we *mean* by things being *realised* in the world of nature?"[14] It is interesting to note that put in this way, the question is *ontological* in character, for it aims to determine *how* the entities in nature objectify themselves. In concentrating on certain passages of Berkeley's *Principles*, for example on sections 23 and 24, Whitehead is seeking to answer his *ontologically* formulated question. This is a typical example of Whitehead's method to invert relations, which he also employs in the reinterpretation of Locke. For him, metaphysics precedes epistemology and determines it. Consequently, he engages in *onto-epistemology*. As we will see later, this shift in emphasis has far-reaching consequences for Whitehead's thought.

Whitehead quotes extensively from sections 23 and 24 of Berkeley's *Principles*. What does Berkeley say and what consequences does Whitehead draw from it? In section 23, the reader is asked to 'represent' to himself trees in a park or books in a case, but under the condition that nobody is present who perceives these objects. This poses no problems at first, but then Berkeley formulates the question: "What is all this, I beseech you, more than *framing in your mind* certain ideas which you call books and trees, and at the same time *omitting to frame the idea of any one that may perceive them*."[15] Suddenly the focus is on the perceiving subject, and this is precisely what makes Whitehead's question pressing. But let us come back once more to Berkeley's description of the perceiving subject. Section 23 closes with the words,

> When we do our utmost to conceive the existence of *external bodies*, we are all the while *only* contemplating our own ideas. *But the mind taking no notice of itself*, is deluded to think it can and doth conceive bodies *existing unthought* of or *without the mind*, though at the same time they are apprehended by or exist in itself.[16]

If these words were indeed correct, the concept of 'material substance' would be superfluous for Berkeley, as indeed it finally happened.

Already in paragraph two of the *Principles* has Berkeley's perceiving subject been characterized as "something which knows or perceives them [i. e. ideas or objects], and exercises diverse operations, as willing, imagining, remembering about them. This perceiving, *active being* is what I call mind, spirit, soul or myself."[17] This perceiving subject is an *active* being that plays a constitutive role in the realization of entities in nature. Berkeley's definition of the 'perceiver' as an *active* being, especially with regard to the cognitive act *as* perception, was of great consequence for Whitehead. But he chose to give his own interpretation to Berkeley's expressions, "the mind taking no notice of itself" and "omitting to frame the idea of any one that may perceive them." What Berkeley really means to say is that in the perceptual act the perceiving subject usually suppresses its own mental activity and therewith also suppresses the explanatory context in which the perception takes place. Berkeley draws rather radical consequences from this, which lead him to the conclusion that the ideas and objects of human cognition owe their existence *exclusively* to the perceptual act of the perceiving subject. He is thus able to affirm that "the existence of an idea consists in being perceived."[18] Whitehead regards this as too radical and too one-sided a result, although he acknowledges that Berkeley has drawn attention to a crucial epistemological problem, namely the determination of which role in the cognitive act is to be attributed to the 'perceiving mind' *as* perception.

In order to correctly explain Whitehead's strategy of the 'third way', we need to clarify the notion of the perceived *objects*. The most important passages in this context are section 24 of the *Principles* and section 9 of the fourth of the *Alciphron* dialogues[19], which is cited at length in *Science and the Modern World*. The passage from *Alciphron* makes no secret of Whitehead's intentions. It runs:

> Euphranor: Tell me, Alciphron, can you discern the doors, windows, and battlements of that same castle?
> Alciphron: I cannot. At *this* distance it *seems* only a small round tower.
> Euphranor: But I, who have been at it, *know* that it *is no* small round tower, but a large square building with battlements and turrets, which it seems *you do not see.*
> Alciphron: What will you *infer* from thence?
> Euphranor: I would infer that the *very object* which you strictly and properly *perceive by sight* is *not that* thing several miles distant.
> Alciphron: Why so?
> Euphranor: Because a little round object is one thing, and a great square object is another. Is it not?[20]

Euphranor then comes to the conclusion, "neither the castle, the planet, nor the cloud, *which you see here*, are those *real ones* which you *suppose exist* at a distance."[21]

This leads to the obvious question of how it is possible to maintain that a small round tower and a large square building can be identical. Berkeley is faced here with a contradiction because it cannot be said that we are dealing with one entity, yet with two different perceptions. Whitehead is thus compelled to clarify what Berkeley understands by entity or 'thing'. In the very first section of the *Principles*, Berkeley cites the example of the 'apple' that signifies a thing that respectively has taste, odor and form in a determinate way, which together are 'collections of ideas' or 'sense impressions', that is "constitute a stone, a tree, a book, and the like *sensible things.*"[22] According to Berkeley, these 'sensible things' cannot exist without mind, which leads him to the famous conclusion in section 3 of the *Principles*: "*Their esse is percipi, nor is it possible they should have any existence, out* of the minds or thinking things which perceive them."[23] This also explains Berkeley's view that, as he puts it in section 24 of the *Principles*, "the absolute existence of sensible things in themselves, or without the mind"[24] is a contradiction in itself. He expresses his opinion that 'real things' are constituted by God in section 33 of the *Principles*:

> The Ideas imprinted on the senses by the Author of Nature are called *real things*; and those excited in the *imagination* being less regular, vivid and constant, are more properly termed *ideas, or images* of things, which they copy and represent.[25]

Whitehead, however, found it impossible to follow Berkeley in this regard. He writes: "For him [Berkeley] mind is the only *absolute reality*, and the *unity of nature* is the unity of ideas in the mind of God."[26] Whitehead's only option is therefore to pursue his 'third way', which he also calls 'provisional realism'. The ontological problem that he sets out to solve is located within the triangle of the *relations* between 'perception', 'mind', and 'entity'. Whitehead's original question about the actualization of things in nature is answered thus: "He [Berkeley] contends that what *constitutes* the realization of *natural entities* is the *being perceived within* the *unity* of mind."[27]

Whitehead decides on a new beginning: Concepts like 'perception', 'mind', and 'entity' must be redefined and this redefinition must take place within a larger context of explanation. Appropriate determinations of concepts and new categories must be developed in order to restructure the whole set of Berkeleyan problems. It was Whitehead's conscious decision to design this new formulation as a *metaphysics of nature*; for he was aware that his conception, too, would be unable to solve these problems within the framework of natural philosophy. For this reason, he adopted his very own strategy of transforming the classical concept of sense perception into the new theory of prehensions.

Whitehead introduces the concept of 'prehension' in the following way:

> The word *perceive* is, in our common usage, shot through and through with the notion of *cognitive apprehension*. So is the word *apprehension*, even with the adjective *cognitive* omitted. I will use the word *prehension* for *uncognitive apprehension*: by this I mean *apprehension* which may or may not be cognitive.[28]

Applied to the conclusion of Euphranor noted above, this means that the castle, the planet, or the cloud that we see *here and now* represent an 'actuality' constituted by the act of *prehension* of entities *here* in this *place*, which stands in relation to *other places*. The objective reality is constituted by the *relations between places* that arise through the prehension of entities, because things are associated with their places. Prehension is a cognitive act that underlines the *ontological relation* between places. This prehension can take place unconsciously as well as consciously; according to Whitehead, cognition is possible even without consciousness. His stress is no longer on 'natural entities', but rather on the actualization of entities by means of the 'unity of prehension', as is demonstrated in the following statement:

> This *unity* of a prehension defines itself as a *here* and *now*, and the things so gathered into the *grasped unity* have essential reference to other places and other times. *For Berkeley's 'mind', I substitute a process of prehensive unification.*[29]

The last sentence is remarkable in that it shows that the concept of prehension is aimed at resolving Berkeley's dilemma. At any rate, we are convinced that Berkeley was of crucial importance to Whitehead in developing his own concept of prehension. In *Science and the Modern World*, it is still only a notion, but in *Process and Reality* prehension has advanced to the status of a 'category of existence'. Whitehead is now confident that he has found the answer to the question about the realization of entities in nature, a question to which he had originally been led in his discussion of Berkeley. He proceeds henceforth to transform Berkeley's perceptual act into an *ontological process* of *self-constitutive* entities. The process of 'prehensive unification' is the first step in this direction, which Whitehead describes as the 'third way'. With amazing simplicity, reminiscent of Berkeley's style, he explains:

> Note that the idea of *simple location* has gone. The things which are grasped into a realised unity, *here and now*, are not the castle, the cloud, and the planet simply in themselves; but they are the castle, the cloud, and the planet *from the standpoint*, in space and time, *of the prehensive unification*. In other words, it is the perspective of *the castle over there from the standpoint of the unification here*.[30]

The unity is actualized by means of space and time; this is the realistic element in Whitehead's 'provisional realism'. Berkeley's 'mind' now becomes a concrete entity in space and time. This attempt of

Whitehead's is similar to the conception developed by Samuel Alexander in *Space, Time and Deity* 1920.

Whitehead speaks of a sense object as an entity that we *grasp* through our sense perception. Such entities in the sense of Berkeley's 'sensible objects' are, for example, the color green with certain shades, a sound of certain quality and pitch, a certain odor and the quality of touch and contact. The relation of these sense objects to space and time is described by Whitehead as 'ingression', meaning that a sense object 'enters into space and time'. The *cognitive aspect* of perception of a sense object is constituted by 'prehensive unification.' This can be a standpoint A, which is understood as a spatiotemporal region. Whitehead says of this:

> The standpoint A is, of course, a region of space-time; that is to say, it is a volume of space through a duration of time. But as *one entity*, this standpoint is a *unit of realised experience*.[31]

We have made a long digression from the question posed by Berkeley and from his conception. We have seen that there is a direct connection between Berkeley's analysis of the perceptive act, for example in *Alciphron*, and Whitehead's later theory of prehension. *Science and the Modern World* still represents a transitional phase that precedes the mature theory Whitehead put forward in the "Gifford Lectures" and published as *Process and Reality*. The following definition of *perception* gives an indication of what will later be elaborated in *Process and Reality*:

> Perception is simply the cognition of prehensive unification; or more shortly, *perception is cognition of prehension*. The *actual world* is a manifold of prehensions; and a '*prehension*' is a '*prehensive occasion*'; and a prehensive occasion is the most concrete finite entity.[32]

It appears that Whitehead has found his own way to answer the question about the reality of nature. The transition from epistemology to metaphysics is completed. The context of explanation is extended. 'Reality' is no longer confined to 'ideas' or 'sense impressions on the mind', but encompasses a network of 'prehensive unifications' that are determined by the relational structure of prehensions. Berkeley's perceptual acts are transformed by Whitehead into 'acts of prehension', which in turn are to be understood as 'processes of unifying'. As Berkeley had correctly maintained, the perceiving subject is an *active* being, a *constitutive* element in the *process of actualization* of a sense object. The perceiving subject and the sense object are to Whitehead constitutive elements of a 'region of space-time' and thus elements of 'prehensive unification' as a natural process.

Berkeley's importance for Whitehead's philosophical development is obvious. As we have seen, Whitehead had, since his early works, been concerned with Berkeley's philosophy and was particularly interested in the acute analyses of sense perception in Berkeley's writings such as the *Dialogues*, the *Principles*, and especially *Alciphron*.

In the transitional work *Science and the Modern World*, Whitehead realized that he would have to incorporate Berkeley's analyses in an expanded context of explanation. By removing Berkeley's theory of perception from the *epistemological* context and placing it in an *ontological* context, Whitehead finds the lever for his own theory of the constitution of sense perception, which is then systematically developed in *Process and Reality* as the theory of prehension. This philosophical shift from Berkeley's position enables Whitehead to make a new philosophical beginning. He was aware of the potential of the Berkeleyan doctrine, as C. S. Peirce had been earlier. Peirce recognized that beginnings of a pragmatic epistemology can be found in Berkeley. In order to surpass Berkeley, Whitehead had to enter into a critical discussion of the fundamental concepts of Newtonian cosmology. Also in this respect, Berkeley provided a certain guidance for Whitehead: Berkeley's criticism of Locke's theory of sense qualities and of Newton's concept of absolute motion became components of Whitehead's own criticism of scientific materialism, and hence also served to determine his conception. Whitehead carried Berkeley's criticism of Newton further in a consistent and systematic manner. The criticism of Newton and Locke in *Process and Reality* part 2, chapters 1, 2 bears witness to that. In this work, Locke assumes the role previously occupied by Berkeley, because Whitehead now attempts to interpret Lockean empiricism *ontologically*. This is perhaps one of the strokes of philosophical genius in *Process and Reality*. Whitehead transforms Locke's fundamental positions into a theory of the constitution of actual entities. It follows that Berkeley and Locke are the most important philosophical sources for Whitehead's accomplishment of the transformation of the traditional empirical doctrine of sense perception and of the mechanistic Newtonian conception of 'bodies'. The Berkeleyan act of perception is changed into an *action of nature*. This is achieved by stressing the coming-to-awareness of the body in nature, whereas Locke's 'sensible objects' are remolded into constitutive actual entities. Hume plays a role inasmuch as Whitehead emphasises the feature of process that figures in his analysis of 'mind'.

In summary, it can be said that Whitehead's great philosophical achievement consists of the *ontological* transformation of the traditional empiricism of Locke, Berkeley, and Newton. Whitehead's original *philosophical* problem was the doctrine of the bifurcation of nature. In Berkeley, he found the point of departure from which to submit sense perception to a new interpretation and to overcome bifurcation. In Locke, he found the theory of the constitution of objects, and in Hume the feature of process of mind. Ultimately, though, it is Berkeley who must stand as the predecessor of Whitehead's criticism of scientific materialism. Berkeley's search for the true nature of sense perception provided the basis that Whitehead could draw upon in order to develop his own metaphysics of nature as a *metaphysics of experience*. In this respect, it can be said that it was not Plato, Aristotle, Descartes, Locke, or Newton who were the predecessors of the philosophy of organism, but rather Berkeley. Whitehead owes to Berkeley the impulse for his *critical and philosophical* reconsideration of Newton's basic categories and, hence, of the basis of mechanistic philosophy. This was the decisive step towards Whitehead's own philosophy of nature as metaphysics of experience and as philosophy of organism.

Notes

1. James Boswell: *Life of Johnson.* Edited by R. W. Chapman. (Oxford: Oxford University Press, 1970), 333-334.

2. *Proceedings of the Aristotelian Society* 22 (1922), 215-233.

3. *Proceedings of the Aristotelian Society* Suppl. Vol. 3 (1923), 34-41.

4. PNK VII. Emphasis added.

5. PNK 8-9. Emphasis added.

6. PNK 12-13. Emphasis added.

7. PNK 14. Emphasis added.

8. CN 28. Emphasis added.

9. CN 4.

10. CN 53.

11. PNK 202. Emphasis added.

12. *Proceedings of the Aristotelian Society* Suppl. Vol. 3 (1923), 40.

13. SMW 84. Emphasis added.

14. Ibid. Emphasis added.

15. Quoted from *The Works of George Berkeley*. Edited by T. E. Jessop (London: Nelson, 1949), 2:50. Emphasis added.

16. *Works* 2: 50-51. Emphasis added.

17. *Works* 2: 41-42. Emphasis added.

18. *Principles*, Section 2; *Works* 2: 42.

19. We must note here that Whitehead cites incorrectly an important source in Berkeley's *Alciphron*. In both *Science and the Modern World* and *Principles of Natural Knowledge*, *Section 10* of the Fourth Dialogue is mentioned. However, *Section 9* must be the correct citation. The various editions of *Science and the Modern World* (both in English and in translation) have repeated this error. This is an indication of how completely Berkeley has been ignored by Whitehead scholarship.

20. *Works* 3: 153.

21. *Works* 3: 154. Emphasis added.

22. *Works* 2: 41. Emphasis added.

23. *Works* 2: 42. Emphasis added.

24. *Works* 2: 51.

25. *Works* 2: 54. Emphasis added.

26. SMW 85. Emphasis added.

27. SMW 86. Emphasis added.

28. Ibid. Emphasis added.

29. SMW 87. Emphasis added.

30. Ibid. Emphasis added.

31. SMW 88. Emphasis added.

32. SMW 89. Emphasis added.

3.

Whitehead's Interpretation of Locke in *Process and Reality*

Rainer Specht

I consider my paper as a footnote to the theme of this conference. My starting point is Whitehead's conviction that, in essential points, the philosophy of organism reaches back to philosophic positions of the seventeenth and eighteenth centuries. In this connection, Locke plays a special role. In *Process and Reality* he is mentioned on one-sixth of all the pages, that is on 64, and is the second most frequently treated philosopher after Hume, whose name appears on 75 pages.[1] Moreover, Whitehead pays a special tribute to Locke by calling him the British counterpart to Plato.[2]

Among other things, Whitehead values Locke's objectivity: This author would cite the facts dispassionately even when they did not suit his theoretical preferences,[3] and he would never explain inconvenient aspects away (as did later 'a priori sensationalists').[4]

I wish to concentrate for the moment on the textual accuracy of the interpretation of Locke offered by *Process and Reality*, leaving aside the task of evaluating Whitehead's transformation of Lockean terminology within the framework of a systematic discussion of the philosophy of organism—if only because I am not sufficiently familiar with Whitehead. I shall criticise Whitehead's interpretation of Locke on almost every point, assuming that this, too, is a way of taking him seriously. For taking an author seriously means taking his assertions seriously. At the time when the book was written, the basic conception of Locke as it appears in *Process and Reality* was probably not uncommon. It is somewhat distressing to see how much the perception of a classical text has changed within two generations. Whitehead's interest in Locke was acute and immediate. He must have been an attentive

34

reader of Locke because he discovered features in the *Essay* that to the present day seem to have been partly overlooked in the evaluation of Locke. This is particularly true for the interpretation of the passage in 4.6.11, which is referred to in the preface to *Process and Reality*.[5]

I shall first deal with Whitehead's interpretation of Locke's relation to metaphysics as well as with the supposition of a Lockean sensationalism or subjectivism. Then, I shall examine some theses and concepts that Whitehead regards as Lockean anticipations of theses and concepts of the philosophy of organism. Third, I shall discuss the alleged inconsistency of the *Essay*. Fourth, I shall comment on Whitehead's transformation particularly of the Lockean concept of substance. Fifth and last, I shall make some general remarks about Whitehead's adoption of Locke.

The Relation to Metaphysics: Sensationalism and Subjectivism

According to Whitehead, Locke explicitly excluded metaphysics from his work (at any rate, his investigation pursued only a limited goal).[6] He was a rationalist inasmuch as he hoped to achieve ultimate clarity with his analysis of human understanding, but insofar as he distanced himself from metaphysics, he was an antirationalist.[7]

As a matter of fact, however, Locke was convinced that there are narrow boundaries of human clarity that cannot be overstepped. Similarly, Whitehead's suspicion with regard to metaphysics does not hold true. 'Metaphysics', 'metaphysicians', or 'metaphysical' are mentioned in the *Essay* in five places, three of which are neutral (those with 'metaphysical truth')[8] and two pejorative. In this latter sense, schoolmen and metaphysicians are referred to in 3.10.2 as very skillful in coining phrases that correspond to no clear and distinct ideas. Locke emphasises, however, that this comment also refers to disputatious natural and moral philosophers. Section 4.8.9 explains that books of metaphysics and school theology are mines of uninformative assertions about God, spirits, and bodies, but they are combined with "some sort of natural philosophy." Locke's intention to abolish metaphysics is nearly as difficult to derive from these references in the text as it is to derive an intention to abolish natural or moral philosophy or theology. A study of their content yields a similar picture. Locke's theology in 4.10 treats a classical theme of metaphysics in the classical way of metaphysical thinking. The general considerations about the knowledge of existence in 4.9 are metaphysical, at least according to the terminology of the Cartesians, which Locke was familiar with. That Locke's relatively scanty metaphysics has a different function from the Cartesian metaphysics does not alter the fact that it *is* a metaphysics.[9] In a modern sense Locke did not even practice his analysis of human understanding "in divorce from metaphysics,"[10] for the acceptance of Gassendi's doctrine of *tabula rasa* (which Robert Boyle did not accept precisely for metaphysical reasons) is a metaphysical option with far-reaching consequences.[11] I believe that one comes closer to the truth by regarding Locke neither as eliminating metaphysics nor as a rationalist in Whitehead's sense.

Whitehead considers Locke as a sensationalist empiricist,[12] albeit not consistently sensationalist.[13] He and David Hume, Whitehead says, are the great leading figures of this movement. Every school needs two leading philosophers: the first has a reasonably adequate grasp of the realm of experience, the second later renders the scholastic theory consistent. For sensationalist empiricism Locke played the first role, Hume the second[14]—just as for Cartesianism Descartes played the first and Spinoza the second role.[15]

I shall not discuss the expression *empiricist*, which is ambiguous and was unknown to Locke. In fact it is almost impossible to establish the precise meaning of this word with regard to the seventeenth century. I shall, however, speak about the expression *sensationalist*, which was likewise unknown to Locke. According to common terminology, Locke is not a sensationalist because he coordinates with the external sensibility the inner faculty, which he calls 'reflection'. However, Whitehead employs 'sensationalism' in a more specific sense to denote a habit of thought, which he rejects already in the preface to *Process and Reality*.[16] He maintains: (a) *that emotional feelings necessarily stem from sense perception*[17], or in somewhat different words: (b) *that our prehension of other entities depends on the mediation of private sense perceptions*,[18] or *that the primary activity in the act of experience is the merely subjective prehension of the datum free from any subjective form of reception*.[19] According to Whitehead, sensationalism is often combined with a subjectivism which maintains that *the datum in the act of experience can be adequately analyzed purely in terms of universals*.[20]

Generally speaking, Whitehead's appeal to 'universals' in respect to Locke is misleading, to say the least. For Locke, universals are products of the understanding that arise by means of abstraction and presuppose particular ideas. The real correlate of universals is the similarity between things (similarity presupposes difference). Locke's doctrine of universals points, even in its wording, back to scholastic models, namely to conceptual models with provenance from Ockham.

As I shall demonstrate later in section 3, Whitehead assumes that in the first half of the *Essay* Locke was a sensationalist, but that in the third book he tacitly introduced a new doctrine of ideas that is incompatible with sensationalism,[21] and that in *Essay* 1 and 2 he accepted subjectivism (except for a few lapses), but tacitly abandoned it in *Essay* 3 and 4.[22]

This ascription of Whitehead's is not confirmed in the text of the *Essay.* To be sure, 2.1.4 attributes passions such as pleasure and pain that arise on the occasion of thought, to reflection, but 2.7.1 completes this statement with the information that pleasure and pain reach our mind by all the means of sensation and reflection. Thus, they also arise immediately by affections of our senses from without (or "through something that affects our bodies" 2.7.2). This is corroborated in section 2.7.4 and complemented in 2.7.5, where it is said that God has apportioned pleasure and pain to all the things that surround and affect us. Finally, section 2.8.13 adds that God has combined the idea of pain with the motion of a piece of steel through our flesh. These texts show that Locke was not a sensationalist in the sense of Whitehead's formulation (a); for in addition to feelings of reflection, which arise on the occasion of thought, he also admits feelings of sensibility that the affecting objects produce immediately in us.

Moreover, the doctrine of sensitive knowledge demonstrates that Locke was not a sensationalist in the sense of Whitehead's formulation (b) either. Sensitive knowledge, a successor to the Ockhamistic *notitia sensitiva,*[23] pertains, according to Locke, to the existence of things present to our senses.[24] The claim, *A body, S, exists* is certain when S makes certain its existence to us by affecting our senses;[25] and we know that S exists for precisely so long as it exercises this effect on our sense organs,[26] which effect we often experience in the ciphers of pleasure and pain.[27] The very fact that we perceive so many ideas through pleasure and pain, which we later remember without pleasure and pain, makes it clear to us that existent external things were initially involved.[28] Examples of pleasure and pain abound in this section: pleasure at the scent of a rose or the taste of sugar, pain through heat and cold, or the pleasure that accompanies many actual sense perceptions.[29] The most striking example is that of fire: Whoever perceives a fire and yet doubts its existence ought to hold his hand in it and be convinced of the existence of the fire by means of his feeling.[30] Quite contrary to Whitehead's suppositions, such passages make it clear that for Locke the primary factor in the apprehension of existent external things are certainly not the naked sense data, but rather the special feelings that directly produce objects in us. The mere givenness of sense data, on the other hand, provides no information about existence or nonexistence. This implies that Locke is also not a subjectivist in Whitehead's sense.

Now, Whitehead based his assumption of sensationalism and subjectivism in Locke not so much on the fourth, but rather on the second book. Locke had proposed the theory of sensitive knowledge, at least in outline, already in 1671, and he only developed it in the fourth book of the *Essay* for systematic reasons. For it is only in this book that Locke deals with the doctrine of truth, the definition of which immediately presupposes his definition of knowledge.[31] At any rate, the influence of particular external objects on the mind, which is imputed here, is often and explicitly dealt with also in the second book.[32] I know of no textual or systematic justification for describing such passages as 'lapses' (as Whitehead does on page 157). Their relative infrequency can easily be explained by the fact that their theme really belongs to natural philosophy, whereas Locke considers his *Essay* as natural history.[33]

After these reservations, what remains of Whitehead's suppositions about the relation of Locke and Hume is of a relatively general character. It needs to be said that, in particular, it is of little help to place both authors in the same philosophical line, and modern scholars have increasingly tended to reject too direct a genealogical interpretation of the triad Locke, Berkeley, Hume.

Anticipatory Theses and Anticipatory Concepts

Locke's significance for the philosophy of organism rests, according to Whitehead, on the fact that its presuppositions are illuminated in the *Essay* in an exemplary fashion through passages that correspond to the undeniable positions of common sense,[34] and that especially in the third and fourth books the main positions of the philosophy of organism are anticipated in the most comprehensive way.[35] Whitehead gives the following list of Lockean thoughts, which can be developed in the direction of the philosophy of organism: (1) *The ideas of particular existents are the fundamental data.* (2) *Particular existents possess powers for the conditioning of other conditional particulars.* (3) *All qualities contain a relational element which is illustrated in 3.9.14, among other places.* (4) *Time is something perpetually perishing* (though, of course, Locke had not grasped that actual entities cannot alter but perish with the passing of time).[36]

I would only like to indicate that the roots of the philosophy of organism are in any case not here where Whitehead thinks to find them. For the tendencies mentioned certainly do not represent original contributions of Locke. That the ideas of particular existents constitute the fundamental data was true long before Locke for every philosophy that provided a doctrine of abstraction, be it external or internal. That particular existents possess powers for the conditioning of other conditional particular existents is supposed by every realistic philosophy that admits transient causality, that is, by the great majority of philosophies until the early seventeenth century.[37] That all qualities possess a relational element is a common notion in scholasticism, which distinguishes relative from absolute accidents ('qualities'), and then observes that this distinction does not pertain to actual genera, because every created 'absolute', including the qualities, encompasses relations.[38] Finally, that the parts of a duration are "something perpetually finishing" (2.14.1) is a theme that by its nature belongs to the scholastic determination of an *ens successivum* which is only present "*quando unum iam non est, sed fuit; aliud vero est, vel futurum est*" ("whenever something is no longer, but has been; something else is really existing or will exist in the future").[39] The substitution of "*corruptum esse*" ("to be perishing") for "*iam non esse*" ("to be no longer") is common usage.[40] Now, it is possible to regard the successive, which according to Ockham is something midway between being and not-being,[41] in terms of its developing or of its perishing parts. In the first case, it is something which successively develops, in the second something which successively perishes. The second aspect has been highlighted in our tradition, perhaps because of a difficult and much discussed passage in the fourth book of the *Physics*, where Aristotle had explained that "*phtoras gar aitios kath' hauton mallon ho chronos*" ("time is by itself more the cause of perishing").[42] Within the sphere of Locke's literary circle, Gassendi's description of time as *essentia transitoria* ("transitory essence")[43] and Walter Charleton's contrast of eternity and time as 'perpetual duration' and 'perpetual flux'[44] correspond most closely to the impressive formulation of *Essay* 2.14.1, which Whitehead repeatedly quotes. However, Whitehead's belief that in essential points Locke was drawing on philosophers of the seventeenth and eighteenth centuries is mistaken since the themes in Locke, which can be developed in the direction of the philosophy of organism, were really taken over from much older philosophies. I am not certain that this is an important observation, but as it may well be, I have thought it wise to mention it here.

Whitehead finds all the basic concepts of his philosophy of organism explicitly preformulated in Locke or Descartes: system, process, creative advance into novelty, *res vera*, stubborn facts, individual unity of experience, feeling, time as perpetual perishing, endurance as re-creation, purpose, universals as forms of definiteness, and particulars as the ultimate agents of stubborn factuality.[45] But for some of these fundamental concepts, the identity of their specific author needs to be established. A partially negative answer would indicate that here, too, Whitehead draws on authors earlier than the seventeenth century. Whitehead notes that Locke lays emphasis upon the morphological structure of understanding and of ideas, although morphology constitutes only the lowest level of understanding.[46] That is accurate, and such emphasis on morphology is consistent with Locke's intention to compose a natural history of human understanding; in the eyes of tradition, too, history certainly occupies a lower level than philosophy. Hume, who hoped to surpass natural history,[47] sought for something which could perhaps really be translated by 'process',[48] and which belongs at the center of natural philosophy.[49] Whitehead's explanation that Locke did not approach the concept of process because of his unfortunate application of words such as 'cabinet'[50] is improbable, for Locke was not unaware of the ambiguities that such metaphors (which he knew from La Forge among others) could suggest. How far they were from his intentions is shown by the notes to chapter 2.10, which he added to the second edition of the *Essay*.

I shall mention a few more of Whitehead's observations about Locke, most of which are in principle convincing and which ultimately reveal that the philosophy of Locke is not that of Whitehead. An evaluation of the content of these observations would at the same time amount to a systematic discussion of the philosophy of organism. According to Whitehead, Locke (as Descartes) does not bring together into a coherent cosmological system the dispersed individual concepts that point towards the philosophy of organism.[51] Insofar as he is systematic, he relies on alternative concepts that finally lead to Hume's extreme sensationalism.[52] He remains caught in the traditional biases, which he did not revise radically enough and which render his philosophy vulnerable and inconsistent.[53] The substance-quality scheme, which appears linguistically as the subject-predicate scheme and insinuates a representationalist theory of perception,[54] is the first of these biases. Although Locke initiated a revolution against the Aristotelian concept of primary substance, he nevertheless adhered firmly to the traditional view of the mind and its perceptions, which appears against the background of the substance-quality scheme.[55] He also degraded the concept of substance, but without indication of any alternatives.[56]

A second bias of this sort is the universal-particular scheme with its implication of substances simply standing next to one another that renders the 'problem of the solidarity of the universe' insoluble. ("How can actual entities, each with its own formal existence, also enter objectively into the perceptive constitution of another actual entity?")[57] However, Locke had his own way of conceiving of the solidarity of the universe. He indicated it, among other places, in 4.6.11 of the *Essay*, a passage that only a few authors, including Whitehead,[58] have noted, and whose contents is in agreement with Boyle's work on the cosmic qualities. Furthermore, Whitehead reproaches Locke for overlooking that the acceptance of internal relations in actual entities excludes the concept of change, which is only a description of the adventure of eternal objects in the self-developing universes of actual entities.[59]

Despite his criticism of the concept of substance, Locke, therefore, remains Aristotelian here, too, without understanding particulars as historical routes.[60]

A third traditional bias, which is at least implicitly upheld by Locke and which prevented his formulation of a philosophy of organism and rendered his philosophy inconsistent, is that of Cartesian dualism[61] with its views that the nature of the mind is more easily recognized than that of the body, thought constitutes the nature of the thinking substance, and everything mental is a form of thought.[62] In Whitehead's view, this dualism prevents Locke from recognizing the constitution of the conscious actual entity, which is disclosed to its own consciousness in the complex of conscious ideas.[63] In this expression, Whitehead probably pays too little attention to the fact that Locke had considerable difficulties with the Cartesian division of the world into thinking and extended substance, which were expressed, among other places, in his controversy with Stillingfleet.[64] He explicitly rejected the presumption that the nature of the mind is more easily known than that of matter,[65] as well as the thesis that thinking constitutes the nature of the thinking substance and that everything mental is a form of thought.[66] In this regard, he belongs almost to a scholastic tradition that began with Gassendi's *Objections* to Descartes' *Meditations*. The difference in his interpretation of the complex of conscious ideas from that of the philosophy of organism can thus hardly be attributed to the reason cited by Whitehead.

The Thesis that the 'Essay' is Inconsistent

Whitehead presumes that the merit of the *Essay* is its adequacy and not its consistency.[67] In particular, the two halves of the work are not compatible with one another: books 1 and 2 present ideas in the sensationalist mode as mere qualifications of the substrate mind[68] and in some sections suggest the claim that there is no perception of particular actual entities.[69] By contrast, books 3 and 4 relate ideas to particular existents[70] and propose that there is an immediate conscious prehension of external things.[71] (According to Whitehead, this view is consistent with common sense, but not with the sensationalist theory of knowledge of other parts of the *Essay*.)[72]

I suppose that, as in any great philosophic text, there are inconsistencies in the *Essay*. I cannot see, however, that the one alleged here by Whitehead belongs among them. So far as I can make out, Locke's work is oriented mainly toward two literary species, Boyle's *Natural History* and Gassendi's *Institutio Logica*. With regard to the analogies between sections of the *Essay* and sections of the *Logique de Port-Royal*, which have been mentioned occasionally in recent years, it will be necessary to examine in detail whether they could both go back to a common Gassendian predecessor.[73] Since the *Institutio Logica* does not understand itself as a part of philosophy (in the tradition of Diogenes Laertius, X. 31),[74] it remains in the antechamber like natural history. This *Institutio* has four parts corresponding to the usual plan of construction: concept, judgement, inference, and method. Adopting the Epicurean application of *phantasia*,[75] the first bears the title "*De simplici rerum imaginatione.*" 'Imagination' can be substituted by words like *cogitatio, conceptio, apprehensio, intellectio,* and *notio.*[76] Basically, we are dealing with what is commonly called *simplex apprehensio*, that is a study of ideas so far as they have not yet become parts of mental judgments, as well as[77] with the consideration of the words used to designate them, provided they do not yet serve as subjects or predicates of verbal judgments. Singular ideas and universals, ideas of experience and mediated ideas, words in their relation to the ideas, definitions, potential subsumption and relations are considered.

For Locke, who is much impressed by the importance of language for thought, the matter of this prejudgmental part of logic branches off into two different books, the former treats ideas as such (from the very outset complex as well as simple ones), while the second treats words as such. The particularly close connection between generalizing and speaking impresses Locke; he treats the universals not in the second book, which explains ideas, but in the third. This caused Whitehead to allege that only in the third book does Locke realize that general ideas are not primarily given. The three final parts of the *Institutio Logica*, the doctrine of judgment, of inference, and of method, are all discussed in the fourth book. Locke precedes the doctrine of judgment with the doctrine of knowledge although, as *simplex apprehensio*, knowledge belongs in the previous systematic context. There is a good reason for that, of course, because for Locke the object of knowledge becomes the matter of judgment. The extensively presented theory of inference is developed in 4.14-20. A precise methodology is not proposed, but relevant observations are offered. The scheme by which it is constructed confirms the accuracy of Krüger's division into the empiricism of ideas and the empiricism of statements, according to which the dividing line must be placed between the third and fourth books. To place the division in a different way, namely between the second and third Books, as Whitehead proposed, can, in my view, not be justified either on its own grounds or by Locke's exposition.

Whitehead says that with his naive 'good sense' Locke observes that conscious perception is more than something conceptual, but he does not notice that this assumption is incompatible with an extreme subjectivist sensationalism.[78] Since sensible perception is probably intended here, the first part of the statement is confirmed by Locke's doctrine of sensitive knowledge. It is not apparent from the text what passages of "extreme sensationalism" Whitehead has in mind; perhaps, it is a case of misinterpretation. In his concept of prehension, Whitehead sees the heritage of the Cartesian *cogitatio* and of the Lockean 'idea'. 'Prehension' serves as the expression, free of any suspicion of dualism, for the most concrete mode of each level of individual activity.[79] It consists of two phases: first, the objectification of an actual entity as a datum for another, and second, the inclusion of this datum into the subjective satisfaction of an actual entity through feeling.[80] The concept explicated this way bridges, Whitehead says, the gulf between the representing ideas and the actual entity represented, a gulf for whose closure Descartes as well as Locke proposed a theory of the representation of things by *objective* things present in the mind. Thereby they tacitly fell back into the assumption of private ideas or qualities of mind that have no noticeable connection to the actual entities represented.[81] Here, too, Whitehead fails to cite passages as his evidence. In addition he also seems to overlook that for Locke the certainty of the existence of external things does not rest, as it does for Descartes, upon mediated demonstration, but is rather acquired immediately in sensitive knowledge. Perhaps Whitehead's reluctance to rely on this Lockean theory is due to the fact that, like the majority of interpreters, he considered it incompatible with Locke's general theory of knowledge, although there are good reasons in favor of their compatibility.[82] The case is similar for Whitehead's assumption that Locke understood sensible ideas as purely mental accretions to physical facts and believed the physical world to be essentially independent of the mental (in spite of the poorly defined relations between the two).[83] I see no interpretative reason or advantage that would speak in favor of such a reading of the Lockean texts. The theory of secondary qualities in Boyle and Locke, which corresponds largely to Descartes' theory of unclear cognition, may be problematical in many respects, but it is certain that for Locke the perception of secondary qualities is integrated in the context of the doctrine of sensitive knowledge, and at least in this regard it is not advisable to claim that his secondary qualities lie halfway towards the rejection of the Cartesian *realitas objectiva*.[84]

In Whitehead's theory of prehension the component of feeling is distinguished from the component of presentational immediacy. I have indicated that Locke's theory of sensitive knowledge proceeds in a fundamentally similar way. According to Whitehead, Locke misunderstands the relation of the two components and (borrowing from medieval positions) takes emotional feelings for mere responses to sense ideas, although really we prehend actual entities primarily more as emotional than as sensible.[85] As it were, Locke does not proceed this way, the reason being that he has adopted almost verbatim the *notitia sensitiva* doctrine of conceptualism.[86] This position, which Locke took over from the Middle Ages, does precisely not tend in the direction that Whitehead assumed.

In translating the term 'idea', one must bear in mind that for Locke an idea is always something conscious.[87] According to Whitehead, in most of *Essay* 1 and 2 'idea' signifies something like 'eternal object',[88] the final ingression of an eternal object or an abstract quality in a conscious mental actual entity.[89] Thus, it is primarily a matter of simple ideas[90] that, as Locke has it, are called "phantasms, notions, species" (1.1.8) in common parlance.[91] Locke erroneously believes here, in Whitehead's view, that logical simplicity and priority in the process of concrescence are identical.[92] In the predominant linguistic use of *Essay* 3 and 4, however, *idea* stands for the "objectification of actual entities,"[93] or "objectified actual entities and nexūs."[94] Here prevails, according to Whitehead, the conception of particular ideas, that is the conception of earlier actual entities that infuse the first phase of the real internal constitution of an actual entity with their own particularity and possess a vector function,[95] or the conception of the felt components of the constitution of actual entities.[96] While, according to Whitehead, the first two books confound logical simplicity with priority in process, this is then corrected by the later books (but already in passages like 2.23.1), which presumably do so unconsciously. (However, they tie the processes of comparison and analysis which produce universals to consciousness.)[97] Now it is accepted that, at first, there is the complex externality of particular things with their jumble of forms of determinations, which the mind gradually isolates:[98] Universal ideas develop only by means of abstraction of the circumstances of time, space, and of other ideas that determine a particular existence.[99]

The text of the *Essay* does not show the inconsistency Whitehead feared. The very beginning of 2.2.1 says (initially without temporal gradation) that some of our ideas are simple and others complex. The qualities that affect our individual senses, the section continues, form a complex within the affecting objects. But because our senses are specialized, this complex must be dissolved in sense perception so that the qualities enter us in a "simple and unmixed" way through the individual senses. For Locke there is thus something in the order of an original abstraction by means of the individual senses. This doctrine, however, is not new, and the elimination of individualization has been one of the traditional tasks of the *sensus communis*. For Locke, on the other hand, it becomes the task of the active understanding about which I will make a few observations later. Theses of this type already appear in 2.1.3: The senses convey different perceptions of things singly into the mind corresponding to their affection by perceivable objects.[100] The point is that whatever the specialized senses separated is finally united again in the audience chamber of the mind. Section 2.2.1 explicitly says that in the experience of objects entire *groups* of simple ideas enter simultaneously into our mind; for example in the case of liquid wax motion, color, softness, and warmth. These are precisely the same groups as are spoken of later in the chapter on substance of the second book (2.23.1): "The Mind being, as I have declared [for example in the passages just mentioned] furnished with a great number of simple Ideas, conveyed in by the Senses, as they are found in exterior things ... takes notice also, that a certain number of these simple Ideas go constantly together." When that involves time, a new problem arises, which the active understanding deals with by forming ideas about substance. Of course, this is a step further in comparison with 2.1 and 2.2, but not an inconsistency. For this reason it is inappropriate to describe the passage at 2.23.1 as a 'lapse'.[101] At the beginning of 2.1, the elements of complex ideas appear separated because the specialized sense organs separate them. In the perceiving mind to which the sensory nerves immediately convey them, however, (as is already shown by the beginning of the second book) they are together again as collections of ideas.

Locke, who wants to write a natural history of human understanding, is therefore compelled to write also a natural history of human ideas—that is, something that would a little later be called *idéologie*. A detailed description of human ideas also requires the description of the components of those collections of ideas that reach the mind through the senses. For the purpose of such a description, the *Essay* forms (by way of a new abstraction) classes of such components, which it terms 'simple ideas'; such classifications belong to the usual tasks of a natural history, as Locke's teacher Sydenham had already emphasized. The fact that we are dealing with classifications is connected with the peculiar abstract character of the Lockean simple ideas, which Krüger has also pointed out and which Whitehead misinterprets as a confusion of logical with temporal priority. In support of his thesis, Whitehead refers to a few passages in *Essay* 3 and 4 that even speak of ideas in perceived objects and thereby tacitly assume their identity with corresponding ideas in the perceiving mind. This way of speaking may be negligent or philosophically inconsistent, Whitehead says, but nonetheless it alone holds the Lockean system together.[102] Passages with the same content as that sketched by Whitehead, however, can already be found at the outset of the second book.[103] His remark is therefore rather an argument against his thesis.

One possible translation of the Lockean word 'idea' into the terminology of the philosophy of organism is 'feeling',[104] the expression for the operation of the transition from the objectivity of data into the subjectivity of an actual entity,[105] which likewise concerns the domain of the Lockean ideas of particular things, for these may correspond to the *felt* components of the constitution of an actual entity.[106] Whitehead's statements can *mutatis mutandis* be confirmed by reference to Locke's doctrine of sensible knowledge, although it is not correct to say that Locke would describe the feelings that are under investigation here as ideas of reflection.[107] Their vector character is, according to Whitehead, mentioned by Locke only later, in 2.23.1,[108] but in fact, it comes already into play at the outset of the second book.

Substance

It is particularly the concept of substance in its rendering by Locke that has, according to Whitehead, affinities with the philosophy of organism. The philosophy of organism, however, employs the term *actual entity* in place of *substance* so as not to suggest the subject-predicate scheme, which implies that substances undergo adventures of changing qualifications.[109] Whitehead admits that Locke does not doubt that external things are identifiable in successive moments and that he seeks the principle of the identity of bodies over temporal periods, without understanding them as the historic routes of a society of external things.[110] Yet, Locke's 'mind' remains for him, as does Hume's 'soul', a possible expression for actual entities.[111] It is even an expression of perennial truth.[112] Knowledge, however, is not a necessary element of actual entities but rather corresponds to what Locke calls 'capacity'.[113]

The transformation of Lockean substances into Whiteheadian actual entities entails some difficulties, which are most easily seen in the light of the doctrine of perception. (It is to be noted here that Locke has not explicitly treated the knowledge of other subjects.) According to 4.11.2, sensible knowledge makes us certain that *something does exist at that time*, but *something* is less than a substance. Section 4.11.9 is more precise in saying that sensible knowledge pertains to collections of simple ideas and, in the words of 2.8.8, makes us certain of the perpetually continuing existence of the collections of qualities that are their foundation. Hence, sensible knowledge is a certain, temporally limited and particular knowledge of the factual togetherness of sensations and qualities, and no more. 'Qualities' signify here anything that can affect us towards such sensations. It follows that sensible perception is not perception of the determinations of body as substantiality or causality is, and this is certainly a weak point in the rendering of 'substance' as 'actual entity'. Locke's texts emphasize that ideas corresponding to such determinations as substance do not belong with those items of information that we receive immediately through sense perceptions, but rather that the active and structuring understanding introduces them on its own account into pre-existing collections of sensations. The beginning of the chapter on substance, 2.23, quoted several times by Whitehead, describes how the understanding detaches the concepts of bearing and of resting upon something, which it receives from reflective experience, from their original context of reflective experience so as to transplant them into collections of heteronomous sensible experience. Thus, the understanding almost spontaneously imagines in addition to the pre-existing sensations the ordinary concept of substance as a bearer of qualities that, according to Locke, due to its opacity reveals little about the actuality of the body and is only a pathetic attempt of limited brains to represent to themselves the ever-hidden constitution of body.

This real internal constitution of body, a central theme of Gassendistic physics, is the order of their atoms, and its concept is represented as the idea of an atomic structure that always remains concealed from us human beings because our senses cannot perceive atoms. Knowledge of this formula, as well as of the translation rules for substitution of primary qualities by secondary ones, would enable us to deduce the properties of body and their ideal representation within the framework of a genuine science; but because both are withheld from human intellect, our knowledge of nature is never necessary and general. This is not due to a defect on the side of nature that, as such, acts in a predictable way, but is rather a consequence of the sensory inadequacy and temporal limitation of human knowledge. In view of the contemporary situation of science, this position is immediately acceptable to the circle of British physicists, physicians, and chemists to which Locke also belongs.

In the real internal constitution of body, Whitehead recognizes one of the two sorts of *fluxus* that philosophers had discovered at the time of Newton: concrescence and transition from one particular existent to another.[114] (These kinds of *fluxus* had probably already been developed within the framework of the traditional theories of motion.) In Whitehead's view, Locke's real internal constitution corresponds, in the language of the philosophy of organism, to the process that is the constitution of an actual entity.[115] In addition to the consideration of these real essences with respect to a complete analysis of the relations and interrelations within actual entities in the condition of concrescence, the philosophy of organism (perhaps under the influence of Locke's 'nominal essences') also postulates an abstract essence in which the specified actual entities are replaced by notions of unspecified entities that are correspondingly combined.[116]

Here, too, there are limits to what can be translated. The Lockean real essence or inner constitution is in principle concealed from the human mind, so that correspondences between it and Locke's nominal essences can by no means be established. I believe further that, even within the framework of a program for substituting substantial entities by entities in process, the transformation of the real internal constitution into concrescence as intended by the philosophy of organism is not without difficulty because such a transformation imparts into the theory of the constitution of an actual entity the notion of a mechanically grounded universality and necessity, which seems to be alien to the philosophy of organism.

Power is another concept from the domain of the Lockean doctrine of substance with affinity to the philosophy of organism. According to Whitehead, in his introduction in 2.21.1, Locke clearly emphasizes the decisive moments: the principle of relativity, the relational character of eternal objects, the composite character of the actual entities and the concept of power as its chief ingredient.[117] The latter of these emphases makes it clear that the foundations of things always reside in the composite nature of actual entities;[118] according to *Process and Reality*, the concept of power is so important for Locke's individual substances or enduring things because each uniformity of successive actual entities in an historic route presupposes a corresponding identity of their contributions to the datum of a successive actual entity.[119] ('Perpetual finishing' is creation of the present corresponding to the power of the past.)[120]

According to Whitehead, the concept of power, too, stands for two things that the philosophy of organism makes distinct: for the ontological principle in the sense of causal objectification, and for the principle that in its constitution an actual entity can objectify an earlier actual entity (presentational objectification).[121] As far as I can see, this observation concerns a central point of the Lockean doctrine of qualities and of sensitive knowledge in the context of which *quality* and *power* can mean the same thing. Yet, there seem to be profound differences between the Lockean concept of power on the one side, which, like the customary Lockean concept of substance (and in contrast to immediate sensible experience of existence), is only conceived and not perceived, and its correlatives in the philosophy of organism on the other. The understanding derives it, as is shown in the beginning of the chapter on power, 2.21, which is frequently quoted by Whitehead, from reflective experience apprehended in voluntary motion and choice of thought, and then thinks of it on its own initiative as entering given complexes of heteronomous sensitive experience. That sounds almost Kantian, although the source of the concepts of understanding is not pure apperception but rather reflective experience, and Alois Riehl has already drawn attention to this analogue. Whitehead himself seems to have this in mind when he says that the early intimations of the position, which was first *explicitly* introduced into philosophy by Kant, are to be found in Locke and Hume, who interpreted the act of experience as constructive activity of the transformation of subjectivity into objectivity or of objectivity into subjectivity.[122] As a consequence of the Lockean assumption that power cannot be perceived as such neither in the mode of presentation, nor in the mode of feeling, there seem to arise problems in translating Locke's thought here, too.

Locke's Presence in 'Process and Reality'

In my criticism of the interpretation of Locke provided by *Process and Reality* I have perhaps succeeded in showing that it cannot be sustained textually, or that it is either too optimistic or too pessimistic. Locke's actual theory of sensation, for example, is much more in line with the philosophy of organism than Whitehead's sensationalist construct. To my knowledge, these interpretations, which cannot be sustained textually, do often not even contribute to the understanding of Locke by revealing concealed features in the author that would otherwise have gone unnoticed — to stress that so explicitly only in order to blame an important author would be time wasted. It may be profitable to gain a clear understanding of the way in which Locke is treated here, and this is the fifth part of my paper.

Certainly with *Process and Reality* it is a question of the phenomenon of how Locke is transmitted, and thereby also of the retention of Locke. For philosophies can survive only through tradition, and tradition always involves assimilation, that is deformation of meaning or of textual appearance. This is the price philosophies have to pay in order to survive. Nevertheless, there certainly are different modes of an author's presence through tradition, such as the *institutional presence* of Thomas Aquinas during a certain period in my Roman Church or the presence of Karl Marx today in the domain of the Soviet Union. In this case, the institution, for reasons that can be reconstructed, identifies itself with an author to such an extent that an attack on him is also an attack on the institution that needs to be punished politically or through disciplinary sanctions. In addition, there is also the more individual option of the *scholastic presence* or the *presence of direction*, which implies that the adherents of the school or direction must relate their own philosophy to the model authors of the school; in this case, deviations are either made difficult or are punished within the school. Further-more, there is a *presence by means of education* in which the authors serve as conventional objects of instruction and admiration or of deg-radation within the group so educated without there being any more definite sort of obligation. Public presence through education can be transformed into other sorts of presence by private decision, for exam-ple, into that which I provisionally call *working presence*. This type of presence arises when someone within the framework of his own reflec-tion takes literally an author handed on by education, and either accepts or rejects individual theses of that author as he understands them, when he takes them as occasions for the movements of his own thought, and rearranges terms and patterns of thought at his dis-cretion. This working presence inherits from the presence by means of education the freedom with respect to text and author but, due to its spontaneity, it can become a unique and intensive form of the presence of an author. Clearly distinguished from this is another sort of presence, which likewise arises from the domain of education and which can be termed as *presence of meaning*. This case is quite different from the working presence in that precise wording and contexts are carefully respected and are interpreted and attributed a certain mean-ing from the perspective of life-world and from a doctrinal point of view, without the application of philological methods and without obligation towards the intention of the author. One is not in control of texts in this case, but rather binds oneself to them in a definite way, and the wide spectrum of possibilities for private interpretation is a indication of the freedom of the domain of education. The *philo-logical presence* of an author clearly stands out from the five that have been sketched, if only because it is not immediately occasioned by the life-world or by doctrine, but originates rather from a general interest in reconstructing an author's intentions according to textual criteria. It is mainly under this aspect that I have developed my argu-ment, because the philological presence in principle allows the defor-mation of an author's reception to be ascertained and judged. However, each form of transmission in its own way enables the dead to be rendered present, and in each the dead are made to pay a typical price. In principle, each has its own circumstances, its right, its profit, and its advantages, and it is in principle impossible to question it as much as it is impossible to question any form of organization or of life. The view that the philological presence is the only admissible form of presence of an author can as little be sustained as the view that a museum is the only appropriate place for a madonna. Nonetheless, in some cases a philological approach is a necessary precondition for an appropriate description.

But to come back to the point: Whitehead reads Locke not as a philologist but rather in the mode of a working presence. In *Process and Reality*, Whitehead relies on Locke, having both the author and the text at his disposal. Locke is assigned part of the burden of thought and presentation, but at the same time by the bonus of his educational presence given a certain protection to Whitehead. One could almost say that by means of this service, Locke repays the hospitality of being accommodated by Whitehead, much in the same way, I imagine, as, in bygone days older people chopped wood or looked after the rabbits. Whitehead's way of actualizing and exploiting the educational presence of his classic author is clearly different from an entrenchment in, or an arming oneself with, classical authorities[123] within the framework of an institutional or scholastic presence, but it is also different from the delicate and stabilizing presence of a classical figure of culture. Nevertheless, Whitehead's approach corresponds to a typical and viable form of tradition, only that it has the peculiar characteristic of emphatically ceding the place to Whitehead's intentions. This is the reason why *Process and Reality* conveys much better information about Alfred North Whitehead than about John Locke.

The frequency of this sort of presence in the history of philosophy, especially in modern philosophy, seems to me comforting and convincing. I assume that this is good as it is. On the other hand, however, a certain degree of impropriety seems to attach to this procedure, which may only be reconciled by philosophic greatness. Yet the reminder that *Quod licet Iovi, non licet bovi* (What is permitted to God is not permitted to oxen) is sometimes of little help in a decisive case, for (other than with our example) the difference between gods and oxen can be most difficult to establish. If find no adequate categories in the history of philosophy for the working presence discussed above. Here, perhaps, Whitehead's remarks on immortality and the presence of perished entities in concrescing entities may open up a way.

Notes

1. The number of pages in *Process and Reality* on which other philosophers are named (Index: 355-387): Descartes 51; Plato 32; Kant 31; Newton 21; Aristotle 17; Spinoza 12; Bergson 10; Bradley 9; Santayana 9; Leibniz 7; Zeno 4; Berkeley 2.

2. PR 60. As background to the evaluation cf. the famous passage at PR 39.

3. For example PR 51, 60, 145, 146.

4. Generally PR17. Here especially PR 145.

5. PR XI.

6. PR 145, 146.

7. PR 153.

8. Locke: An Essay Concerning Human Understanding 2.23.2 and 3 and 4.5.11.

9. See my paper, "Erfahrung und Hypothesen" ("Experience and Hypotheses") Philosophisches Jahrbuch 88 (1981): 46.

10. PR 153.

11. See my paper, "Zur Vernunft des Rationalismus" ("On Reason in Rationalism") in Rationalität: Philosophische Beiträge. Edited by H. Schnädelbach. (Frankfurt: Suhrkamp 1984), 70-93.

12. For example PR 57, 147. Especially in relation to the assignment of sensa and feelings PR 141 (with conjectural reference to medieval archetypes) and PR 146.

13. PR 157.

14. PR 57. Cf. PR 147.

15. PR 73, also PR 6.

16. PR XIII.

17. PR 141.

18. Ibid. Illustrated by PR 146.

19. PR 157.

20. Ibid.

21. PR 146, 147.

22. PR 157.

23. Cf. my paper "Sinnliches Wissen bei Locke" ("Sensible Knowledge in Locke") in Physik, Philosophie und Politik (Physics, Philosophy, and Politics). Festschrift for C. Fr. von Weizsäcker. Edited by K. M. Meyer-Abich (Munich: Hanser 1982), 257-259.

24. For example, Essay, 4.2.14, 4.3.5, 4.3.21.

25. Essay, 4.11.1.

26. Essay, 4.11.2.

27. Essay, 4.11.3.

28. *Essay*, 4.11.6.

29. *Essay*, 4.11.5 and 6.

30. *Essay*, 4.11.7 cf. 4.2.14.

31. Cf. my paper "Über Wahrheit und Wissen bei Locke" ("Truth and Knowledge in Locke") in *Logisches Philosophieren* (*Logical Philosophy*). Festschrift for A. Menne. Edited by U. Neemann and E. Walther-Klaus (Hildesheim: Olms 1983), 135-152.

32. For example in 2.8.11-22.

33. Cf. for example the allusion in *Essay* 2.8.22.

34. For example PR 51.

35. PR XI. "The writer who most fully anticipated the main positions of the philosophy of organism is John Locke in his *Essay*, especially in its later books." This is followed by the reference to *Essay* 4.6.11. Weaker is PR 130.

36. PR 147.

37. Peter of Ailly and Gabriel Biel accept the causal doctrine of Al-Ghazali and Ockham and are handed on as outsiders. Sebastian Basso, who at the beginning of the seventeenth century was one of the first within the framework of Christian philosophy to reject creative transeunt causality of the creatures, recalls them. It is only with Cartesianism, which presages Hume's critique of causality, that this rejection, which has such significant repercussions, becomes fashionable in philosophy. In the formulation of his doctrine of power and in his theory of causation Locke unmistakably takes the relevant authors into consideration.

38. For example, F. Suárez: *Disputationes Metaphysicae*, 5.8.15 and 47.3.12. Whitehead's illustration of the Lockean thesis by reference to 3.9.14 is a good indication.

39. Ibid 50.5.10.

40. For example P. de Fonseca: *In Arist. Metaph.* 5.13.12, 4; II (Cologne, 1614), 747 c.

41. *Rep.* 2.9 X.

42. *Physics*, IV, 221 b 1. Translation by Hardie and Gaye.

43. *Physics*, 1.2.7; I (Lyon, 1658) 226a. Corresponding F. Bernier: *Abregé de la philosophie de Gassendi*; I (Paris, 1678), 78.

44. *Physiologia* (London, 1654), 1.3.1, 78.

45. PR 128.

46. PR 139-140.

47. Hume intended to achieve this with "mental geography,"which he regarded as a *science* in the *Enquiry Concerning Human Understanding* I, 8.

48. PR 140.

49. *Enquiry* I, 9: "the secret springs and principles, by which the human mind is actuated in its operations . . ." This includes references to those domains of natural philosophy in which comparable discoveries have already been successfully made.

50. PR 54.

51. PR 128, 210, concerning the two types of flux.

52. PR 128.

53. PR 51. PR XI-XII points in a somewhat different direction. "These philosophers were perplexed by the inconsistent presuppositions underlying their inherited modes of expression. In so far as they, or their successors, have endeavored to be rigidly systematic, the tendency has been to abandon just those elements in their thought upon which the philosophy of organism bases itself."

54. PR 54, 56.

55. PR 137-138. More generally PR 147.

56. PR 146.

57. PR 56.

58. PR XI.

59. PR 58-59.

60. PR 55-56.

61. For example PR 19, 53-54.

62. PR 50.

63. PR 53.

64. That is expressed in the *Essay*, for example, in the somewhat ambiguous passage at 4.3.6.

65. According to 3.3.27 in comparison to bodies minds are, ". . . yet more remote from our knowledge." Most passages insist that our knowledge of minds is quite as inaccessible as that of bodies. For example, *Essay*: 2.23.5, 15, 16, 22, 23, 29, 30 and 31, and also 4.17.10.

66. Principally in *Essay* 2.1.9-23.

67. PR 51,57.

68. PR 147.

69. PR 49.

70. PR 146-147.

71. PR 242, 53.

72. PR 52-53.

73. Bernier: *Abregé* (see note 43), Preface, 7-8.

741. Ibid., 6-8.

75. For example Diogenes Laertius, X.50. The beginning of Gassendi's *Institutio Logica* refers to that in I 92a.

76. Ibid.

77. Consistent with suggestions such as those of Diogenes Laertius X.37, 38 and 75.

78. PR 243.

79. PR 19.

80. PR 52.

81. PR 76.

82. I list some of them in "Sinnliches Wissen bei Locke" (see note 23), 255-256.

83. PR 325.

84. PR 325-326.

85. PR 146, 153, 173.

86. Cf. "Sinnliches Wissen bei Locke" (see note 23), 257-258.

87. PR 113, 139, 140-141.

88. PR 52.

89. PR 59, 149.

90. PR 59.

91. PR 138.

92. PR 54, 143.

93. PR 149.

94. PR 52.

95. PR 213.

96. PR 53.

97. PR 54-55, 152.

98. PR 315-316.

99. PR 138.

100. *Essay* 2.1.5.

101. PR 157.

102. PR 113.

103. For example in *Essay* 2.8.7 and 8, Locke says that if he speaks of ideas "... sometimes as in the things themselves, I would be understood to mean those qualities in the objects which produce them in us."

104. PR 25.

105. PR 40.

106. PR 53.

107. PR 155. See text above, immediately following note 23.

108. PR 55.

109. PR 75.

110. PR 55-56.

111. PR 141.

112. PR 54.

113. PR 161.

114. PR210.

115. PR 219, which shows that my paraphrase is not formulated exactly enough.

116. PR 60.

117. PR 58.

118. PR 19.

119. PR 56.

120. PR 210.

121. PR 58.

122. PR 156.

123. "... Ultimately nothing rests on authority; the final court of appeal is intrinsic reasonableness." (PR 39) This sentence seems to help no further, for in those cases where one can argue with authorities, intrinsic rationality is transmitted socially in a particularly intense fashion.

Part II

Metaphysics and Science

4.

Creativity and the Passage of Nature

Dorothy Emmet

In *Process and Reality* 'creativity', along with 'one' and 'many', is called the category of the ultimate.[1] These three are said to be "the ultimate notions involved in the meaning of the synonymous terms 'thing', 'being', 'entity' ". I take this as meaning that anything which can be said to be a 'thing', 'being', 'entity' exemplifies these notions, but every-thing that exists is not a 'thing', 'being' or 'entity'. These are items in Whitehead's eight categories of existence, for instance eternal objects, which are not characterized by creativity. So creativity is not a predi-cate of everything quantified over by an existential quantifier. It is, he says, "the universal of universals characterizing ultimate matter of fact". I take this to mean whatever other characters any matter of fact may have, it must have this one.

He continues that 'it' (i.e. the category of the ultimate) "is that ultimate principle by which the many, which are the universe disjunc-tively, become the one actual occasion which is the universe conjunc-tively." An actual occasion is distinct from the many entities in response to which it becomes a new 'one', which can be referred to as 'a', 'an', or 'the'. The three elements, creativity, one and many, in the category of the ultimate, give matters of fact as outcomes of a process in which each new actual entity is a synthesis of inputs from its environment, which contains many entities. This fits with the notion of an organism, as a unit maintaining itself by inputs from its environment. The total environment — the world as a whole — is not itself an organism. It is a milieu within which organisms arise. For this to be able to happen it must have some structure, and I shall say more about this later.

The purpose of this paper will be to look at the notion of creativity in connection with the notion of the 'passage of nature' in Whitehead's earlier books and with what in *Science and the Modern World*[2] he calls the substantial activity at the base of things. I shall suggest that this is obscured by some of the views in *Process and Reality*. I accept the designation of creativity as ultimate. When it is said to be "the universal of universals characterizing ultimate matter of fact," I take this to mean that, whatever specific characteristics particular matters of fact may have, any matter of fact will have that of creativity, not that it is the universal, or, as Whitehead would say, eternal object, under which other universals can be subsumed.

Nevertheless, there is a point in calling creativity a universal. It is not itself a thing, but a character or property of things. It 'exists' as realized in matters of fact, which are the syntheses making up the processes of the world. These are called its 'creatures', but this must not be taken to mean that creativity is something temporally prior which then produces them. Creativity only exists in its 'creatures'. In itself it is said to be 'protean', which should mean that it has no structure of its own. Yet his combining it with notions of 'one' and 'many' as making for a continual process of forming 'ones' out of 'many's', does give some basic ordering to the category of the ultimate. Creativity as 'protean' might be likened to Aristotle's prime matter (*hyle*). Whitehead does not make this analogy, perhaps because prime matter is pure potentiality, and he wants to give potentiality to eternal objects. There is also the notion of creativity as *activity*, which *hyle* is not. He says that, along with 'many' and 'one', it replaces Aristotle's primary substance. This may have some point, as primary substance is an individual and creativity exists in syntheses of individual 'ones' out of disjunctive 'many's'. However, Whitehead's propensity to find analogies with views of great philosophers of the past can be misleading, both as to what he himself is saying and as to what the philosophers were saying. This applies to the analogy he draws with the "Receptacle" (*hypodoche*) of Plato's *Timaeus*.[3] This was an analogy not with creativity, but with his extensive continuum, which is the world as the potential field of a community of organic actual entities. This, however, is not just 'formless', like the "Receptacle." It has a fundamental topological structure of relations of "whole-part," "overlapping" and "contact." Whitehead had been reading A.E. Taylor's *Commentary on Plato's Timaeus*, and he liked the idea that Plato's Demiurge got the world going by inserting geometrical forms into the "Receptacle." This was congenial to his view of geometrical structure in an extensive continuum. But Plato's *hypodoche* itself had no structure.

I return to this question of structure. Whitehead certainly thinks that a basic structure is necessary if there is to be an actual world, and in *Process and Reality* he assigns the function of providing this to the primordial nature of God (p. n. G.), which is the 'first creature' of creativity. Since creativity is not temporally prior to its creatures which are its actualizations, 'primordial' should be taken as an ordering underlying other more particular orderings. I find it very difficult to see how God can be an actual entity, albeit the first one, but I shall not go into this here. I should want to take 'primordial' as referring to a basic order in the creative process itself, going beyond the bare notions of 'many-one' and the topological relations of extensive connection in the extensive continuum. When Whitehead speaks of the p. n. G. as an 'accident', I think this may be taken to mean that this ordering is not *necessary*, as one which must obtain in any possible world. It is contingent, as an ordering which in fact obtains. I think, however, that Whitehead would hold that the category of the ultimate must obtain in any possible world, and so also must extensive connection (with the topological relations of whole-part, overlapping and contact), so that any possible world would be what he calls an organic extensive community.[4]

Extensive connection was an ordering by which events can always extend over other events, giving the relation of whole-part, overlapping and contact. This is a structuring by geometrical divisioning, and may be the reason why he found the picture of world construction in the *Timaeus* so congenial. Here, however, a note added to the second (1924) edition of *The Principles of Natural Knowledge*[5] is highly significant. Of course the p. n. G. had not then made its appearance, but the relation of extensive connection was very much to the fore. In this note Whitehead says that "the book is dominated by the idea that the relation of extension has a unique pre-eminence and that everything can be got out of it. During the development of the theme, it gradually became evident that this is not the case, and cogredience had to be introduced." Cogredience is the association of events in a duration with a token-reflexive 'here-present' event, called a percipient. 'Percipience need not be conscious perceiving; it could be like the 'observer' as point of reference in relativity theory. The important point, however, for my present purpose is that he continues: "But the true doctrine, that 'process' is the fundamental idea, was not in my mind with sufficient emphasis. Extension is derivative from process, and is not required by it."

So we now have process as fundamental, and the ordering called 'extension' is derivative though necessary. This may mean that we start from the primitive fact that something, the 'passage of nature', is going on (as in *The Concept of Nature*) and this is divisible into events. As there can be no event at an instant or at an unextended point, there can always be a shorter event over which a longer event extends. From this space and time are derived: space from the duration of events contemporaneous from the standpoint of the event called the "cogredient," and time from the transition in the passage of nature from one duration to another.

If the fundamental character of the passage of nature is to be called *creativity*, how much more needs to go into it besides the relation of extensive connection? The note in the second edition of *The Principles of Natural Knowledge* said that this was insufficient to give *process*. Still less would it give process seen not only as "the temporal passage to novelty," where 'novelty' is in effect analytic, since any succeeding event by definition was not there before, but a passage seen as what he calls "the creative advance into novelty." Here I think we shall need to build into creativity another element which Whitehead derived from the p. n. G., and which he called, not very happily, 'appetition'. This was defined as "an urge towards the future based on an appetite in the present,"[6] and so as directed towards the realization of some particular possibility (eternal object). It is not necessarily conscious. Divested of the psychophysiological terminology, I take this as saying that there is a basic teleology, and I should want to put this into creativity itself. This could mean that the process is not just one of events, but one in which there is an immanent activity, and it would thus be possible to think of it as *creative*. Events cannot be creative, or even, I think, active, though their participants may be. (This may have something to do with Whitehead's switch from an ontology of events to one of actual entities, and I do not think he altogether saw how much it was a change.)

I have already said that the conjunction of creativity with the notions of 'one' and 'many' in the category of the ultimate is a way of saying that there is a process in which new syntheses are continually being formed. If this process of synthesis formation is an active one, the notion of events must give way to that of 'organism'. This transition was indeed happening in *Science and the Modern World*. Creativity does not appear in the index, but there is what Whitehead calls "a substantial activity expressing itself in individual embodiments, and evolving in achievements of organism," and he also speaks of "a selective activity akin to purpose."[7] This selective activity seems to answer to what he later called 'appetition'; here it is put into the basic activity.

I have said that activity cannot achieve anything, still less be 'selective', unless it is structured. Whitehead says that "the only endurances are structures of activity, and the structures are evolved." A structure limits pure potentiality, so that something may be actually possible. In *Science and the Modern World* he speaks of "God" as "the Principle of Concretion," the limitation necessary for there to be any actual matter of fact. This limitation is given as "among the attributes of the substantial activity."[8] The substantial activity does not only have the property of extensive connection, which was appropriate to an ontology of events extending over other events, but of producing what he calls "organized systems of vibratory streaming of energy."[9] This picks up a view which he says had first impressed him when, as a young graduate student, he heard a lecture from Sir J. J. Thomson on the "Poynting Flux of Energy," traced originally to Clerk Maxwell.[10] This showed energy as flowing with recognizable paths through space and time. Dr. Mays, in his book *The Philosophy of Whitehead*, thinks that Whitehead in fact meant by creativity the transmission of energy from event to event in nature, and that he failed to see that 'energy' is simply a term used by physicists to describe work done, or, where potential, as capacity to do work, and that it is not an activity, still less something which can be described in psychophysiological language.[11] There is always a difficulty here over the use of the word *energy*. It is an old word, and a good one, and there is no reason why it must be restricted to the physicist's technical use, so long as we watch what we are doing in using it more widely, for instance in speaking of 'mental energy'. Instead of using 'flux of energy' for the x of the passage of nature, it is better perhaps to speak of 'energetic activity', a richer something of which the physicist's energy can be the measurable aspect. Whitehead speaks of an element in nature as an "organized system of vibratory streaming of energy," from which the physicist's energy is an abstraction.

'Organized system' brings us to the notion of *organism*, which was already coming to the fore in *Science and the Modern World*, where there is the highly significant remark that "Biology is the study of the larger organisms; whereas physics is the study of the smaller organisms."[12] The link is that of patterns, and the patterns are carried by energy which goes in an oscillatory or vibratory manner. We shall conceive "each primordial element as a vibratory ebb and flow of an underlying energy of activity."[13] This view was already emerging in *The Principles of Natural Knowledge* (see the last chapter on "Rhythms"), and it was reinforced by, though not derived from, Whitehead's encounter with quantum theory in the form in which it was appearing in the 1920s. This encouraged a view of fundamental particles as manifesting energy in distinct pulses or bursts, as well as their paths having a wave-like pattern.

'Organisms', as 'one-many' syntheses in an ongoing process, are thus shown as structures continuing over time in rhythmic patterns. This may not be the universal pattern of every possible form of process; Whitehead suggests that it goes with the particular character of our 'cosmic epoch', which contains what he calls 'electromagnetic occasions'.[14] Be this as it may, he sees rhythmic reiterations of pattern as integral to our passage of nature. A pattern with rhythmic reiterations is not simply uniform: it contains contrasts as well as repetitions. Moreover, if the passage of nature is also a synthesizing activity, new synthe-

ses may be made, so that there are variations in the pattern, and sometimes a leap to a new one. In any case, a view of structures of energetic
activity exhibiting reiterative patterns, and patterns within patterns,
goes with the notion of systems functioning over time.

I think that up to, and including, *Science and the Modern World*,
Whitehead was working towards a view of the evolution of systems of
activity, issuing in a generalized view of organism. It was a view of the
passage of nature as made up of structures of activity whose patterns
were transmitted either through the same organized units enduring
over a temporal spread, or in the budding off of new units which
would develop a similar pattern. In all cases, there is a transmission of
pattern in a succession from phase to phase. In the earlier books the
transmission was spoken of in terms of the 'flux of energy', following
paths in which patterns were maintained. In the later books the successive phases are given atomicity, and continuity is provided by the
'conformation' of each successor to the pattern, or the aspects of the
pattern, of its predecessors. Also the internal self-development of the
atomic system becomes prominent; so much that 'transition' becomes
a matter of development from phase to phase *within* each atomic system, and not one of continuity between it and its successors. The
emphasis is now on the atomic system as a process of self-development.

Lewis Ford, in his paper "From Transition to Concrescence,"[15] given
to the Seminar *Whitehead und der Prozeßbegriff* in Bonn in 1981, says that
he thinks there was a genuine shift in Whitehead's view, more than just
a change of emphasis, and that it came when he was writing *Process and
Reality*. I think it is foreshadowed in the paper "Time," given to the Sixth
International Congress of Philosophy in Havard in 1926, and also in the
view of 'prehensions' in *Science and the Modern World*. Certainly in
Process and Reality 'concrescence' has won over 'transition', in that the
latter now becomes the conformation of a new concrescence to its predecessors, and not a passing over from predecessor to successors. In *Process
and Reality* Whitehead speaks of two kinds of 'fluency', attributing the
distinction, with doubtful historical accuracy, to Locke. "One kind is the
fluency inherent in the constitution of the particular existent. This kind I
have called 'concrescence'. The other kind is the fluency whereby the perishing of the process, on the completion of the particular existent, constitutes that existent as an original element in the constitution of other
particular existents elicited by repetitions of process. This kind I have
called 'transition'."[16] The passage from one existent to another is now
called 'supersession'. Put bluntly, this is a 'picking up' and not a 'passing
on' view of transition. Whitehead says that each actual entity perishes
and its pattern is reiterated in its successor because the successor "feels
the feelings" of its perished predecessor. This is called 'conformation'.

'Feeling' is normally something which calls for subjective awareness of affective tone. Whitehead says he uses it as a technical term, not implying conscious sentience, but even waiving the problem of unconscious sentience I have the greatest difficulty in seeing how one thing can feel the feelings of something which has actually perished. For if it really has perished, how can it be felt, whether literally or technically, by something else? 'Feeling' is here an intentional term, referring to something felt, and not to the subjective affective state. What is felt are the feelings of the perished entity, or some aspect of them, which have now become an objectified datum, synthesized by the new entity into its own concrescence. The nearest analogy I can see is in memory. Memories of things, people, happenings, now gone, can be integral elements in our own development. But for the memories to have been acquired, there must at some time have been a relationship in the present to something actually there to be related to. And in the most telling example Whitehead gives of conformity of feelings, that of an angry man,[17] he refuses to allow that memory explains "how does (the man) now know that a quarter of a second ago he was angry," and says that the feelings of the new occasion conforms to the past one. It is not that the anger flows over from phase to phase in the angry man, but that the angry man becomes a route of occasions each one of which perishes, and its feeling is reproduced in the next. I find this most implausible as a view of the macroscopic continuity of a mood of anger in an angry man, and still less of the macroscopic continuity of the man himself. Nor does it do justice to Whitehead's contention against Hume, that we experience the derivation of a present experience from that of the immediate past. This experience is much more like one of the passing over of one phase into another in a macroscopic experience than it is like a string of microscopic experiences each of which picks up from its predecessor, and each of which is apparently very short-lived. (Whitehead gives each of the occasions which make up his angry man about a quarter of a second.)

What I miss here is an adequate account of macroscopic subjective aim, e.g. when an angry man is trying to knock down his opponent. I do not think this is adequately provided for by seeing this as the outcome of actions in a society of actual occasions, even a society with what Whitehead calls a 'presiding occasion'. This is not a sufficient view of the unity in directedness in a macroscopic organism. Nor is it a sufficient view of its historic continuity, if this is to be seen as the outcome of the conformation of a vast number of actual entities, each very short-lived and picking up the feelings of its predecessors who are dead and gone. I think that Whitehead has transferred Locke's remark about time as 'perpetual perishing' to the histories of actual things in such a way as not to give them genuine continuity.

It might be said that the notions of extension would allow any entity to be as large as you like, through its being extended over others. This however is a view which goes with that of *events*, which can always extend over other events. It could only apply to the later ontology of actual occasions in their aspect of superjects, that is to say, to their 'feelings' as objectified in others, and this indeed seems to me a very different notion from that of events extending over other events. In any case, the atomicity of an actual entity gives it a limited life span, and in his later books Whitehead insists on this.

There may indeed be atomicity in the world, and quantum theory suggests this. Also a particle may disappear and another one may appear without detectable continuity. Nevertheless there has been a transmission of energy, though it may happen in discrete bursts. In Whitehead's later books, however, 'prehension' seems to have taken the place of transmission of energy. Each entity prehends, picks up, the feelings of its perished predecessors. Moreover, there is no contemporary action and reaction of one entity on another—nor can there be, since there is no causal relation between contemporaries in the same duration. This produces, I think, a difficulty over his later view of space. While he allows temporal successions (albeit in relativistically different time series) he does not provide for a public space for movements in which his plurality of entities can meet each other with actions and reactions. (I went further into this in my paper "Whitehead's view of Causal Efficacy"[18] at the 1981 Seminar in Bonn.) Whitehead's later space, as a potentially divisible extensive continuum, seems to me to be space as cogredient with a percipient occasion, and so in effect a space in presentational immediacy, not a public space which can be a forum for interactions.

Professor Leclerc, in his paper to this present seminar, refers to a passage in *Adventures of Ideas*,[19] where Whitehead speaks of *creativity* as a "factor of activity" in the origin of each new occasion. It is also in the 'actual world' relative to that occasion, providing 'objects' requisite for the new occasion, and is "also expressive of its conjoint activity." Leclerc takes this as saying that there is an activity both of the prehender and of the prehended, and so a genuine meeting and interaction. I should like to think that this could be so. But I cannot reconcile it with Whitehead's continual insistence that there can be no causality (and so no meeting) between contemporaries. I think *conjoint* here means that the activity in the new occasion is only what it is because there have been other occasions active in the world of its immediate past. This is not the same as reciprocal action and reaction.

To sum up: In looking at Whitehead's view of creativity, I want to connect it directly with the 'passage of nature' of the earlier books. I want to see it as realized in a process in which there are genuine transmissions, 'passing on', and not only 'pickings up'. This would accord with his insistence that our experience always comes to us with a sense of derivation and anticipation (a causal efficacy of which we are directly aware). Thus the passage of nature is not as atomized as it becomes in the later books. There are indeed distinct organized systems, but these have spatiotemporal spread with a direction, and there is a transmission of energy through them. This is shown in the reiteration of patterns, and this is an activity of imprinting and re-imprinting, and not just the repetition of a form over a spatiotemporal route. Also the imprint is actively and not passively received, so that there is a possibility of variations, and thus the passage can be an 'advance into novelty' in more than a trivial sense. This stress on creativity as activity could accord with what Whitehead in *Science and the Modern World* called the substantial activity at the base of things. This activity could be ultimate in a way in which creativity as a universal could not. I realize that in *Process and Reality*, the category of the ultimate also contains the notions of 'one' and 'many', and that this gives it some structure and also suggests a process of synthesizing unities out of diversities. I should want to see further structuring which Whitehead provides for through the primordial nature of God as a structuring *within* creativity. I should also want to see the element of 'appetition' which Whitehead assigns to God as a teleological tendency within the creative process itself. If the deepest level of teleological creativity in nature is seen as an activity of divine immanence, I should welcome this. But it would be within the process, not something inserted to it. Whitehead speaks of the entities within process as having 'subjective aims' derived from God. I would rather say that each may have its own subjective aim, as its way of shaping its creativity; yet it may also be able to bring this into harmony with the deepest level of cosmic teleology. This immanent view would allow potentialities to be opened up from within the process itself, as alternative paths which things may take, always of course within the constraints of what has already been realized. We should not then have a separate realm of eternal objects (if Whitehead indeed has this), and that, I think, would be an advantage.

I may seem to be pulling Whitehead into a more familiar and less original, even if also into a less idiosyncratic, type of view. But I think that even with these modifications, we can be left with a genuinely original view. The original elements which I find productive, and which I should want to preserve, are 1) the view of nature as a community of interrelated activities, centering in individual "unities functioning with spatiotemporal spread." 2) This could yield a generalized concept of organism, which might span physical and biological units. 3) These units are never fixed, but are always passing on. 4) The processes which are their histories form patterns which get reiterated, with possibilities of variation. 5) Some of these variations are not just matters of chance, but come because the activity realized in their units is integrative as well as conformative.

The crucial question in all this is whether there is a passage of nature with active properties, issuing in a community of organisms of this kind. For this we need both concrescence and transition. I think that their combination gives richness to the passage of nature, so that it can be not just productive of novelty, in the sense that things happen which had not happened before, but it can be "the creative advance into novelty." It will then be possible to fill out Whitehead's saying in *The Concept of Nature*[20] that "the passage of nature is only another name for the creative force of existence."

Notes

1. PR 21.

2. SMW 152, 231.

3. AI 171-172.

4. PR 288.

5. PNK 202.

6. PR 32.

7. SMW 152.

8. SMW 249.

9. SMW 51.

10. AI 238.

11. W. Mays: *The Philosophy of Whitehead*, New York: Macmillan 1959, pp. 65-66 and 212.

12. SMW 145.

13. SMW 51.

14. PR 98.

15. In: H. Holz/E. Wolf-Gazo (eds.): *Whitehead und der Prozeßbegriff/Whitehead and the Idea of Process*, Freiburg/München: Alber 1984, pp. 73-101.

16. PR 210.
17. AI 235.
18. In: Holz/Wolf-Gazo: op. cit. pp. 161-178.
19. AI 230.
20. CN 73.

5.

Whitehead's Concept of Creativity and Modern Science

Friedrich Rapp

If I could know just how this leaf grew from its twig I would be silent
for all time: For then I would know enough.

Hugo von Hofmannsthal

The category of creativity occupies a central position in Whitehead's speculative cosmology. It is the ultimate universal concept expressing both the
process of becoming, which is characteristic of all events, and the origination of novelty. Modern science, by contrast, seems to manage its explanations and predictions without employing the concepts of novelty and
creativity. Yet, philosophy and science deal with the same range of discourse – the processes of the physical world. Thus the question arises of
how this difference is to be explained, and how speculative natural philosophy and modern natural science are related to one another with
regard to the origination of novelty. To investigate this question, first the
category of creativity in Whitehead's process philosophy will be compared
to the explanatory scheme of modern science. That will be followed by a
discussion of the systematic dilemma that arises for any formulation of
the concept of novelty. The following section treats Whitehead's critical,
and yet simultaneously affirmative, attitude toward science. This is
related to the distinction between different aspects of his concept of creativity in the fifth section, and possible approaches to reducing complexity in a theoretical way will be discussed in the concluding section.

Creativity as Key Concept

In *Process and Reality*, Whitehead describes 'creativity', 'many', and
'one' as the ultimate universal categories that define the universal

process of the creative combination of many disparate beings into new unities.[1] All the more specialized categories of his 'philosophy of organism' presuppose these three most general categories.[2] The fundamental concept of this philosophy of organism is based on a speculative generalization of the notion of power.[3] The atomistic view of a merely mechanical aggregation of parts is replaced by Whitehead with the conception of the universal relatedness and reciprocal prehension of all real occasions, factors that are expressed in the concrete elements of 'actual entity', 'prehension', and 'nexus'.[4] In this context, the category of the actual entity is designed to replace the traditional concept of substance and to avoid the fallacy of misplaced concreteness. The actual entities that reciprocally experience one another so as to realize highly diverse structures are in Whitehead's words, "the final real things of which the world is made up. There is no going behind actual entities to find anything more real."[5]

Despite their diverse functions and the difference in their significance all actual entities are uniform in principle so far as their real existence is concerned. God is an actual entity too in Whitehead's cosmology, which is deliberately kept on one level and formulated according to what he terms "the ontological principle."[6] God as a transcendent creator is replaced by Whitehead with the supreme principle of creativity, which determines all being and is conceived as purely immanent. Creativity is the source of novelty and of the creative advance, which leads to the concretion of actual entities that have not previously existed: "The ultimate metaphysical principle is the advance from disjunction to conjunction, creating a novel entity other than the entities given in disjunction."[7]

Because of its universal and fundamental significance, creativity comes close to the traditional concept of God. As Whitehead has it, "the primordial nature of God" is a necessary completion of creativity, for without a principle that decides between possible alternatives, and therewith determines the direction of the effect of creative power, no concrete event would ever be actualized. God's function consists in establishing which of the timeless 'eternal objects' (forms or ideas) are in fact to be realized in the creative process. The primordial nature of God is the principle of concretion.[8] Yet, within the framework of his metaphysical principles, Whitehead does not wish to assign to God the special status of a keystone or foundation.[9] He is no more and no less than the most important instance of an actual entity.[10] Thus it is true of God that: "he is not *before* all creation, but *with* all creation."[11] However, God's essence is not exhaustively described by this conceptual primordial nature; rather, it is complemented by his physical 'consequent nature' in which the world exercises its efficacy on God. God's coming-into-being is connected not only to the beginning, but also to the continuation of the universal process: "his derivative nature is consequent upon the creative advance of the world."[12]

Whitehead objects emphatically to any static or mechanical conception that interprets change as a mere reorganization of passive elements.[13] All actual entities demonstrate an immanent creativity and striving for self-actualization. "Self-realization is the ultimate fact of facts. An actuality is self-realizing, and whatever is self-realizing is an actuality."[14] Whitehead undertakes to express the process character of all events and of fleeting becoming in his cosmology: "the flux of things is one ultimate generalization around which we must weave our philosophical system."[15] Creativity is accorded the key position in this dynamic process of becoming: "Neither God, nor the world, reaches static completion. Both are in the grip of the ultimate metaphysical ground, the creative advance into novelty."[16]

For Whitehead, process thought is tied to consistent and thorough historization of all events. Specific actual entities can only be adequately understood in the context of their coming-to-be and with reference to their further development.

> All actuality involves the realization of form derived from factual data. . . . But no actuality is a static fact. The historic character of the universe belongs to its essence. The completed fact is only to be understood as taking place among the active data forming the future.[17]

Whitehead's speculative cosmology is conceived as an alternative to rival Descartes' mechanistic conception of nature, which abstracts from all relations that do not fit into the physicalistic world view.[18] Whitehead, by contrast, invokes the plethora of elements characteristic of a concrete process of becoming, all of which are to find their expression in the comprehensive concept of creativity:

> If we stress the role of the environment, this process is causation. If we stress the role of my immediate pattern of active enjoyment, this process is self-creation. If we stress the role of the conceptual anticipation of the future whose existence is a necessity in the nature of the present, this process is the teleogical aim at some ideal in the future. . . . It thus effectively conditions the immediate self-creation of the new creature.[19]

Reduction to the Known

In view of Whitehead's explicit emphasis upon the concept of creativity one would expect that creative advance and the principle of novelty also play a significant part in modern science, but this is by no means the case. One seeks in vain for the categories of creativity, of novelty, or of creative advance in the conceptual system of the natural sciences. Consequently, they are not found in epistemological investigations of the nature of scientific explanation and the formulation of scientific theories.[20] Nor is this merely a question of terminology: No synonymous concepts or concepts related in meaning are apparent in the natural sciences.

This situation is more readily understood if we examine the interpretations of similar categories offered by Whitehead and modern science. The traditional fundamental concepts of the philosophy of nature such as space, time, matter, and causality are of major importance here. The first three concepts do, of course, appear in modern science in their operational form under the guise of units of measurement of the basic physical quantities, centimeter, gram and second.[21] It is vital here that these three basic concepts can in principle be understood quantitatively inasmuch as their magnitude is established by comparison to a conventionally determined unit of measure. These fundamental concepts appear in science, then, along with the other quantities derived from them, as variables in mathematically formulated relations of dependence. This can be generalized: traditional concepts of the philosophy of nature play an (explicit) role in modern science only insofar as they can be made operational by use of experimental method and mathematical description. There is no place in mathematical physics for the concept of cause or for the corresponding notion of causal relations. Only the mathematical description of functional dependencies between quantities directly or indirectly observed is relevant. Nevertheless the causal concept is not entirely eliminated from modern science. Immediate effects, such as the transfer of energy or impulse, are interpreted in terms of the model of cause and effect.[22] However, it is always a quantitative description of relations of dependence between variables observed that serves as the point of reference in doubtful cases.

Now the phenomena Whitehead centers his argument on are obvious. If therefore an analogy between causality and creativity is taken for granted, it ought to be possible to determine at least a functional substitute for the concept of creativity in modern science, even if it does not appear explicitly. The process character of all events is as little subject to doubt as the fact that novelty constantly arises in the world by means of the creative process. The modern sciences must also take account of these givens in some way. On closer examination, however, it turns out that the conceptual understanding of the phenomena in question is always dependent on their interpretation. The point is that mathematical and experimental science understands, conceptually articulates, and interprets them differently than Whitehead's philosophy of organism does. This is further proof for the general insight that the world by itself remains virtually mute and inaccessible to discursive knowledge; it is only with the help of an accessible, revelatory theoretical understanding and a certain categorial grid that it can be grasped and its theoretical implications can be described.

The experience primarily oriented on everyday life referred to by Whitehead stands in stark contrast to the great success of science (as some critics would even insist today, it is too great a success) with its theoretical explanation and technical exploitation of natural processes. This success was achieved without taking into account the phenomenon of creativity Whitehead speaks of. Indeed, the achievement and potential of modern science rests firmly on the methodological device of paying no attention to the sorts of phenomena highlighted by Whitehead and forming the basis of his speculative cosmology. Rather, it systematically excludes them. This raises both the question of how such an exclusion is possible in general and of the procedure it rests upon in particular. The answer to these problems requires a closer examination of the methodological and epistemological principles science rests on. Four points need to be mentioned here, which we will briefly discuss: the experimental procedure, the analytical method, the mechanistic model, and the mathematical rendering of science.

By means of the *experimental procedure*, processes that take place spontaneously in nature are dissected and analyzed in accordance with a certain cognitive interest. In contrast to the integral phenomena that offer themselves to the disarmed senses in virgin nature, in scientific research the relevant object of investigation is abstracted from the current of natural events in the laboratory by means of 'artificial' technical apparatus and measuring instruments so that the connection between theoretically conceived variables is presented in the purest form possible. These variables are chosen with regard to the specific formulations of a question and a specific research program that attends to the present state of knowledge and, if possible, leads beyond it. By means of this procedure, the field of scientific knowledge is systematically expanded and the various particular areas involved support and complement each other. The devices and apparatus, with which the test conditions are produced and experimental results are amplified and transferred, are technical in nature. This makes the systematic and reciprocal relation between modern science and technology manifest: In principle, every experimental setup is a technical system, and every physical discovery can be used technically. The difference between science and technology consists in their respective purposes. Whereas the natural sciences strive for knowledge that is as universally valid, systematically ordered, and formulated with as much mathematical precision as possible, in technology the concrete results, such as the easing of labor, transportation, or the transmission of information are what matters. This means that, for technology, theoretical knowledge is of interest only inasmuch as it serves this immediate goal.

The universal principle the experimental procedure is based on, is the *analytical method*. Achievement of the most comprehensive understanding possible, in which the phenomena under examination are prominent in their unrestricted totality and entirety, is not the aim of this method. The conscious choice is rather to undertake a theoretical and conceptual analysis, which then is made concrete by the experimental setup. Now, because it depends on demarcations and inferences and not on an immediate, intuitive, and integral apprehension of the whole, all discursive knowledge is, by its very nature, analytic in its wider sense. To this extent modern science can justly claim to stand in the tradition of Western philosophy. Yet, there is an obvious difference in this regard between the positions that were occupied by, say, Aristotle and Descartes. Descartes developed the analytical method as a perfect instrument of mathematical scientific knowledge;[23] to him, the world can be analyzed in terms of mind and a mechanical agglomeration of matter that is open to experimental and technical interference. For Aristotle, on the other hand, the analysis into irreducible elements remained limited to a merely conceptual analysis of something that retained its unrestricted totality.[24]

The *mechanistic mode of thought* sets the background of the modern understanding of nature. The model for the conceptual understanding, theoretical interpretation, and empirical examination of natural processes is provided neither by purposively organized living beings in their totality, nor by human acting oriented by value and directed towards goals, but rather by functional aspects of mechanical systems. These systems are technical artifacts, the performance of which rests exclusively upon combined activity of their components. This corresponds to the reductionistic, and to that extent materialistic, approach of modern science. The physical world is regarded as a collection of elements that possess exclusively material properties. In this view, organic, biological, and mental phenomena can be explained solely by the functional aspects of their material components and the forces acting between them.

The *mathematical* rendering of science consists in the quantitative description of the functional relations of dependence between the quantities under investigation. Such restriction to the numerical value of operationally defined variables facilitates exact prediction of the effects to be expected under the conditions concerned, a prediction which is also significant for the practical or technical application. Furthermore, this mathematical rendering provides the possibility of formulating scientific theories as deductive systems of statements from which more specialized laws, or the characteristic features of specific individual instances, can be obtained by specification of the axioms and the more general laws. The price for the facile management of such universally valid mathematical formalism is the introduction of theoretical concepts that can be traced only indirectly to the results of observation and the abstraction from all combinations that cannot be incorporated into the preformulated conceptual scheme.

A close connection exists, both historically and systematically, between these four characteristics of modern science. They have developed gradually through a complex historical process and are so well-adapted to one another in their concrete manifestation that today there seems to be a pre-established harmony between them. With its analytic dissection and mechanistic models, the experimental method permits investigation of well-defined dependency relations, which then can be presented in mathematical form. In doing this, the mathematical variables, which have suffered from a loss of content, serve as a methodological guidance for reducing the wealth of the physical world to a few, univocally defined and experimentally confirmable dimensions of observation.

This understanding of nature in modern science and the theoretical framework within which it is presented leave no categories for discussion of the origin of novelty and creative advance. In terms of this approach, one can in principle only come up against what is already known. The conception of novel objects, properties, or relations, which have not previously existed, and the phenomenon of creative coming-to-be are from the very beginning conceived of as manifestations and variations of what is already well-known both empirically and theoretically. They are not granted a unique, specific, and irreducible character. From the perspective of the natural sciences, novelty—but not creativity—simply consists in the repetition of what has hitherto happened in another time and under other circumstances, or it is merely a relatively insignificant particular combination of elements that make up a new form.

In this way, the focus is directed away from creative coming-to-be and from the full concreteness of novelty toward the combination of already existing and known elements. What results here is a sort of reduction, that is, the explanation of new and complex objects and phenomena by the combination of the elements out of which they are formed. This applies to the scientific theories of the development of the universe as well as to the explanation of biological evolution (phylogenesis) or of individual development (ontogenesis). Accordingly, the biological theory of evolution explains the origin of new species by invoking spontaneous mutations and with reference to selection in the struggle for survival. Novelty or creativity appear nowhere as independent concepts. This same reductive strategy is applied in order to explain the development from a fertilized seed to a fully grown living being. The procedure applied is analogous to the one employed to deduce the production of the physical properties of a macroscopic body, or the chemical properties of a compound, from the constitution of their respective elements.

Abstraction from full concreteness is another characteristic feature of scientific concepts. Very general idealized concepts, which are correspondingly deprived of content, are introduced in terms of experimental method and mathematical description. The result is conceptual standardization. Although the objects, processes, and properties falling under these concepts exhibit quite different features to immediate sensation, these differences are disregarded. This can be illustrated by the examples of the center of mass, temperature and energy. For science, the function of these concepts is to serve as variables in mathematically formulated physical laws. These laws also provide implicit operational definitions of the variables since a prescription for determining their respective numerical value can be derived from them. This can best be illustrated by the concept of energy. The mechanical, electric, thermal, or chemical energy of a closed system manifests itself in highly diverse phenomena. From the vantage point of everyday understanding, and without any conception of the conservation of energy, one would never suspect a relevant or well-defined connection between them — the winding path to discovery of the law of energy bears witness to that.

The formulation of scientific concepts is either directly or indirectly aimed at their empirical verification. Yet, the concrete definitions provided for them are far removed from ordinary understanding. Since they preserve no connection to spontaneous observation, but are established instead with a view to abstract, universally valid and mathematically formulated laws of nature, scientific concepts are more 'unnatural' for spontaneous apprehension than, for example, the conceptions of Aristotelian physics. Novelty and creative production — such as in the case of the transformation of energy — are not regarded by modern science as phenomena of their own. Rather, they are emasculated by subsumption under an abstract quantity, the 'energy' conserved. Novelty *qua* novelty, and a productive force as a creative principle, are not even considered in a classification of this sort.

In essential features, this systematic analysis coincides with the results of *contemporary philosophy of science*. One of the central issues in this field is the logical reconstruction of scientific explanations. What is considered here is neither the accurate description of concrete psychological acts of thought, nor the formulation of heuristic procedural prescriptions, but rather the ideal logical scheme that all scientific explanations are supposed to follow. Concerning the issue of creativity, the commonly accepted nomological (or covering-law) model of scientific explanation is of particular relevance. The fundamental idea of this model is that the events to be explained are deductively subsumed under general laws that express an invariable relation between events. According to Hempel and Oppenheim, an explanation consists of two types of statement: the initial conditions I, which describe the specific characteristics of the phenomenon for which an explanation is desired, and the universal law L, according to which in the case of a particular variation of the initial conditions I, a certain predictable result R always ensues as a consequence.[25] A simple example is provided by the law of freely falling bodies $s = \frac{g}{2} t^2$. The equation describes the relation betwen the height from which a body falls, s, and the time it falls, t, whereby the resistance of the air is ignored. From a known I (s here), R (t here) can be calculated.

As can be seen from this deductive-nomological model of explanation, new phenomena and the capacity for creative production are accorded only an accidental role in the conceptual system of modern science. They appear only indirectly and in a subordinate manner, as expressions of the relevant initial conditions I. What is considered essential is the law L, which expresses invariable, universally valid functional relationships. The concrete spatiotemporal phenomena are only taken as contingent instantiations of L. In this view, the genuine substantial element consists in the nontemporal mathematical relations that are identical in all cases. Such Platonism is the theoretical counterpart of the empirical and experimental direction of modern science.

These fundamental observations are not affected by the contingent, historical development of the sciences. Such changes in the conceptual systems and paradigms as were investigated by Pierre Duhem[26] and Thomas Kuhn[27], for example, certainly led to new theoretical conceptions and new models of the natural order (for example Newtonian mechanics, electrodynamics and the theory of relativity). Still, the fundamental view of explanation as subsumption under universal laws remained unchanged. The change was a matter only of the concrete shape, but not of the logical structure of the explanations in question. In every epoch, the laws thought to be universally valid formed the reference point for scientific explanation. The 'conservative' tendency of normal science, i.e. its tendency to stay within the framework of a given paradigm and to rely on a fixed model, is set out clearly by Kuhn:

No part of the aim of normal science is to call forth new sorts of phenomena; indeed those that will not fit the box are often not seen at all. Nor do scientists normally aim to invent new theories, and they are often intolerant of those invented by others. Instead, normal-scientific research is directed to the articulation of those phenomena and theories that the paradigm already supplies.[28]

To him, the most striking characteristic of ordinary research problems lies in "how little they aim to produce major novelties, conceptual or phenomenal. . . . Even the project whose goal is paradigm articulation does not aim at the *unexpected* novelty."[29]

As Kuhn argues, the transition to new paradigms is only an 'anarchistic' interlude that must lead as soon as possible to the formulation of a new model of explanation, which will then again become obligatory. In short, the aim of science is not investigation of novelty *in concreto* as unique spatiotemporal events, but rather its subsumption under established lawful patterns. Yet, because the newly discovered laws are exempt from temporal change, novelty is dissolved into an abstract, temporally invariable conceptual framework.

This by no means suggests that the procedure of the sciences is fruitless or even irrational. The empirical limitation to experimentally demonstrable relations between idealized and mathematically representable variables, the derivation of the properties of more complex, integral wholes from the constitution of their constituents, and the explanation or prediction of new phenomena by instantiation of general laws, have proved to be highly successful principles. By firmly adhering to this program, theoretical knowledge, empirical research, and the possibilities of technical application have continuously been expanding. The immanent progress of the natural sciences and of the technology based on it is obvious. These increases in theoretical explanatory power and in the practical applicability of modern science cannot be the result of random achievements. They must have a factual foundation. In terms of its program, modern science can legitimately claim to understand the structure of physical processes.

A Dilemma of Explanation

There is no irresolvable opposition between Whitehead's understanding of novelty and creativity and that of modern science, either logically or from the perspective of what is investigated. Both are, from a material point of view, occupied with a common object of investigation, namely the physical world. Thus a comparison of the two positions is possible and necessary. However, because of their diverse approaches, different objects are involved from a formal point of view. The same thing is discussed, but from different perspectives so that neither logically excludes the other. Without the creative development of novelty, which Whitehead emphasized, that is, without unexpected and hitherto unobserved phenomena, there would indeed be no *need* for scientific research, apart from providing the greatest possible economy of thought in summarizing the knowledge already achieved. And without some sort of homogeneous, recurring and law-like structures in nature, which modern science relies on, scientific research would have no *factual* foundation. The known and the unknown, constancy and change are correlative concepts as Kant saw so clearly. For him the synthetic proposition: "In all change in the world substance remains and only the accidents alter . . . (is) the first of the completely *a priori* laws of nature."[30]

Furthermore, with respect to the ancient formula: "*Gigni de nihilo nihil, in nihilum nil posse reverti*"[31] ("From nothing, nothing comes; nothing can be turned into nothing") he maintains that change can only be perceived in substances, that is in something permanent because "it is just this permanence which makes possible representation of the transition from one condition into another and from non-being into being."[32]

The notion of coming-to-be from non-being is in fact absolutely inconceivable when every coming-to-be is at the same time regarded as having been caused by some preceding state of affairs. The temporal and ontological tie to an earlier stage relieves the being concerned of its isolated monadic existence and places it in a (supposedly intelligible) relation to an earlier state. This presupposes substantiality and permanence in a very general, and still indefinite form. This general permanence is by no means restricted to the traditional conceptual scheme of substance and inherent accidents. The laws of conservation that are crucial for modern physics (energy, impulse, spin, and parity) also represent a specific, mathematical formulation of the logical and ontological connection between permanence and change. In this context, the quantities conserved constitute the abstract and formal analogue to the classical concept of substance, and their concrete and numerical manifestations correspond to the traditional accidents.

The same issue can also be tackled from the perspective of the relation between the universal and the particular. The place of substance and permanence is then taken up by an invariable universal which *ex hypothesi* retains its permanent, yet still largely unspecific features and is only concretized by the specific characteristics of the particular at hand. The notion that all discursive scientific knowledge occurs through subsumption of the objects being investigated under universal concepts—under variable recurring elements—comes equally to the fore in Plato's theory of forms[33] as in the classification by genus, species, and specific difference, and in the system of comprehensive classification provided by the Porphyrian Tree. For such a scheme of subordination the ultimate, specific traits that constitute the unique character of a particular existent elude exhaustive description by universal concepts. As St. Thomas says: "*Individuum . . . est, quod est in se indistinctum, ab aliis vero distinctum*" ("The individual is that which is undivided in itself and yet distinct from others").[34] For this reason, Duns Scotus introduced the concept of the irreducible "*haecceitas*" as an analogue to proper names, which, as ultimate "*differentia individuans*" ("distinguishing difference"), was intended to express the relevant particularity.[35] But a universal concept that is applicable to the most diverse individuals when taken as the relevant *differentia individuans* still requires a concrete determination.

Thus the ultimate, specific, and unique character by which a concrete existent is distinguished from other analogous beings cannot be completely captured by subsumption under universal concepts. This is *a fortiori* true for that novelty, which has come into being by a creative process. This novelty cannot, by definition, be completely characterized with concepts already common—for otherwise it would not be new. Only the known features that have already been encountered, or some combination of them, can be positively characterized. Any hitherto unknown characteristics can initially only be described in a negative way, by providing them with the label 'new'. On the other hand, there are concepts available for known phenomena which facilitate their description and classification in terms of regular well-known relations. Logically, however, as hitherto unknown, whatever is novel is entirely incomprehensible.

New phenomena can be identified as new by comparison with recurring, and thus already known, events. By invoking this contrast, Hume excluded the possibility of miracles since they would breach already known laws of nature.

> There must, therefore, be a uniform experience against every miraculous event, otherwise the event would not merit that appellation. And as a uniform experience amounts to a proof, there is here a direct and full *proof*, from the nature of the fact, against the existence of any miracle; nor can such a proof be destroyed, or the miracle rendered credible, but by an opposite proof, which is superior.[36]

The pragmatic part of this argument corresponds to everyday understanding and to the practice of scientific investigation. Nevertheless, it should be noted that this argument does not conform to the postulates of empiricism. For the decisive factor is not the immediate testimony of the senses in doubtful cases when the existence of facts is at stake, but rather reflection based on rational theoretical arguments.

The task of conceptualizing and explaining novelty by tracing it back to what is already known leads to a dilemma. *Either* one invokes what is already known — and then genuine novelty is explained away because it is declared to be a mere repetition and/or combination of already known elements, *or* novelty is taken seriously to the full extent as something hitherto completely unknown. Then it is completely different from what has been experienced and for which appropriate concepts have been minted. Except for the merely negative definition that it has not yet existed, there would be no positive theoretical grip by which positively to apprehend novelty as novel. Whitehead quite correctly reproaches modern science for having chosen the first alternative so that novelty and the creative advance are played down or ignored altogether. New phenomena are explained by relation to combinations that are already known; any given novelty is traced back to common elements and relations, and thereby conceptually deprived of its uniqueness.

Yet, neither Whitehead nor anyone else is in a *fundamentally* better position.[37] Anyone who raises the issue of novelty and its creative development will find himself confronted with the second alternative: If there can be absolutely no reliance upon what has been known previously and accordingly is common, then clearly there is no reference point and no possibility of conceptually articulating novelty so as to explain it by incorporation into what is already known. Formally, Whitehead also reverts to general, recurrent, and regular structures, exactly as modern science does. In formulating his speculative cosmology, he even invokes the latest theoretical position of modern science. His categorial system is supposed to have the same character of universal validity as the absolutely universal relations he proposes between actual entities, creativity, prehensions, and eternal objects.

Fortunately, however, the dilemma only occurs in this sharp form when a simplified logical scheme is presupposed. In reality, neither of the alternatives mentioned is entirely adequate. Novelty is not entirely ignored by modern science, nor does Whitehead treat it as an absolutely incommensurable quantity. In actuality, we always experience novelty in connection with states of affairs and properties already known. A historically developed system of concepts in which the relevant new states of affairs or characteristics can be classified is at our disposal in all concrete everyday or scientific cognitive situations. This is true notwithstanding the fact that the Hempel-Oppenheim scheme has been applied in quite diverse ways during the course of the historical development of the scientific disciplines. Indeed, even in the course of a single research project both the *explanans* and the *explanandum* undergo constant reinterpretations in the course of which old concepts gain new nuances of meaning and, should the occasion arise, completely new concepts are also introduced. Surely, the logical, nontemporal dilemma formulated above is not entirely discharged by the continuous conceptual development and creation of new categories and theories in scientific practice, but it is extensively mitigated.

Thus the mere fact that there is reference to what is already known, or to a definite view or theoretical context is not fully conclusive. Conclusive is rather the way in which this happens in particular cases and what significance is thereby granted to novelty and creativity. The comparison between Whitehead and modern science shows that each interprets and evaluates the same phenomena quite differently, depending on their respective theoretical background. It is important to note that for Whitehead novelty is, in the first instance, an ontological category, which can subsequently also be accorded epistemological significance. The aim of his cosmology is to overcome the 'bifurcation of nature' by ascribing to every actual entity both a physical and a mental pole at the same time.[38] Whitehead's basic concepts are chosen in such a way that the universal reciprocal prehension of the actual entities that they express also includes conceptual knowledge as a special case. In the philosophy of organism all actual entities are, by their very nature, new in every instant and at the same time they are creative because they develop in the creative process of becoming and in turn contribute themselves to that process.[39]

A natural scientist would hardly raise fundamental objections to any of this. But to reflect the position of his subject, he would describe Whitehead's view as being of little value because it makes no cognitive contribution to the formation of scientific problems. It would seem that Whitehead stresses phenomena and relations that science does not deny, but simply regards as unproductive for its progress of knowledge. Whitehead emphasizes the significance of novelty and creativity and elevates them to the rank of fundamental philosophical categories, while science undertakes to provide theoretical explanations and therewith predictions. Science endeavors to reduce novelty to what is already known.

Rejection and Affirmation of Science

But that does not exhaust the differences. For Whitehead's speculative cosmology and modern science not only stress different aspects, they also differ in their objectives, the range of their validity, their degrees of abstraction, and their procedures for verification. The sciences attempt to establish operational mathematical, functional relations between idealized variables. For Whitehead, as for common understanding, verifiability under well-defined experimental conditions (and correspondingly also predictive force and technological applicability) is not a substantial objective. He strives for a greatly expanded understanding that recognizes all the natural processes in their complete concrete determination, and to that extent it corresponds to the ideal of a "unified science"[40] on the speculative level, but of course without the reductionist program of physicalism. Consistent with the inverse relation between the scope and the content of concepts, his theoretical system must necessarily be highly abstract despite the intended proximity to what is given in fact. Since he has undertaken to subsume the plenitude of being from the level of the inorganic world up to human consciousness under the same categories and to explain all the phenomena in question in one and the same scheme,[41] he is forced (in a way analogous to that of the sciences) to introduce technical philosophical terms into his cosmology, terms whose range of meaning is then necessarily stretched to the uttermost.

It must be noted that despite his explicit thematic treatment of creativity, Whitehead is by his recourse to the scheme of deductive subsumption closer to traditional metaphysics than, for instance, Hegel or Bergson. By the explanation of dialectical opposites and the representation of the *durée réelle*, these thinkers provide a less formal analysis of creativity that is more intimately related to the immediate events. Obviously, the tension between universal concepts and concrete phenomena cannot be obviated by such alternatives, but an account that is closely related to the phenomena considered, and relies on the analysis of characteristic examples and on the use of analogies rather than on general concepts, may lead to an enriched, saturated understanding that is as close as possible to the specific type of concrete experiences in question, though not to universal classifications.

Whitehead's attitude towards modern science is clearly ambivalent.[42] The indisputable value of his philosophy of organism consists in its attempt to combine science and philosophy into a single speculative synthesis. His philosophy offers one of the few serious endeavors to formulate a comprehensive system aimed at harmonizing the thoroughness and universality of philosophical questioning with the state of knowledge attained by modern science. Certainly, as an expert in modern science, and in particular in mathematical physics, Whitehead was also competent enough to question the foundations of modern scientific thought. He rebukes science for its limited idiosyncratic perspective, which screens out everything that does not fit into a previously formulated scheme. "They canalize thought and observation within predetermined limits, based upon inadequate metaphysical assumptions dogmatically assumed."[43] Theoretical curiosity and the desire for technological produceability have induced science to pay attention only to the mechanism of "causal efficacy."[44] Whitehead contrasts this abstraction of science to the full sensible concreteness, the constant flux of appearances, and the potentiality of natural processes, which invariably lead to novelty. In the light of these phenomena, the viewpoint of natural science is utterly inappropriate:

> Matter-of-fact is an abstraction, arrived at by confining thought to purely formal relations which then masquerade as the final reality. This is why science, in its perfection, relapses into the study of differential equations. The concrete world has slipped through the meshes of the scientific net.[45]

According to Whitehead, "the disastrous separation of body and mind which has been fixed on European thought by Descartes" is responsible for the blindness of natural science.[46] The result is a seriously impoverished understanding of nature: "Science can find no aim in nature: Science can find no creativity in nature; it finds mere rules of succession."[47]

Along with this acute and apposite criticism, Whitehead also endorses science. The fact that he incorporates and integrates the positive results of science into his system of thought, and that he partly derives his philosophic assumptions from the theoretical foundations of science, shows how involved the relations are here. Since modern science provides a continuation, refinement and deepening of everyday experience, philosophical reflection cannot bypass the results science has achieved. On the other hand, it undertakes to scrutinize these results and to criticize and correct them if need be. As anybody else, Whitehead is also caught in this dilemma. His philosophy of organism is the result of the enormous effort to capture the undiminished totality of human experience in a philosophical system and at the same time to combine it with the results of scientific research. He admits that his philosophy of organism is the result of a generalization of the basic concepts of modern physics.

> *Mathematical physics* presumes in the first place an electromagnetic field of activity pervading space and time. The laws which condition this field are nothing else than the conditions *observed by the general activity of the flux of the world*, as it individualizes itself in the events.[48]

The vigorously criticized conceptual scheme of modern physics appears here as the starting point of, or at least the impulse to, the formulation of a nonphysicalist cosmology. Such a cosmology is intended to offer a "synoptic vision" in which the fundamental concepts of mathematical physics can by "imaginative generalization"[49] be conjoined to immediate experience, which is not yet conceptualized nor restricted by theory.

Aspects of the Concept of Creativity

The difficulty in attempting a synthesis between natural science and philosophy (while at the same time maintaining a distance) must be taken into account when one attempts analytically to isolate the different functions Whitehead attributes to the concept of creativity.

In relation to the special categories, creativity is a *meta-theoretical key-concept*, which together with the 'one' and the 'many' forms the zenith of his system;[50] to that extent, it is analogous to Spinoza's *deus sive natura*. More precisely, the basic concept of creativity takes into account that every process is active in and of itself without the intervention of a transcendent creator.[51] Whitehead remarks in this context:

> My point is that any summary conclusion jumping from our conviction of the existence of such an order of nature to the easy assumption that there is an ultimate reality (the Absolute, Brahma, the Order of Heaven, God) which, in some unexplained way, is to be appealed to for the removal of perplexity, constitutes the great refusal of rationality to assert its rights.[52]

It is a philosophical commonplace that, in order to avoid an infinite regress, all understanding, and more so every explicit explanation, must employ ultimate categories, principles, or axioms as final and absolute reference points. It is precisely this function that Whitehead attributes to creativity:

> In all philosophic theory there is an ultimate which is actual in virtu_ of its accidents. It is only then capable of characterization through its accidental embodiments and apart from these accidents is devoid of actuality. In the philosophy of organism this ultimate is termed 'creativity'; and God is its primordial, non-temporal accident.[53]

Comparing these two quotations, it is difficult to avoid the impression that Whitehead, too, has not really solved the problem. Instead, he has merely allocated it a different systematic position, because for him it is creativity that becomes the "ultimate reality . . . to be appealed to for the removal of perplexity." Whitehead's creativity is thus understood as the ultimate 'Absolute' in the same way as God conceived as *causa sui*. Both reveal themselves only through their manifestations; no reference can be made to anything *beyond* them.

Whitehead attempts to escape this problem, which can hardly be avoided from a strictly logical perspective, by not confining the concept of creativity to the theoretical level, but rather linking it to *immediate experience*. Like Hegel, Whitehead gives his abstract speculative categories a preconceptual or intuitive meaning. He answers the rhetorical question "How do we add content to the notion of bare activity?" by stating that "This question can only be answered by fusing life with nature." Accordingly, the starting point for the formulation of a speculative cosmology lies for him in the fact "that the energetic activity considered in physics is the emotional intensity entertained in life."[54] Whitehead reproaches physics for studying only "half the *evidence* provided by human *experience*."[55] He contrasts the one-sided and misleading perspective of the natural sciences to the range of poetic experience known to the Romantics. "Wordsworth, to the height of genius, expresses the concrete facts of our apprehension, facts which are distorted in the scientific analysis."[56]

But Whitehead was well aware of the clash between this all-embracing vision and the Cartesian ideal of clear and distinct perception. His endeavor to synthesize science and logic with immediate, intuitive understanding comes up against severe difficulties. He therefore proposes that nature must explain itself and postulates that the mere ascertainment of what things are must already contain the elements for their explanation. "Such elements may be expected to refer to the *depths* beyond anything which we can grasp with a *clear* apprehension."[57] This is obviously intended to apply equally to the category of creativity concerning which one is always referred to inner experience that escapes definite conceptual analysis. Apparently, there is no unproblematic golden middle between the limitation and operational precision of the natural sciences and the universal validity, and hence relative indeterminateness, of speculative cosmology.

Seen from the *subjective, epistemological* perspective, creativity corresponds to the innovative knowledge of novelty. A characteristic of this novelty is that it cannot be reduced to, nor deduced from what is already known. In science, the frame of reference against which new phenomena are measured consists of: the historically defined state of knowledge of the searching individual or group, the relevant formulation of the question, the basic approach to the problem, and the *explanans*, which in the case of scientific explanations is accepted as the final point of reference. The creativity of artistic or scientific activ-

ity can be investigated only *ex post facto* with regard to its preconditions, but it cannot be systematically planned in advance or forced; the
creative ability of genius remains a mystery that ultimately escapes
conceptual understanding.

The *objective, ontological* aspect of creativity comes clearly into focus
when temporal modality is considered. Concerning phenomena that
have not previously existed, but now actually appear, two conditions
apply. They can only come into being if they are possible, and if according to the principle of sufficient reason they are actualized by some
cause, however this creative power may be interpreted in detail. It is in
this sense that Whitehead says:

> The creativity is the actualization of potentiality, and the process of
> actualization is an occasion of experiencing. . . . The process of crea-
> tion is the form of unity of the Universe.[58]

This modal analysis of the transition from potentiality to actuality led
Whitehead to develop the conception of eternal objects as the forms of
possible determination.[59]

Modes of Reducing Complexity

If one attempts to evaluate Whitehead's concept of creativity and
the interpretation of novelty offered by modern science, one remarks
a striking difference. On the one hand, in science, there is a systematic
conceptual structure worked out to the last detail that is theoretically
and experimentally confirmed and technologically productive. This is
a structure of scientific theories and interrelated disciplines, which has
gradually evolved into its present form in the course of a convoluted
historical process through the combined efforts of many generations of
scientists. Within this reductionistic and thus mechanistic conceptual
structure, scientific theories describe experimentally reproducible phenomena and mathematical relations between well-defined variables.
By contrast, Whitehead's speculative cosmology is the intellectual
accomplishment of a single individual, even though the collective heritage of philosophy and the history of science is, occasionally in a most
unconventional way, accommodated. While the sciences manage to
get along without explicit reference to novelty or creativity, an adequate understanding of natural processes can, in Whitehead's view,
only be achieved if creativity is accepted as the ultimate key concept.

It is more than just coincidence that today the linguistic analysis of
scientific language and the logical reconstruction of the methodological procedural rules of modern science have replaced traditional phi-

losophy of nature. The gulf between ordinary, everyday understanding and the abundance of detailed and highly technical scientific data has become so great that no convincing philosophical conception can be developed, neither on the basis of ordinary language concepts nor on the basis of scientific categories alone. Whitehead is therefore perfectly justified in choosing (similar to Descartes, Leibniz, and Kant) the sciences as a point of reference, and yet desiring to surpass them. The accomplishments and problems of Whitehead's efforts thus offer an instructive setting for the question of whether it is still possible today to formulate a metaphysics of nature that goes beyond a more or less obvious popularization of the state of scientific knowledge while at the same time retaining a certain distance from natural science.

This much is certain: the variety and complexity of phenomena in the inorganic and organic world, and of man and his history, can only be conceptually understood if one is prepared to accept a simplifying scheme. Viewed from the perspective of concrete phenomena and relations, creativity, which according to Whitehead is always involved, is always heterogeneous in its particular manifestations, for example in chemical reactions, in the ontogenesis and phylogenesis of life forms, in cosmic evolution, in intellectual and artistic creation, and even more in the constantly changing combinations of contrary intentions and actions in history. Whitehead has set out to explain all these phenomena by one and the same categorial system, which is inspired by the model of event or process philosophy. Inevitably, his conceptual system leaves a broad space for interpretation and requires detailed exegesis. This is especially true for his universal concept of creativity.[60]

The empirical method and the mathematical precision of modern science guarantee a theoretically mediated examination of the physical variables that are consciously defined to maintain a certain distance from the profusion of concrete sensibility. No similar univocal corroboration of Whitehead's interpretation of creativity is possible. One can perhaps answer with Nietzsche that subjectivity is the highest form of objectivity. Whitehead's speculative cosmology cannot, by its very nature, provide the same degree of conceptual precision and empirical verifiability as modern science. Yet, to say that Whitehead's metaphysics eludes examination, is too strong a verdict.[61] Surely, Whitehead's cosmology, like any other metaphysical conception, is not formulated so as to permit such empirical tests as are common to science. The relatively vague character of Whitehead's philosophy, which also entails the aptness and need for interpretation, is inevitable in view of the plenitude and complexity of concrete experience. This leads to a paradoxical situation: The more one pays due consideration to the concrete plenitude of the world in view of a universal conceptual system, the more indeterminate and metaphorical the propositions intended to conceptualize this plenitude must become.

Abstraction from this plenitude, and reduction of the investigated phenomena to a few well-defined and theoretically conceived qualities, which are then investigated in terms of certain physical variables, is the price modern science has to pay for its experimental and theoretical successes. Whitehead, in his comprehensive cosmology, has to pay the price of applying highly abstract and general concepts that necessarily lack precision. The comparison of mathematical-experimental science and speculative cosmology shows that in the effort to comprehend the mystery of creativity, one is torn between the Scylla of a detailed and exact, but lifeless uniformity, and the Charybdis of a universal, but not fully analyzable power of creativity, which is full of life. Whitehead's advice applies to both theoretical procedures: "Seek simplicity and distrust it."[62]

Notes

1. PR 21.

2. PR 18 and 31.

3. PR 18-19.

4. Ibid.

5. PR 18.

6. PR 18-19.

7. PR 21.

8. PR 343-345. This conception which is developed in *Process and Reality* is investigated by R.M. Palter: *Whitehead's Philosophy of Science* (Chicago: University of Chicago Press 1960), 11-12. Calling on notions that Whitehead had formulated in his earlier work, Dorothy Emmet suggests positing concretization in the creative process itself, as a universalization of the concept of organism and the immanence of God and not as an element introduced from without (59 above). Jan Van der Veken argues to the same effect (78 below). A.H. Johnson proposes the contrary position. By calling upon its universal character (and without attending to its special status) he interprets creativity as an idea, that is as an eternal object, which manifests itself in concrete actual entities. He takes creativity to result from the primordial nature of God creating himself: *Whitehead's Theory of Reality* (New York: Dover 1962), 70.

9. PR 343.

10. PR 18.

11. PR 343.

12. PR 345.

13. PR 208-209.

14. PR 222.

15. PR 208.

16. PR 349.

17. MT 122.

18. MT 211-212.

19. MT 228.

20. For example, W. Stegmüller: *Probleme und Resultate der Wissenschaftstheorie und Analytischen Philosophie* (*Problems and Results in the Philosophy of Science and Analytic Philosophy*) (Berlin: Springer 1969 ff.) and F. Suppe (editor): *The Structure of Scientific Theories* (Urbana, Ill.: University of Illinois Press 1974).

21. G. Joos: *Lehrbuch der theoretischen Physik* (*Textbook of Theoretical Physics*) (Leipzig: Akademische Verlagsgesellschaft 1954), 775. See also D. Bender and E. Pippig: *Einheiten, Masssysteme, SI* (*Units and Systems of Measurement, SI*) (Braunschweig: Vieweg 1973), for the basic variables introduced as a supplement for reasons of teleology.

22. G.H. von Wright: *Causality and Determinism* (New York: Columbia University Press 1974), 57-61; C.G. Hempel: *Aspects of Scientific Explanation* (New York: Free Press 1965), 348-350 as well as G.A. Svečnikov: *Kategoria prinčinnosti v fizike* (*The Causal Category in Physics*) (Moscow: Socekgiz 1961), 88-116.

23. Descartes' *Discourse on the Method* (1637) gives a programmatic outline of the new method of procedure.

24. Aristotle: *Metaphysics* I, 1.

25. Hempel provides more detail about this in his *Aspects of Scientific Explanation* (see note 22), 331-496.

26. P. Duhem: *La théorie physique, son object et sa structure* (Paris, 1914). *The Aim and Structure of Science*, translated by P. Wiener (Princeton: Princeton University Press 1954).

27. T.S. Kuhn: *The Structure of Scientific Revolutions* (Chicago: Chicago University Press 1962).

28. Kuhn: *Structure* 24.

29. Kuhn: *Structure* 35.

30. Kant: *Critique of Pure Reason*, First Analogy of Experience, A 184/B 228; compare C.F. von Weizsäcker: *Die Einheit der Natur* (*The Unity of Nature*) (Munich: Hanser 1971), 383-404.

31. *Critique of Pure Reason* A 185/B 229.

32. *Critique of Pure Reason* A 188/B 231.

33. *Meno*, 75 a.

34. Thomas Aquinas: *Summa theologiae*, I, 29, 4c. Cf. A. Pieper "Individuum" in H. Krings (editor), *Handbuch philosophischer Grundbegriffe* (*Handbook of Basic Philosophical Concepts*) (Munich: Kösel 1973), 2: 728-737.

35. A. Geulincx: *Opera philosophica*, 626a.

36. David Hume: *An Enquiry Concerning Human Understanding*, Part I, Chapter 10.

37. As Francis Bacon explains (*The Advancement of Learning*, ed. Spedding, II, 1): "History is properly concerned with individuals, which are circumscribed by place and time. For though Natural History may seem to deal with *species*, yet this is only because of the general resemblance which in most cases natural objects of the same species bear to one another; so that when you know one, you know all. . . . Philosophy discards individuals; neither does it deal with the impressions immediately received from them, but with abstract notions derived from these *impressions*." And in his detailed investigation, *Identité et réalité* (fourth edition, Paris: Alcan 1932) E. Meyerson explains: "La force explicative des théories provient uniquement du principe de l'identité dans le temps qu'elles cherchent à faire prévaloir, en d'autres termes de ce qu'elles font subsister quelque chose, la nature intime de la chose qui subsiste étant tout à fait secondaire." ("The explanatory power of theories comes exclusively from the principle of identity in time which they attempt to have dominate, in other words it comes from the fact that they cause something to subsist, the internal nature of the thing which subsists being completely secondary.") Paul Henle's argument in "Scientific Method and the Concept of Emergence," *The Journal of Philosophy* 39, (1942): 491 points in a similar direction: "In a universe in which emergence was the rule or in which every event involved emergence, rational thought could at best give a partial and inadequate account."

38. PR 289-290.

39. Ibid.

40. Otto Neurath propagandized the linguistic and methodological unity of the sciences in the sense of the Logical Empiricism of the Vienna Circle, and (in association with Rudolf Carnap and Charles W. Morris) founded the *International Encyclopedia of Unified Science*. Kuhn's work, cited in note 27, appeared as Volume 2, Number 2 of this encyclopedia.

41. PR 17.

42. In SMW 51 Whitehead describes his goal as being "to trace the philosophical outlook, *derived from* and *presupposed by* science." Emphasis added.

43. AI 151.

44. PR 169.

45. MT 25.

46. MT 211.

47. Ibid.

48. SMW 190. Emphasis added.

49. PR 5.

50. PR 21.

51. PR 222.

52. SMW 115.

53. PR 7.

54. MT 229 and 231-232.

55. MT 211. Emphasis added. In this connection F.S.C. Northrop argues in his paper "Whitehead's Philosophy of Science" that Whitehead's application of macroscopic concepts, for example to an electron, is *postulated* and does not rest upon immediate *sense experience:* "But the moment this distinction between the sensed and the postulated is admitted, Whitehead's doctrine that 'nature is only what is disclosed in sense awareness' is rejected and bifurcation cannot be escaped." P.A. Schilpp (editor), *The Philosophy of A.N. Whitehead* (La Salle, Illinois: Open Court 1951), 191.

56. SMW 104.

57. SMW 115. Emphasis added.

58. AI 230-231.

59. PR 22-23 and 45-46.

60. This is worked out in detail by Reiner Wiehl: "Zeit und Zeitlosigkeit in der Philosophie A. N. Whiteheads" ("Time and Timelessness in Whitehead's Philosophy") in *Natur und Geschichte (Nature and History)* Festschrift K. Löwith. Edited by H. Braun and M. Riedel. (Stuttgart: Kohlhammer 1967), 373-405.

61. A. Shimony: "Quantum Physics and the Philosophy of Whitehead," in Max Black (editor), *Philosophy in America* (Ithica, N.Y.: Cornell University Press 1965), 256-257, criticized the lack of empirical precision in Whitehead's philosophy and suggested regarding actual entities as quanta of a generalizable "field of feeling."

62. CN 163.

6.

Whitehead's Cosmology as Revisable Metaphysics

Hans Poser

Our metaphysical knowledge is slight, superficial, incomplete. Thus errors creep in. But, such as it is, metaphysical understanding guides imagination and justifies purpose. Apart from metaphysical presupposition there can be no civilization.

AI 164

Introduction

Cosmology, as Whitehead defines it, "is the effort to frame a scheme of the general character of the present stage of the universe."[1] It presupposes the particular sciences, yet, it is not a unified science as that enterprise was conceived by logical positivism, nor is cosmology the sum of the particular sciences. Whitehead's conception of cosmology is also far removed from that of contemporary physicists with their theories of the big bang, steady state or the pulsating universe. All such extrapolations, which remain within the domain of physics, are a part—but correctly understood, a negligible part—of a much more comprehensive system, a system that assigns a particular place to "God, the world, the human soul, indeed everything," to speak with the full title of Christian Wolff's *German Metaphysics*. In *Process and Reality*, Whitehead even identifies cosmology with what he terms speculative philosophy, which he defines as "the endeavour to frame a coherent, logical, necessary system of general ideas in terms of which every element of our experience can be interpreted."[2] Such a cosmology is intended to accomplish what in Wolff's view was the task of metaphysics. Its statements are not part of the empirical sciences, but are metaphysical.[3] I call 'metaphysical' such statements whose truth or falsity cannot be decided on formal grounds, and which cannot be verified by experience, but which nevertheless have the world as their object.

The definition of cosmology as a part of metaphysics, yet as retaining a relationship with the particular sciences, already implies an indication of the levels on which we have to tackle the question of the epistemological status of such reflections, namely the level of metaphysics and the level of the common foundation of all empirical sciences. They are interdependent in the following sense: Rationalist thought, on the one hand, sees the foundation of the unity of the empirical sciences in metaphysical principles, which in their absoluteness are the foundation of all knowledge, while empirical tradition, on the other hand, criticizes such metaphysics as meaningless and refers to experience and its exclusively formal treatment as the foundation of all scientific knowledge. Now, Whitehead's cosmology requires a theory that encompasses the empirical sciences, and also demands an answer to the question of the foundation of such a universal theory. This is the subject of the following inquiry. The aim in this undertaking is not merely to describe Whitehead's metaphysics *qua* cosmology, but to attempt an explication of the preconditions of a metaphysics that is non-absolute (because it depends on empirical science). Whitehead's argumentation provides the starting point and background for our inquiry, but central issues of the contemporary discussion about the sciences, from Carnap to Popper and Kuhn, will also have to be considered. The most suitable point of departure is empiricism's criticism of metaphysics, for if this criticism can be shown to apply, then a cosmology such as the one postulated and developed by Whitehead could only be conceived as an empirical, and not as a metaphysical theory. This will be followed by a discussion of the rationalist (op)position, which in turn will allow for an elaboration of the notion of a revisable metaphysics and of cosmology in continuation of Whitehead's thought.

Is Metaphysics Meaningless?

Contrary to Kant's caricature of metaphysics, the old matron who once wept like Hecuba now enjoys a nostalgic popularity. 'Metaphysics today' is no longer a taboo subject, and Whitehead is not the only thinker to have profited from a revival. But how is that possible? Were metaphysical systems not until recently considered by Rudolf Carnap and Franz Kröner, for example, not only as dated, but also as meaningless and anarchic deliberations?[4] Has not linguistic analysis revealed once and for all that confusion over language games is the only source of the illusory problems of metaphysics, so that any serious attention to them almost attests to a deplorable incapacity for analytical thought? After all, philosophy of science is often considered as the successor of ontology and philosophy of nature, which is free from metaphysical confusion. And 'ethics without metaphysics' has also been recommended. Only out of an obligation to critical reason, Hans Albert proposed,[5] metaphysics may still be permitted in the form of refutable theories. Could this be another instance where we have followed our inclination to look for the answer in the wrong place? Is it possible that we do not only have an obligation to myth, as Odo Marquard claims,[6] but also to metaphysics?

Kant described metaphysics as the battleground of endless strife, as the domain of questions that reason poses for us but we nevertheless are incapable of answering. Now the critics of metaphysics, from Hume to Carnap, and from Bayle and Comte to Popper and Topitsch, have not only always insisted upon the meaninglessness of the answers; from this, they also concluded the meaninglessness of the questions and proposed categories for their replacement. Each renaissance of metaphysics, however, rests upon the fact that these categories have proved to be too narrow. This is the point of departure for the contemporary interest in metaphysics and cosmology, and this is what legitimizes a discussion of Whitehead and his philosophy of nature.

In support of this argument, it is not only necessary to indicate those questions where the philosophy of science has trespassed its boundaries, but, further, to demonstrate that this step was inevitable for epistemological reasons. In other words, we have to show that the claim that metaphysics is meaningless—in whatever form it may be proposed—does not in fact destroy metaphysical thought, but on the contrary presupposes it. These two themes will be combined in what follows, for the intention here is not to reopen the discussion about the criterion of meaning, but to develop a new approach through which the metaphysical system is itself conceived as open to revision.

The Escape from Empiricism

Consistent with the increased intensity of skepticism from Bacon to Locke and Berkeley, the basic principle of Hume's *Treatise* announces clearly what was to become the unquestioned foundation of the philosophy of science in logical positivism. Our intellectual representations are only images of sense impressions. These sense impressions have an atomic structure in the form of the simple impressions, which are the basis of simple ideas.[7] Consequently, the only firm foundation of all the sciences is "direct observation."[8] So it is no surprise that the empirical sciences became the example of all positive scientific thought and that later logical positivism, which adopted Hume's program, understood the unitary knowledge sought by unified science as a program of physicalistic reduction. Conversely, metaphysical statements are meaningless and therefore unscientific, as Carnap put it, because in the first place there is no criterion of their truth; that is to say, no one can ever decide whether they are true. If the meaning of a statement lies in the method by which it can be verified (that is to say, we only know what a proposition means when we know how to verify it), any statements that can be tested neither formally nor by experience must be meaningless. This is the *verification principle*. In the second place, the positivists argued that metaphysical statements are meaningless for the mere reason that already metaphysical concepts cannot be attributed any meaning inasmuch as they cannot be reduced to something given in experience. This is the *principle of reduction*. So Whitehead can sum up positivism accurately by saying that it offers "no starting point for speculations that transcend the domain of immediate observation."[9]

The empirical criterion of meaning with the two principles just mentioned rests on three decisive philosophic presuppositions: First, on its own account, reason is unable to provide any content in relation to reality and disposes only of a formal ability to combine that has been provided by logic. Second, the concept of truth depends on correspondence theory so that the notion of meaning of a sign and of a statement must be consistent with that theory. Third, all the facts or states of affairs that are observed can be understood in themselves, in isolation from everything else and without any previous theoretical assumptions.

As it is reflected in its criterion of meaning, the empiricist approach also implies that science progresses cumulatively on the basis of inductive generalizations. Such a conception of science has not been immune to criticism. For example, Whitehead mocked Bacon's inductive method, which "if consistently pursued, would have left science where it found it."[10] The difficulty is that the principle of induction cannot itself be demonstrated, so that there can be no verification of natural law. Moreover, the principle of reduction cannot be fulfilled in the case of dispositional predicates (and therewith in the case of any of the material constants of physics). The very concepts that are supposed to provide content for physical theory, it follows, do not satisfy the criterion of meaning. Not even the epistemological lapse into physicalism, by which Carnap attempted to avoid the issue, resolves the problem of meaning. It merely attempts to eliminate the difficulty in a dogmatic way, simply by postulating that there are manifest characteristics that precede the simple impressions. This postulate is nothing but a variation on the third presupposition of the empirical criterion of meaning mentioned above. In opposition to this, and in defense against Bacon, Whitehead insists that "there are no brute, self-contained matters of fact, capable of being understood apart from interpretation as an element in a system."[11] We will see how he avoids this difficulty by transforming the concept of the actual entity into a fundamental ontological concept.

The same refutation of the possibility to isolate observations from theories led Popper in his criticism of Carnap to substitute his falsification principle for the principle of meaning. Initially, Carnap replaced the principle of reduction with his principle of translation, which he watered down in the course of the discussion to his theory of reductive propositions and to an emphasis of the difference between observational and theoretical language. But this was not the end of the matter. In place of cumulative scientific progress, Popper institutes progress in the knowledge of how nature is *not*, knowledge, that is, of what we perceive as false on the basis of observations. In this regard, Popper stands in the empirical tradition. He was by no means inclined to embellish his borrowings from rationalism with elements from the false prophets of metaphysics. Historians of science and paradigmatists from Kuhn to Laudan were brought up in arms by this; they set out to show that despite all their indisputable successes, scientists have never been falsificationists, but—if anything—that they employed auxiliary hypotheses in order to make repairs to theories in the course of normal science. Even Feyerabend's philippic tirade against 'proper' empiricism proceeds on the assumption that it is *empirical* success or failure that decides the suitability of hypotheses, whether or not they are achieved inductively. It is of great importance, however, to note what has emerged in the course of this development, namely, that it is not observation that provides the sole foundation of all the empirical sciences. As Schelling saw clearly when he joined the rationalist's chorus in mocking unreflective empiricism (sad to say, in his *Journal of Speculative Physics*), "Experience would be excellent, if only we could make out what it really says. This can only be achieved through theory." And, "Whoever does not have a correct theory cannot possibly have correct experience . . . Facts in themselves are nothing." Indeed they "*appear* to one who grasps them with concepts quite differently than they do to whomever glances at them without such concepts."[12] Schelling may well have taken this insight from Spinoza, who argued against Boyle in exactly the same way. Whitehead came to the same conclusion. The claim that science is "a description of observation together with the intervention of a mere formula" is a "magical incantation."[13] Of course, "theories are based on fact," but "conversely every ascertainment of fact is shot through and through with theoretical interpretation."[14] This requires a logical scheme or a system of thought to supply the "fundamental concepts or categories," which allow for the classification and interpretation of the observation.[15]

This insight, characteristic of rationalism, that every observation and every experiment is guided by theory, is one of the focal points of the Popperian methodology, and has meanwhile become common stock in the theory of science, where it appears either as 'Kuhn's paradigm' or as 'Lakatos's research program' or as 'Laudan's tradition of research'. The availability of a scheme of order is the essential prerequisite, first and foremost, for the identification and establishment of the facts, and then also for the classification and structuring of the phenomena and their assignment to a particular context. As a system of thought, however, the ordering scheme cannot be derived from experience. To the contrary, all experience presupposes the scheme. Thus it is *a priori*, and since it is not analytic it must be synthetic. Now, in contrast to the *demonstrationes more geometrico* offered by Descartes and Spinoza, contrary to Kant's transcendental reflections concerning the metaphysical foundations of science, and in opposition to Fichte's claim that the principles proposed by the doctrine of science are absolute truths, this conceptual scheme is anything but absolute or self-evident. Indeed, according to the historians of science, this scheme is changeable and is thus a *relative apriori*. Most important, the ordering scheme is not subject to the correspondence theory of truth. The attitude that 'anything goes' is certainly an exaggeration, but, on the other hand, alternatives for the formulation of hypotheses or the conceptions of theories are available (and not only as theories by scientific outsiders, as Goethe's theory of color or Schelling's speculative physics had been in their day). The choice between them is not much helped by a principle of economy in line with Avenarius, or by a pragmatic orientation towards utility because the *practical* utility of classical mechanics, for example, is still greater than that of relativistic mechanics. It is therefore necessary to recur to the notion of *theoretical* utility, which can pertain only to the present stage of science, and which, second and more important, presupposes a normative evaluation and decision of whatever is considered to be the knowledge of wider scope. This is how the philosophy of science had to pass through the history of science in its search for the foundations of the empirical sciences outside the realm where the meaningful is restricted to whatever can be reduced to observation. The surmounting of empiricism has become inevitable.

The Rationalistic Claim that Metaphysics is Indispensable

The Popper-Kuhn-Feyerabend paradigm, which accepts a change of a theoretical stance only on the ground of contradictory experience, is unable to accommodate the characteristics of the debate between Leibniz and Newton: namely their discussion not about the formulae of physics, but solely about the understanding of these formulae, about the nature of space and time, about whether laws of action at a distance can be admitted once the law of sufficient reason is conceded, a discussion where, as Whitehead put it, each accused the other of "the error ... of mistaking the abstract for the concrete."[16] We have to acknowledge that this is a debate about nonempirical problems, about problems of the formulation of fundamental concepts and principles, in short, about problems concerned with schemes of thought. A theoretical discussion of these conceptual frameworks invoked in order to structure actuality goes, then as well as now, beyond the empirical sciences and the philosophy of science. This is an old theme of rationalistic thought that is relevant to recall again. Indeed, this was the systematic reason for undertaking an excursion into the history of philosophy in the preceding section, and that purpose mirrors Whitehead's in his discussion of the development from Descartes via Leibniz to Kant.

While empiricism proceeds from atomic units of observation, the rationalistic tradition proceeds from a conceptual atomism of absolute, simple concepts thought to be innate, the content of which is apprehended in an act of intuition. The argument in support of the existence of the absolute, simple concepts is in its form identical with the empiricists' argument for simple impressions, and to that of Wittgenstein for elementary propositions: since there are composite concepts, there also must be simple ones to provide us with the content. Otherwise, there would be an infinite regress, and it would be impossible to think anything substantive. Rationalism, just as empiricism (and particularly Carnap in *The Logical Structure of the World*) formally maintains that each concept of our thought is either a simple concept or can be generated by the combination of simple concepts. As an unadulterated coherence theory, Leibniz's analytical theory of truth with its universal characteristic and complete alphabet of thought was the result of a consequent and logical development of this line of thought. The individual substance belonging to one particular of all possible worlds is characterized by the complete concept of all its attributes. (We will not discuss here the ontological transformation, namely the fact that this substance is conceived of as an organism, which is determined only by its perceptions and their inner dynamics. The similarities with Whitehead are so overwhelming that Whitehead's endeavor can be read as a new monadology.)

Just as the empirical undertaking fails in the attempt to ascend from mere impressions to theories, classical rationalism encounters severe difficulties with individuation, with the transition from the content of pure thought to the filthy details of the empirical. It is completely irrelevant, Descartes insists in the *Principles*, that his laws of motion do not conform to experience; after all, they cannot be false because they arise from thought. (It should be remembered that Galileo had high praise for Copernicus for having disregarded mere appearance, and that Newton paid heed to all that when he described the force-free homogeneous motion of a center of gravity, both of which never really exist, as being the fundamental form of motion.) For Descartes, the reduction of all the properties of the *res extensa* to extension is a reduction of material properties to geometry and therewith to mathematics; for one of Descartes' great mathematical accomplishments is his analytic rendering of geometry. The book of nature is written in numbers and is thus rational and accessible to knowledge. Whitehead was right in interpreting Descartes' understanding of natural law as that of laws imposed by God on nature (which is certainly true for Leibniz), at least insofar as God had freely established mathematics as it is and thereby also established the laws of nature.[17] This interpretation is fully consistent with the thrust of our argument, namely the insight that the laws of nature and our knowledge of them are removed from experience and observation. Descartes resorts to explaining the quagmire constituted by the empirical world and its deviations from the ideal by invoking subordinate hypotheses about the relevant mixtures of matter. This, however, requires a further criterion of truth, which allows for the assessment of the correspondence between phenomenal matters of fact and statements of fact, so that *truths of matters of fact* can be talked about in more than a merely formal way. Hence, not even classical rationalist epistemology with its differentiation of confused cognition, clear and distinct knowledge, and evident or adequate apprehension is sufficient to overcome the fundamental difficulty of explaining what connection there is between experience and theory.

The problem is more difficult still when we come to Kant, who incorporated the Cartesian and the Leibnizean pattern into what he called the forms of intuition and the forms of thought, and who substituted the categories as forms of thought for the Cartesian *prima possibilia* as innate ideas, thereby achieving a first synthesis of empirical and rationalist understanding. Even if the constitution of objects can be achieved by these forms in terms of the conditions of possible experience, problems arise in explaining how there can ever be any deviations. How, for example, can an actual wheel deviate from an ideal circle, or a real fall differ from what the law of acceleration prescribes? Leibniz's model is more flexible in this regard since for him every deviation from the seemingly ideal law is still lawful. As finite creatures, we can only ever gain a limited or perhaps, under the best of circumstances, a symbolic knowledge (i.e. a finite representation of something infinite) of the infinitely complex matters of fact that we are confronted with in the empirical world. This symbolic knowledge cannot rest upon an absolute, divine alphabet of thought. Instead, it has to rely on concepts provided by the present state of knowledge, in other words, on concepts of the alphabet of human thought. The formulation and alteration of hypotheses is thus possible for Leibniz, since hypotheses depend upon those concepts which are employed in the sciences at a given moment as relative basic concepts. History is thus accommodated in the theoretical interpretation of the process of knowledge. It follows that, in principle, *hypotheses* are *subject to revision*. This result at the same time poses another problem: While for the absolutely simple concepts immediate apprehension of their content was required, this cannot apply to the relatively simple concepts. For if they were absolutely evident, and so atemporal, their revision would not only be superfluous, but impossible.

In addition to its acceptance of fundamental concepts, rationalistic thought is characterized by a second element, which was also absorbed in Kant's transcendental philosophy: no law of nature can be formulated without the presupposition of some definite *universal principles*. For Leibniz, for example, these were the law of sufficient reason, the principle that change is continuous, and the principles of the conservation of living force and of the identity of complete cause and total effect. Such principles made possible what Whitehead regarded as the special achievement of rationalism and yet at the same time expressed reservations about, i.e. an integrated interpretation of nature[18] — which was something Newton had to dispense with. For Leibniz, these principles are contingent, because they are not principles of logic (in Kant's terminology, they are synthetic principles). Yet, they are not *a posteriori*, but inasmuch as they are the conditions of the possibility of any definite empirical knowledge, they are *a priori*. God might have chosen other principles, but at the cost of rendering the world chaotic. Ultimately, we thus encounter in Leibniz a distinctly metaphysical foundation for the possibility of synthetic empirical knowledge. Kant endeavored to secularize, so to speak, this metaphysical foundation and to ground it exclusively in the conditions of human cognition. His result was an *a priori* formula of the forms of thought and intuition. These forms can only be what and as they are, whereas Leibniz always admitted that it was theoretically possible for God to promulgate other laws of nature and other principles (except for those of identity and contradiction). True as the interpretation of natural knowledge is that regards it as grounded in the conditions of the possibility of knowledge (where those conditions are not subject to empirical inspection), and as important as rationalism's insight is that the indispensable achievement of ordering and structuring must be accomplished by cognitive reason through a conceptual system, it is still true that the renewed dogmatism of transcendental philosophy, which arises from the fact that such schemes are immutable in the sense of a basic equipment of the transcendental subject, is highly restrictive.

So rationalism has stumbled into a dead end similar to the one where empiricism is trapped by its effort to ground scientific knowledge on experience alone. Just as it is impossible for empiricism to formulate theories by means of experience alone, it is equally difficult for rationalism to harmonize its absolute principles with the changes in the sciences, and with the multiplicity of conceptual schemes encountered in science. In either case, the relation to reality is lost. A cosmology in the sense intended by Whitehead cannot call to its support neither empiricist nor rationalistic epistemology.[19] Contrary to empiricism, such a cosmology insists on the indisputable primacy of the conceptual scheme by which actuality is conceptualized. In contrast to rationalism, it insists upon the openness of the relevant basic principles and the possibility of their revision. If so, it is a sensible project to carry the notion of hypothesis familiar to the empirical sciences over into metaphysics and to sketch out a revisable metaphysics.

The Concept of a Revisable Metaphysics

Although we have so far followed Whitehead's direction and only expanded in the light of the contemporary discussion what he said, mainly in *Adventures of Ideas*, about the relation between rationalism and empiricism, we now need to distance ourselves from him for the following reason: In the course of his analysis, Whitehead develops two positions that are at first incompatible. On the one hand, he insists that "positivistic doctrine" with its emphasis on the "purely descriptive character" of laws of nature "without a doubt . . . contains a fundamental truth about scientific methodology";[20] but, on the other hand, he stresses the absolute necessity of a 'conceptual scheme'. As he has it, the tension between these two tendencies, through "the urge towards explanatory description" of the world, gives rise to "the interplay between science and metaphysics"[21] and thereby introduces the notion of a metaphysics that can be revised by science. Whitehead proceeds to a certain extent inductively: Instead of presupposing absolute principles and then working deductively from them, he turns to the available empirical sciences and uncovers their necessary presuppositions. So far, his procedure is a methodological guideline for what will follow. He hopes (and this is the main difference) that the development of the contrast and of the coalition of the particular sciences and metaphysics not only follows a particular direction, but he also anticipates that "there is a gradual approach to ideas of clarity and generality. In this way mankind stumbles on in its task of understanding the world."[22] Within Whitehead's cosmology, this goal is tied directly to his concept of God.[23] But we shall not concern ourselves here with the assumption of a converging approach and the far-reaching preconditions it entails. We shall rather undertake to discuss from a Kantian point of view the conditions of the possibility of a metaphysics that can be subject to revision.

Now, to describe metaphysics as revisable may appear a contradiction in terms. It has traditionally been the task of metaphysics to portray what is immutable, certain, and ultimate. To argue historically, the response can only be that not only metaphysical approaches and systems have been revised as a result of the author's own criticism or that of others; moreover, Leibniz, for example, described his *Monadology* as a 'hypothesis' that, although it could not ultimately be proved, was nevertheless able, he thought, to provide coherent answers to all the central and open questions of the philosophy of his time.[24]

This is the place to discuss the systematic reason for the impossibility of granting metaphysical propositions an absolute justification. No proof of absolute principles is possible, because that proof itself would have to be based upon other, even more absolute principles. Accordingly, a justification of these principles can only be undertaken from within, that is to say from an examination of the presuppositions and conditions that make the relevant positions possible. That with this procedure one has actually arrived at the ultimate and absolute elements could then only be explained, first, by demonstrating the clarity and singularity of all the principles thus attained (which Descartes made a central point of his method), and second, by showing that all possible knowledge can be derived from these principles, thus asserting that these principles are complete (which is what Fichte explicitly suggested as the procedure of demonstration in his theory of science in 1795). The former is impossible, since no universal criterion of clarity can be established (because this would involve clarity and would thus lead around in a circle). The latter is unattainable because the starting point always has to be the relevant stage of knowledge at a given time.

Even if there were such absolute principles, we could not know we possessed them, even if we really *did* possess them. In a similar way, Gorgias has reprimanded the philosophers.

The insight into this problem is what constitutes the difference between the claims made by Whitehead on the one hand, and by Descartes and Fichte on the other. Whitehead calls upon similar arguments in the preface to *Process and Reality* for drafting his sketch of a conceptual scheme: "At the end, insofar as the enterprise has been successful, there should be no problem of space-time, or of epistemology, or of causality, left over for discussion. The scheme should have developed all those generic notions adequate for the expression of any possible interconnection of things."[25] A little later, he proposes as the criterion for the success of his cosmology its "adequacy in the comprehension of the variety of experience within the limits of *one* scheme of ideas."[26] This criterion can, of course, only be applied to experiences in any one given historical time. If so, the scheme itself is subjected to alteration.

In the light of similar considerations, Stephan Körner developed the notion of metaphysics as revisable.[27] His basic line of thought, which can also be exploited for our understanding of Whitehead, is that the apparent absolute claim of metaphysical systems arises from their *internal* irrefutability. The irrefutability is internal inasmuch as the systems are constructed so that immunity against criticism is ascertained, in such a way that whatever might seem a contrary instance is either reinterpreted, and then laid claim to, or else it is rejected as somehow not really existing. (Topitsch is a master at unmasking these techniques.)[28] None of that excludes *external* criticism, which leads to an alteration of the fundamental positions, and this is what Körner builds on. The task of metaphysical systems is then to assist our intellectual orientation by creating a formal unity of the fundamental convictions that dominate at a given time without ever claiming to reveal the truth. As a result, metaphysical systems allow us to integrate whatever we accept as true (for example the results of the natural sciences) into a world view. This notion of metaphysics is largely identical with Ayer's concept of metaphysics as a "secondary system" erected on top of the primary systems of the sciences.[29] An external criticism of such a system is possible only when the fundamental assumptions of the world view, which are the source of the unifying conception, are challenged. This is exactly what happens when, for example, a program of physicalistic reduction is rejected in favor of an organic thesis or when the coexistence of both views as equally well-justified is declared (as it is by Leibniz and Whitehead). If this is so, it must still be asked whether this understanding of metaphysics is apt to accommodate Whitehead's intentions.

This question must be addressed before the concept of a revisable metaphysics can be developed further.

Whitehead's understanding of metaphysics is expressed in two fundamental and seemingly contradictory assumptions. The first maintains that philosophy can never hope to procure a formulation of the first principles of metaphysics, which is ultimately valid;[30] the second claims that none of these first principles is in itself unknowable.[31] From this he infers that the progress of philosophy can only consist in "an asymptotic approach to a scheme of principles, only definable in terms of the ideal which they should satisfy."[32] In this context, he does not pay heed to the problem that the value of any approximation can never be established because the ideal required by such a procedure cannot be appropriated from direct insight into the principles. (Whitehead can take no more refuge in immediate insights or "intrinsic reasonableness" as the last instance of justification than could those he reproached for having done so.)[33] The problems he sees are the obstacle of the limitations of language (which is why he rejected any treatment of philosophic questions that proceeds from ordinary language), and problems that belong to the empirical component of philosophy. Once Whitehead's assumption is accepted that the empirical sciences can exert an influence on metaphysics, then theories in the empirical sciences have immediate consequences for the metaphysical theories based on them. Any problems with the formulation of theories in the empirical sciences give rise to problems with the formulation of metaphysical theories. In particular, the hypothetical character of empirical generalizations is transferred to the metaphysical propositions they support. Just as "the special sciences fall short of their aim ... [speculative] cosmology equally fails" as a metaphysics.[34] That the hypotheses of empirical science are then conceived as stages on the path by which the truth is approached may be admitted as a regulative idea. However, since the only criterion of the success of such theories, or of the success of the metaphysical hypotheses they support, is "the applicability of its results beyond the restricted locus from which it originated"[35] as far as the aesthetic and religious domains, the introduction of a regulative idea cannot serve the function to justify truth. The motor that propels theoretical development is rather the "method of imaginative rationalization." This method involves the formulation of systems of thought that both ignite the imagination and delimit what can be accepted as rationalization. Far from being definite, both undergo in Whitehead's view that development which constitutes the adventure of ideas. The metaphysics that results is part of the process, and is therefore never completed but always open to criticism, correction, and further development. The concept of metaphysics as subject to revision does not contradict Whitehead's understanding of metaphysics (such a contradiction could only arise if revisability was confounded with arbitrariness), but in fact corresponds exactly to the hypothetical character Whitehead ascribes to metaphysics. Indeed he explicitly describes the expressions by which speculative philosophy seeks to unify and harmonize the diverse expressions of human experience, as "working hypothesis."[36]

Let us now return to Körner. He enumerates the conditions such a system of metaphysical hypotheses must satisfy. A system of this type has to provide a *categorial framework* within which *categorization* determines what *objects* (either particular things or attributes) are, when they are dependent and when independent, what the ultimate genera of a category of independent particular things are (*constitutive principle*), and, finally, what the individualizing attributes are (*principle of individuation*). It could easily be demonstrated that Whitehead's cosmology does in fact make such determinations, even though it is an event ontology and not a substance ontology. Our concern here is not Whitehead's ontology but its epistemological framework.[37]

Whitehead, too, lists a number of conditions that a cosmology in the sense of his definition cited at the outset must satisfy. Before all, it must be *adequate*. This means, first, that it should not impose any restrictions upon the fundamental concepts of any science, second, it should not have the tendency to 'explain away' whatever is inconsistent with it, and third, "its business is not to refuse experience but to find the most general interpretative system."[38] The principle of adequacy, then, includes the *applicability* of the suggested interpretative system to the content of experience.[39] Together, the conditions of adequacy and applicability constitute the *empirical aspect* of cosmology and at the same time illustrate the obligation toward the historical state of knowledge at a given time. For, as Whitehead insists, "a general idea occurs in history in special forms determined by peculiar circumstance of race and of stage of civilization."[40] Whitehead's additional requirement of *coherence* "means that the fundamental ideas, in terms of which the scheme is developed, presuppose each other so that in isolation they are meaningless." By means of explanation, Whitehead points out the presupposition that "no entity can be conceived in complete abstraction from the system of the universe."[41] Furthermore, the system must be *logical* which means, first, that it must be free from contradiction and, second, that "logical notions must themselves find their places in the scheme of philosophic notions."[42] These two conditions of coherence and logical consistency represent the *rational aspect* of cosmology. They thus make evident theclaimtoovercomethedichotomybetweenempiricismandrationalism.

We now have to discuss how far these conditions are compatible with one another from an epistemological point of view since we have seen that the rationalist and the empiricist positions exclude one another, but individually are too limited in scope. What is required here is an epistemological model, such as the one Kant offered, which permits a synthesis of both sources of knowledge without ascribing whatsoever absolute character to either of the two sides. Whitehead achieves this by expanding his methodological reflection in two directions. On the empirical side, he completes the unsatisfactory theory of *simple impressions*, stretching it *below* as it were, by taking over the Leibnizean non-conscious perceptions of the monads as his theory of *prehensions*.[43] On the other side, he busts the bonds of transcendental philosophy by introducing the concept of a 'system of thought'. He is now confronted with the difficulty of justifying and explaining this concept of a 'logical scheme' (as he calls it) in a way that allows him on the one hand, to attribute the ordering function characteristic of Kuhn's paradigms to it, and, on the other, to conceive of it as originating in reason without succumbing to dogmatism or to the pretense of absolute certainty.

To my mind, a solution can only be found if one understands the proposition of such a system of thought as a *creative production of speculative reason*. Only when spontaneity of reason is understood as not only referring to the faculty of producing representations *qua* concepts, but also to produce creatively what Kant called 'forms of thought', can a foundation for such an effort be laid.

The suggestion that Whitehead's fundamental concept of creativity be combined with another one, namely that of speculative reason, may initially appear strange. It could be argued that as principle of novelty, creativity is related to facts, to actual events, while according to common thought, reason should be distinct from fact. Whitehead, however, establishes just such a connection in the ontological principle: "No actual entity, then no reason."[44] Furthermore, he insists that "the production of a scheme is a major effort of the speculative reason."[45] Also, he describes the method of "philosophic generalization" as "the divination of the generic notions which apply to all facts."[46] But more than this is at stake, and an example may clarify what is involved. The fact that Gödel's procedure and the procedure of transfinite induction are accepted methods of mathematical proof is not itself subject to further demonstration, but is founded only on the decision either to permit or to reject them. As procedures of demonstration, they are the products of the free creative power of the human mind and cannot be deduced from absolute and evident conditions. The same is true for the axioms of modal calculus, for example (or, to chose a provocative example of a completely different kind, for the rules of chess). The idea that these examples illustrate at least to some extent Whitehead's fundamental position is confirmed by his statement that "mathematics has developed, especially in recent years, by a speculative interest in types of order, without any determination of particular entities illustrative of these types."[47]

Now if we focus on Kant's deduction of the forms of thought from the forms of judgement, it becomes clear that these same, presupposed forms of judgement cannot be derived from a *single* (Aristotelian) logic, which is considered to be unalterable. Instead, there is a multiplicity of formal languages, some of which are mutually exclusive. So far as their formal structure is concerned, each of these languages is a suitable candidate to justify the systems of thought in question. According to the discussion about the foundation of mathematics, they cannot be traced back to a more fundamental or absolute basis (if not at the price of prohibiting 'undesired' formal languages, that is, at the price of a previous normative decision about what is admissible in logic). Formally speaking, their ultimate ground is the free creative power of the human mind. Already Heyting appealed to this power, while at the same time severely limiting its range. In his constructionism the limitation is expressed as the requirement that all creative intellectual power be tied to some procedure of construction. This limitation must be superseded by a condition tied only to the *communicability* of relevant formal and constitutive rules. This assumption guarantees the communicability, at a later stage, of the system of thought, and thereby the communicability condition of the empirical criterion of meaning is met. On the other hand, the verification principle of the criterion of meaning becomes pointless because even in systems of logic it cannot be fulfilled in an absolute manner. It makes no sense, for example, to speak of the absolute truth of the propositions in modal logic. Such truth is only relative to the axioms, or systems of axioms, that have been accepted, which means that a coherence theory of truth is applied.

The approach suggested here avoids—as Kant has done—innate ideas in favor of innate powers, but at the same time, it ensures the possibility to fulfill the conditions of coherence and logical consistency for a system of thought built on it. Indeed, this approach enables us to understand Whitehead's synonymous use of 'system of thought' and 'logical scheme'. Similarly, it avoids a hasty way of superseding empiricism or rationalism by an evolutionary or a historical interpretation of the 'systems of thought'. What is to be avoided in this context is immunization by ignorance, namely by ignoring the integrating achievement of creative, speculative reason.

Against all this, it could be argued that the extension of the concept of formal languages that we have suggested is besides the issue.

After all, Whitehead's great achievement in the field of logicism had been the development of an extensional logic and the foundation of mathematics. One could, however, point out that the Whitehead of *Adventures of Ideas* is quite different from the Whitehead of *Principia Mathematica*, that research into the foundations of mathematics has advanced considerably since 1910, and that our proposed approach only follows Whitehead's conviction that the present state of knowledge is the only possible starting point. But what is more, our approach is also justified *immanently*: a condition for cosmology, which we have not yet discussed, is that the system must be *necessary*, in the sense of a guarantee that the scheme of thought can be *universally* applied to all kinds of experience, including ethical or religious experience,[48] and hence that it must be necessary in the sense of portraying an essence of the universe. Yet, the mere description of something as an essence already requires a scheme of modal logic and hence the departure from a purely extensional logic.

The outline of a revisable metaphysics, which we have presented here, is drafted along the lines of Kant's critique of reason because he interprets systems of thought as (relative) *a priori* conditions of knowledge and its objects. In the light of Whitehead's pronounced rejection of Kant, one might be tempted to regard such an endeavour as defective from the very outset, if it claims to be a further development of Whitehead's metaphysics. After all, Whitehead includes "the Kantian doctrine of the objective world as a theoretical construct from purely subjective experience" in the list of "prevalent habits of thought"[49] that must be repudiated. He also does not cease to emphasize that it is precisely not the task of philosophy to explain the emergence of concrete matters of fact from universals.[50] Neither objection affects what is suggested here, because Whitehead's criticism of Kant is directed mainly against the dogmatic claim to be able to discover, or to have actually discovered, the *a priori* conditions of knowledge. Such dogmatism has now lost its foundation because it has been established that it is possible for categoreal schemes to change. The second objection is also invalid because Whitehead continues this passage by saying that: "The definiteness of fact is due to its forms; but the individual fact is a creature, and creativity is the ultimate behind all forms, inexplicable by forms, and conditioned by its creatures."[51] It is particularly this element of creativity that has been assigned its systematic place in the approach we suggested.

Our approach is also able to avoid all three manifestations of what Reiner Wiehl describes as the 'dogma of criticism'.[52] It neither guarantees nor requires the unity of the concepts of knowledge in the sense that they ought to be derived from a single principle. The ultimate concepts cannot be achieved through a critique of pure reason involving transcendental reflection or deduction; they can only be understood as relative conceptual forms. This brings up the epistemological problem of how complete relativity is to be avoided and how the approach to truth advocated by Whitehead could possibly evolve. This problem can be solved, on the one hand, by pointing out that every system of thought responds to a problematic situation in a given hissolved if reason turns to practical matters, i.e. if speculative reason is complemented by Odyssean reason, which, by trial and error, raises short-term expectations and is thereby able to evaluate the suitability of the proposed systems for this or that relative purpose. The problem has thus shifted to a question of the purposes and these are, in Whitehead's view, relatively constant (which may itself be questionable). For Whitehead, the epistemological problem of how to overcome empiricism and rationalism leads away from pure epistemology and into practical philosophy.

Conclusion

A more thorough presentation of these reflections would require a fundamental analysis of the critical application of reason. In this place, however, our aim has merely been to outline a mode of thought that achieves the combination of the conceptual heritage of empiricism with the insights of rationalism into a metaphysics that is subject to revision. This metaphysics as cosmology should be flexible enough to do justice to Whitehead's (apparently unfulfillable) demand that all the conceptions of empirical science must be interpreted. This remains true despite the failure of the Unified Science Movement and despite the bad experiences of sciences that have been metaphysically restricted by the prescriptions of Critical Theory or the clumsy applications of Critical Rationalism in the social sciences. Formal systems can be devised to branch out in such a way that certain parts (as for example Euclidian and non-Euclidian geometry) can be interpreted as branches of a common theory (in our example, of absolute geometry) despite their mutually contradictory statements. The empiricist and positivist requirement (which is impossible to meet) that there be a homogeneous basis of observation for all disciplines has been avoided in the same way as the rationalistic requirement of ultimate or basic unifying principles effective everywhere or, equally, the requirement that all principles be deducible. The idea of such a flexible and unifying power of speculative reason — which is not tied to the myoptic vision of Odyssean reason — was certainly at the back of Whitehead's mind when he devised his metaphysics of nature, that is, his cosmology.

Notes

1. FR 76.

2. PR 3.

3. Cf. PR 4 where the fundamental principles of the universe, thus of cosmology, are described as "metaphysical."

4. Rudolf Carnap: "Überwindung der Metaphysik durch logische Analyse der Sprache" ("The Overthrow of Metaphysics by the Logical Analysis of Language") *Erkenntnis* 2 (1931-1932) 219-241; F. Kröner: *Die Anarchie der philosophischen Systeme* (*The Anarchy of Philosophical Systems*), (Leipzig: Meiner 1929).

5. *Traktat über kritische Vernunft* (*Essay on Critical Reason*) 2nd edition (Tübingen: J.C.B. Mohr 1969), 47-48.

6. Odo Marquard: *Lob des Polytheismus* (*In Praise of Polytheism*) in *Philosophie und Mythos* (*Philosophy and Myth*), H. Poser (editor) (Berlin: de Gruyter 1979); reprinted in O. Marquard: *Abschied vom Prinzipiellen* (*Departure from the Principles*) (Stuttgart: Reclam 1981).

7. *A Treatise of Human Nature*, I.I.1, ed. Selby-Bigge (London, 1888) 1-7. Whitehead emphasizes this connection between impressions and ideas (PR 131) and speaks of Hume's epistemological atomism. (AI 159).

8. Hume: *Treatise*, XVI.

9. AI 159.

10. PR 5.

11. PR 14.

12. "Einleitende Bemerkungen" and "Allgemeine Betrachtungen", in *Zeitschrift für speculative Physik*, I.2 (1800), 133 and 130 respectively. ("Introductory Notes" and "General Observations" in *Journal of Speculative Physics.*); *Werke* 4: 534 and 532; cf. *Werke* 5: 322.

13. FR 57.

14. AI 3.

15. FR 67-68. Whitehead speaks of a "logical scheme," "categorial notions," or "schemes of thoughts."

16. SMW 72; cf. PR 7.

17. AI 144-145.

18. AI 144.

19. Cf. PR 156.

20. AI 147 and 148.

21. AI 164.

22. FR 88 and 89.

23. The connection is apparent from the following doctrines of the philosophy of organism: "(i) The doctrine of God embodying a basic completeness of appetition, and (ii) the doctrine of each occasion effecting a concresence of the universe, including God. Then, by the Category of Conceptual Reproduction, the vector prehensions of God's appetition, and of other occassions, issue in the mental pole of conceptual prehensions. . . ." PR 316.

24. Cf. A. Heinekamp: "Die Rolle der Philosophiegeschichte in Leibniz' Denken" ("The Role of the History of Philosophy in Leibniz's Thought") in *Studia Leibnitiana* supplementary volume 10, 1982: *Leibniz als Geschichtsforscher (Leibniz as Historian)*, 114-141, 139.

25. PR XII.

26. PR XIV. Emphasis added.

27. Especially in his *Categorial Framework* (Oxford: Blackwell 1970).

28. For example, E. Topitsch: *Vom Ursprung und Ende der Metaphysik (On the Origin and End of Metaphysics)* (Vienna: Springer 1958); E. Topitsch: *Erkenntnis und Illusion (Knowledge and Illusion)* (second, revised edition Tübingen: J.C.B. Mohr 1988).

29. A.J. Ayer: *The Central Questions of Philosophy* (London: Morrow 1973).

30. Precisely because, ". . . there are an indefinite number of purely abstract sciences, with their laws, their regularities, and their complexities of theorems—all as yet undeveloped." (AI 177). Or, as he says a bit further on "We cannot produce that final adjustment of well-defined generalities which constitute a complete metaphysics. But we can produce a variety of partial systems of limited generality." (AI 185-186).

31. PR 4.

32. Ibid.

33. PR 39.

34. FR 86.

35. PR 5.

36. AI 286-287, cf. PR 8.

37. Whitehead justifies this in PR 20 ff, where he provides the ontological basis by interpreting actual entities and their *nexūs* in terms of their reciprocal perceptions in order to present them in the categorial scheme in following sections. For a discussion of the special problems of an event

ontology cf. G. Abel: "Einzelding- und Ereignis-Ontologie" ("Individual Entities and Event Ontology") in: H. Poser and H.-W. Schütt (editors) *Ontologie und Wissenschaft (Ontology and Science)* (Berlin: TUB-Dokumentation 1984), 21-50.

38. FR 86.

39. PR 3 and 5.

40. AI 5.

41. PR 3.

42. Ibid.

43. Cf. E. Wolf-Gazo's contribution to this volume pp. 21 above.

44. PR 19.

45. FR 71.

46. PR 5.

47. AI 173-174.

48. PR 3 and 4.

49. PR XIII.

50. PR 20.

51. Ibid.

52. Cf. Reiner Wiehl's contribution to this volume, pp. 127 below.

Part III

Cosmology and Anthropology

7.

What One Thinks: Singular Propositions and the Content of Judgements

Wolfgang Künne

When is whatever a person may think the same as what another person thinks or the same as what he himself thinks at a different time? This is the question I wish to explore here, the question of the identity of what is thought.

Two examples may indicate the kind of answer I am aiming at. The following sentence is ambiguous: (S1) *The night before the election, Jones thinks that he will win, and his opponent Smith thinks so too.* Now just *what* is it that Smith also thinks? Does (S1) mean that Smith "says in his heart" just as Jones does, 'I will win'? If so, both cannot have correctly thought what they thought. Or does the sentence mean that Smith says of his optimistic competitor, 'He will win'? In this case, Jones and Smith are either both right or both wrong. The ambiguity of (S1) reflects, I believe, different aspects that can guide us in determining what it is that a person thinks. Those who defend materialistic theory of thought would be well-advised to adhere to one of these aspects to the exclusion of the other, but I am anticipating the course of the argument.

I promised two examples. Here is the second one: A much debated question in the Middle Ages was whether the belief of the ancients, i.e. the Old Testament prophets, was the same as the belief of the moderns, as the Christians were then called. The prophets believed that the Messiah would appear (*Christum nasciturum esse*). Christians believe that he has already appeared (*Christum natum esse*).[1] The philosophical question I am concerned with is here entangled with a theological one, which the Jewish contemporaries of Aquinas would certainly have answered differently from Aquinas himself. So I will replace the example with another one: First Crito thinks, 'Socrates will die

tomorrow.' Two days later, he thinks, 'Socrates died yesterday.' Does he
think the same thing in both cases? My answer is a clear and confident
'Yes and No'.

In *Process and Reality*, Whitehead writes: "*The same proposition can
constitute the content of diverse judgements.*"[2] Here the term *proposition* is
used as had become customary in Cambridge at the turn of the century:
It does not anymore serve to designate a declarative sentence, a string
of words in some natural language or other, but to denote what is
thought in an act of judgement (and is expressed in a declarative sentence). If one defines a *state of affairs* as something that *might* be the
case, but perhaps is not, as distinguished from a *fact* as something that
actually *is* the case, then it is possible to interpret Whitehead's 'propositions' as 'states of affairs'. "In a proposition the logical subjects are
reduced to the status of food for a possibility. Their real role in actuality is abstracted from; they are no longer factors in fact."[3]

As Whitehead repeatedly emphasizes, not all "propositional feelings" have the "subjective form" of judgement.[4] For example, the shock
over a certain fact is a "propositional feeling", but it is not a judgement.
When a reader grasps the propositions expressed in Hamlet's mono-
logue, he does not necessarily concern himself with their truth values.
Indeed, the anonymous logicians, against whose unduly narrow use of
the category of proposition Whitehead is arguing in this connection,
should always have been aware that a proposition that *p* may be thought
without either accepting it as true or rejecting it as false: In order to
judge that *if p then q* or that *p or q*, one must of course be able to *think*
the simpler proposition that *p*; but one is by no means required to
judge that *p*. Frege and Russell made as clear a distinction as possible
between what they termed 'entertaining a proposition' ('*Fassen eines
Gedankens*') and 'judging' ('*Urteilen*'). I shall discuss the question about
the identity of what is thought with respect to acts of judgement and to
beliefs (i.e. those states that are either initiated or activated by these
acts). Of course our question is concerned with *all* propositional acts
and states (with *all* so-called propositional attitudes), regardless of the
subjective forms they may have.

According to Whitehead a *singular proposition* is the content of a
judgement expressed by a quantifier-free indexical sentence such as:
(S2) *This is spherical.* (S3) *This is smaller than that.* In characterizing
the structure of such propositions he follows Russell's example. If a
sentence contains a "logically proper name" such as the demonstrative
'this', then, Russell insists, what the demonstrative denotes in a given
context is a 'constituent' of the proposition expressed in this context.[5]
This corresponds to Whitehead's statement in the first chapter of *The
Concept of Nature* 1920: The object indicated by the demonstrative in a

sentence is a constituent of the proposition the sentence is intended to express. So when in a statement of (S2) we refer to the moon, the moon itself is a component of the proposition. Within the framework of the metaphysics of *Process and Reality*, the object indicated by a demonstrative is categoreally classified as an 'actual entity' (or a compound of such entities), or it is described as the 'logical subject' of the propositions expressed. A proposition of this sort "is a complex entity, with determinate actual entities among its components."[6] The other component of the proposition expressed in (S2) is the property of being spherical. Whitehead categoreally classifies this component as an 'eternal object', which he also describes as the proposition's 'logical predicate'. Owing to the categoreal heterogeneity of these components, the proposition is an "impure" or a "hybrid" entity.[7] Singular propositions are not themselves 'eternal objects'; they come into being and perish with the 'actual entities' that are their logical subjects.[8]

The category of singular propositions has gained new prominence in analytic philosophy over the last decade. Keith Donnellan regards it as the codification of the "natural pre-theoretical view" of what is expressed by an indexical sentence:

> What I see as the natural pre-theoretical view might be captured as a certain way of representing what proposition is expressed. If . . . Socrates were to say about himself, 'I am snub-nosed', the proposition expressed might be represented as an ordered pair consisting of Socrates . . . and the property of being snub-nosed. Propositional identity, given the same predicate, would be a function simply of what individual is referred to.[9]

John Perry calls propositions of that kind "*de re propositions*,"[10] and David Kaplan uses Whitehead's label 'singular propositions.'[11]

The suggestion by Donnellan and Kaplan to represent what is said in (S2) with reference to the moon by the ordered pair: $<$the moon, the property of being spherical$>$ resists generalization as can be seen in (S3). In an asymmetrical relation, the order of the *relata* is decisive for the identity of the proposition. The following suggestion avoids this difficulty. Let singular propositions be represented by ordered pairs of the form: $\ll s_1, \ldots, s_n >, P_n >$, in which P_n is an n-place logical predicate, or eternal object, and $< s_1, \ldots, s_n >$ is an ordered n-tuple of logical subjects, or actual entities. Now we are able to represent the proposition expressed by (S3) as follows: $\ll$the moon, the sun$>$, the smaller-than relation$>$. And we can represent our singular proposition about the shape of the moon as: $\ll$the moon$>$, the property of being spherical$>$. Of course, I am not saying that Whitehead's singular propositions really *are* such ordered pairs, such classes. As he saw, "the appeal to a class to perform the services of a proper entity is exactly analogous to an appeal to an imaginary terrier to kill a real rat."[12] The *representation* of singular propositions by ordered pairs is intended to expose the fact that the identity of such a proposition is determined by the sequence of objects $s_1 \ldots s_n$ *themselves*, which in some cases may consist of a single element. Accordingly, its identity is not determined by the ways in which these objects are given to the judging subject. Thus the identity of a proposition that is expressed by an indexical sentence is not determined by the sense of the referring terms, but by the objects referred to. This is a fundamental difference between Whiteheadean singular propositions and Fregean '*Gedanken*' ('thoughts').

The content of a judgement expressed by an unquantified indexical sentence is for Whitehead a singular proposition. Were it possible to avoid *indexical* reference to objects, the category of singular propositions would lose some of its relevance. So let us ask: Can a demonstrative always be replaced by a definite description that refers to the same thing but is free from any demonstrative element while the content of the judgement is preserved? The answer is 'No.' Assume that Jones sincerely asserts, 'My birthday is on New Year's Eve'. In this way, of course, he expresses the judgement that his birthday is on New Year's Eve. Now it is quite possible that there is *no* definite description, free from all demonstrative elements, that expresses a property Jones would be ready to ascribe to himself at the time of his utterance. After all, he might be suffering from amnesia: 'Whoever I may be, there is one thing I know for sure: My birthday is on New Year's Eve'.

Whithead does not only believe that indexical sentences cannot be replaced by sentences free of demonstratives while preserving the content of judgement; he also thinks that sentences in which no indexical *components* appear (no words such as 'I', or morphemes such as the ending in the Latin one-word sentence *ambulo*) can nevertheless still be indexical. "Explicitly in the verbal sentence, or implicitly in the understanding of the subject entertaining it, every expression of a proposition includes demonstrative elements."[13] It is at least correct to say that the indexical nature of a sentence does not depend upon the presence of a demonstrative part of the sentence. If somebody expresses his opinion with the sentence 'James Watt invented the steam engine', he need not alter his belief if he discovers that billions of years ago a functional equivalent of the steam engine was invented in some far off corner of the universe by a human-like creature. If somebody believes that Watt was the inventor, he thinks that James Watt invented it on *this* earth and at some time in *our* history. The proposition expressed by that sentence, accordingly, does not only depend on the lexical or grammatical meaning of the sentence alone, but also on the context of its expression. To that degree it is indexical.

Is the content of a judgement that is expressed in an unquantified indexical sentence a singular proposition? I believe that there are three reasons for answering this question negatively.

First, a judgement can be expressed with such a sentence even when *no* singular proposition can be assigned to the utterance. Suppose in his hallucination Macbeth screams: (S4) *That is a dagger stained with blood.* In a situation like this, no object is denoted by 'that', and in the absence of such an object it cannot be said that (S4) expresses a singular proposition. As Russell insisted, "You cannot have a constituent of a proposition which is nothing at all. Every constituent has got to be there as one of the things in the world."[14] (What I have just said of Macbeth's utterance, Donnellan says of sentences involving empty proper names: "If a child says, 'Santa Claus will come tonight' . . . he has . . . not expressed a proposition."[15]) Now Macbeth's utterance of (S4) surely is a good reason for attributing an act of judgement to him. The content of his judgement is, however, not a singular proposition.

Second, inconsistent descriptions of situations that can easily obtain, are evoked when the content of judgement is identified with a singular proposition. Let us consider the following scenario, which dramatizes one of Castañeda's reflections.[16] At time t, Smith sees in a store window the blurred reflection of a man at whose head a gun is pointed. Smith observes in t: (S5) *He is in danger now.* But at t, Smith does not come to believe what he could express with the words: (S6) *I am in danger now.* Yet the man whose blurred reflection Smith sees is none other than Smith himself!

Here, the following *de re*-belief-ascription would be justified: (S7) *There is a man such that he is identical with Smith and Smith believes him to be in danger.* But under those circumstances it would be false to say: (S8) *Smith believes that he himself is in danger.* For (S8) would ascribe to Smith a belief which in principle he should be able to express with the help of the I-sentence (S6)—or else with one synonymous to it. If such a belief is termed an *ego*-belief, then we can conclude from the above story that not every belief entertained by some person x about x is an *ego*-belief. That conclusion, however, should not be seen as supporting a dualistic metaphysics according to which the ego-belief Smith entertains is not at all a belief about *Smith*, about a *soma empsychon* or a Strawsonian person, but is, rather, a belief about something else, perhaps a *res cogitans*. For even if (S8) does not follow from (S7), nevertheless (S7) follows from (S8).

Now if the content of the belief Smith acquires at t is a singular proposition, exactly *which* singular proposition is it? Its identity is determined by whatever the indexical components of Smith's utterance of (S5) at time t stand for. This proposition can be represented as follows: $\ll$Smith, $t\gg$, the property of being in danger$>$. Then of which singular proposition is it true that it is *not* the content of the belief that Smith acquires at t? The answer must be that it is the proposition he would express at t by the I-sentence (S6), in other words, the *same* proposition. With this description, we are caught in a contradiction.

Third, sometimes *different* singular propositions must be assigned to *one and the same* belief. Suppose Jones points towards a book lying in front of him and states at t_1: (S9) *This is my copy of Process and Reality.* While his back is turned for a moment, somebody exchanges Jones's copy for another which looks the same. In t_2, Jones repeats his earlier assertion. But now he points to a different book (-token) he is incapable of distinguishing from the first. The singular propositions expressed by Jones in t_1 and t_2 by sentence (S9) are different from one another because the demonstrative 'that' denotes each time a different object. To the extent, Jones entertained a *different* propositional attitude before the books were exchanged than he did afterwards. Of course, we may also describe his cognitive situation this way: At t_1, Jones has the *same* belief as at t_2. What he believes is true at t_1, but is no longer true at t_2. Aristotle and Aquinas would have described this situation in exactly the same way: This is a case where someone continues to hold on to a *doxa, opinio,* which is initially true, but which "becomes false when a change in the object occurs without being noticed" ("*pseudes egeneto, hote lathoi metapeson to pragma*").[17] A "change from truth to falsity" ("*mutatio de vero in falsum*") takes place, "when opinion remains constant but the thing changes" ("*si, opinione eadem manente, res mutatur*").[18]

Is there necessarily a change in a person if his *propositional* attitude changes? At t_2 Jones believes of a different book that it is his copy of *Process and Reality* than he believed at t_1. Does it follow that *Jones* has changed? Surely it is not he who has changed but his environment.

Plato and Aristotle came up against a problem of similar structure in their reflections concerning the category of change (*metabole*). At first, it is true of Socrates that he is just as tall as Theaetetus. Then Theaetetus grows and Socrates does not. So it is no longer true of Socrates that he is just as tall as Theaetetus. Does it follow that *Socrates* has changed? Aristotle answers 'No', and I find this is a convincing answer.[19]

The general term 'is just as tall as' is a two-place predicate. Equality in height is a relation. We produce a one-place predicate from this two-place predicate when we partially saturate it with a singular term: 'is just as tall as Theaetetus'. To be just as tall as Theaetetus is a *relational property*. From the fact that this relational property at one time pertained to Socrates and subsequently did not anymore, it follows only that one of the *relata* in the relation has changed. *Which* of them has undergone the change cannot be determined from the switch in the relational property. (This may also be the reason why nothing like a change in the category of the 'relative' is included within the Aristotelian—and the Thomistic—classification of the ways of alteration [*metabole, transmutatio*]. If an object first possesses a relational property and subsequently looses it, the object in question need not itself have changed.)

Similarly, it is a relational property of the thinker to think of some given thing that it is thus and so. From the fact that it first pertains to an individual and then does not, it only follows that one of the relata in the relation has changed, but not which one it is—the thinking subject or the object of which he thinks that it is thus and so. This means that a propositional attitude is not a genuine *psychological* property. For it is true of such a property that if a person first possesses and then looses it, that person has *himself* undergone a change. This conclusion follows from two premises whose truth I am fully convinced of: First, if a person's mental state is different at t_2 from that at t_1, then his internal physical state is different at t_2 from that at t_1 (Mental properties are 'supervenient upon' physical properties.) Second, if a person's internal physical state at t_2 is different from that at t_1, then the person himself has undergone a change.

The relational property of thinking this and that of a given thing, for example of this sheet of paper, cannot be identical with a neurophysiological property. At the most, it can be identical with a property borne by a *mixtum compositum* whose components are a brain and this sheet of paper. And heterogeneous compounds of this kind are not, to my knowledge, the object of neurophysiology. (Such a *mixtum compositum* is a Cartesian *res extensa*, just as its components are; considerations of this sort certainly are not arguments in favor of a dualism of substances.) This makes apparent how far my suggestion to distinguish two ways of classifying judgments and beliefs is relevant for the discussion of materialistic theories of thinking.[20]

If we classify judgments or beliefs with the intention of deciding which of them can be expressed in declarative sentences with the same lexical and grammatical meaning, we will obtain a classification that distinguishes genuine psychological properties. In this way, we classify judgments and beliefs according to their meaning-content. The truth value of this content, however, is not stable in the cases I have explored here. At times it is true and at other times false—exactly the way an Aristotelian *doxa* is.

For example, when Crito first predicts, 'Tomorrow Socrates will die', and then two days later reports, 'Socrates died yesterday', his judgments have different meaning-contents. In *this* regard I would join the side of those who answered *negatively* to the medieval question of whether the belief of the ancients was the same as the belief of the moderns. Aquinas answered negatively in this sense, too: Socrates' death "is one thing (*res una*); but the soul which additionally thinks of time (*cointelligit tempus*) . . . thinks of Socrates' [death] in different ways: as present, as past and as future; and accordingly it forms different conceptions (*conceptiones diversas format*) in which different truths are found." These different truths are, at different times, expressed by 'Socrates will die', 'He is now dying', and 'He has died'.[21]

So far as the sentence (S1) is concerned, on one interpretation it identifies the meaning-content of Jones's act of thinking with that of his opponent Smith. Each thinks he himself will win the election.

A meaning-content is, of course, also present in Macbeth's hallucinatory thought when he utters a sentence which is synonymous with (S4). His thinking would have had exactly the same meaning-content, had his reference, made with the help of the demonstrative 'that', *not* failed.

The meaning-content of a person's thinking is of great importance if we are to make sense of his behavior. Remember the story about the reflection in the store window. It may be assumed that the man in danger wishes to preserve his own life, and if we want to explain why at *t* he takes no steps to ensure his own security, we have to take his beliefs into account. His behavior becomes quite understandable when we realize that certainly he would describe the situation by using the third person, but not by using the first person.

We can classify judgements and beliefs from yet another perspective. Which of them represent the same *singular proposition* (or the same singular fact)? A thought expressed by an indexical sentence S represents exactly the same singular proposition as the one expressed by the indexical sentence S' if and only if the demonstrative counterparts in S and S' denote the same entities and if the same thing is said about these entities by S and S'.

When Crito first makes his predictive judgement and then the corresponding retrospective one, his acts of thinking represent the same singular proposition. In *this* regard I would give a *positive* answer to the medieval question about the identity of the prophets' and the Christians' beliefs.

On a second interpretation, (S1) identifies the singular proposition which Smith thinks with the singular proposition Jones thinks. Both think of Jones that he will win the election.

No singular proposition is thought by the hallucinating Macbeth, for there is no object the demonstrative in his use of (S4) denotes.

I will end my plea for a strict distinction between what Whitehead calls *singular propositions*, which are expressed by the judging subject with an unquantified indexical sentence on the one hand, and the *meaning-content* of his judgment on the other[22] with an anecdote that owes its point to this difference.

Reporter: How do you assess the chances for success in the peace negotiations?
Kissinger: I am somewhat optimistic. After all, both sides agree that it would be a good thing for the other to give in.

Whitehead's system of categories provides concepts with whose help one can seek to define more precisely the combination of the categorially heterogeneous components of a singular proposition into the *unity* of a singular proposition. Whitehead was correct in rejecting what some analytic philosophers maintain, i.e. that the set theoretical representation of singular propositions captures their essential nature.[23]

There is still a significant deficiency in Whitehead's categorical system from the perspective of our problematics. In the rendering of Whitehead, two "propositional feelings" may (1) have their "subjective form" in common. (Perhaps two acts of judgment are involved.) (2) They may have the same intentional object. (Perhaps both represent the same singular proposition.) Or, (3) they may have the same meaning-content. Each of these three factors can remain constant while the others vary. Despite the wealth in categorical differences of Whitehead's system, it still blurs the essential difference between (2) and (3), which is of crucial importance to the question of the identity of what is thought and to the psychology of "propositional feelings." There is only one concept for Whitehead — the singular proposition — where two are necessary. The result is that the one concept is systematically overloaded.

Notes

1. Cf. Thomas Aquinas: *De Veritate*, q. 14 a. 12.

2. PR 193. Emphasis added.

3. PR 258, cf. PR 22.

4. PR 25; II, IX, § 1; III, IV, § 2.

5. Cf. Russell: "Knowledge by Acquaintance and Knowledge by Description" (1910) in *Mysticism and Logic* (London: Unwin 1974), 162.

6. PR 257.

7. PR 185-186.

8. PR 22 and 188.

9. Keith Donnellan: "Speaking of Nothing," in *Philosophical Review* 83 (1974): 11-12.

10. Perry: "The Problem of the Essential Indexical," in *Noûs* 13 (1979).

11. Kaplan: "How to Russell a Frege-Church," in *Journal of Philosophy* 72 (1975): "Dthat" and "On the Logic of Demonstratives," in: French, Uehling, Wettstein (editors) *Contemporary Perspectives in the Philosophy of Language* (Minneapolis: University of Minnesota Press 1979).

12. PR 228.

13. PR 43. Cf III, IV, § 6, and J. Searle: *Intentionality* (Cambridge: Cambridge University Press 1983), 221.

14. Russell: "The Philosophy of Logical Atomism" (1918) in *Logic and Knowledge* (London: Allen & Unwin 1956), 242.

15. Donnellan: "Speaking of Nothing," 20-21.

16. Cf. H.-N. Casteñeda: "Reference, Reality and Perceptual Fields," in *Proceedings and Addresses of the American Philosophical Association* 53 (1980) with references to his earlier works on 'quasi-indicators.'

17. Aristotle: *De Anima*, 428b 5-6 tr. J.A. Smith.

18. Thomas: *Summa theologiae*, I, q. 16, a.8.

19. Plato: *Theaetetus* 155 b-c; Aristotle: *Metaphysics* XIV, 1; cf. my *Abstrakte Gegenstände* (*Abstract Objects*) (Frankfurt: Suhrkamp 1983), Chapter 2, section 1.

20. Cf. the discussion of these issues in A. Woodfield (editor) *Thought and Object* (Oxford: Clarendon Press 1982).

21. Thomas: *De Veritate*, q.1, a.5 and 6.

22. Readers of Husserl's fifth *Logical Investigation* will certainly hear an echo of the Husserlian distinction between the 'matter' ('*Materie*') an act of judgement has and the 'state of affairs' ('*Sachverhalt*') it is intentionally directed at.

23. Cf. Schiffer: "The Basis of Reference" in *Erkenntnis* 13 (1978): 171.

8.

Whitehead's Cosmology of Feeling Between Ontology and Anthropology

Reiner Wiehl

The Principle of Unity of Creativity and Rationality and the Four-fold Dualism of Modern Metaphysics

Whitehead explicitly placed his speculative philosophy of feeling within the tradition of European metaphysics, in particular that of the modern period, and he makes it plain that he regards it as a metaphysics of subjectivity. One of its principles is: an actual entity is externally free and internally determined. Whitehead thereby indicated that this metaphysics can be of help in solving the problems connected with determination and indetermination, with determination and freedom, and with ontology and anthropology. He called his metaphysics of subjectivity a cosmology, that is a cosmology of feeling, insofar as feeling and sensation are the basic behavior patterns of concrete subjects. Discussion about a cosmology of feeling may sound strange and reek of panpsychism, but this seems less so if one is prepared to consider Whitehead's idea of a speculative cosmology. This cosmology stands in a marked contrast to the specific metaphysics, which as a pure rational doctrine of the world in general belongs to modern metaphysics. However, only one specific part of it, along with the pure rational doctrine of God and the human soul and with a further, more general part, is ontology or the pure rational doctrine of being *qua* being. In the present case, cosmology rather stands for metaphysics on the whole and as a whole. It is understood—with reference to the original meaning of the Greek word *kosmos*—as a comprehensive doctrine of order and as a rational philosophical doctrine of the conditions of potential order and disorder with regard to the manifoldness of being and its actual and potential worlds. This doctrine of order is also a doctrine of principles in the classical sense of the word. The most universal of all principles of this speculative cosmology is that of *unity*: unity stemming from the manifold and unity in the manifold and of the manifold. Due to the principle of unity, creativity and rationality are operative together in each and every unity. Far from being separate principles, these two powers of origination and formation are inseparable and complement each other in their fundamental efficacy. Whitehead's cosmology enables us to regard as compatible and complementary what had come to be considered as diametrically incompatible by modern philosophy and science, especially since the separation between ontology and theology and since the emancipation of epistemology and philosophy of science. Creativity is unity in manifoldness with regard to becoming and development, to new creation and new formation. Rationality is unity in manifoldness with regard to being and having come into existence, to retention and preservation of unity against all disruptive and destructive influences. Creativity and rationality are engaged in a cooperation that also extends both to identical and to different unities.

Whitehead described creativity as 'the most universal of all universal principles', thus, to a certain extent, conceding its pre-eminence over rationality. One could argue as follows: It is a prerequisite that a unity first comes into being and exists before it can be preserved as an existing that has come into being and that constitutes a particularly defined unity. Seen from this angle, the pre-eminence of creativity over rationality is a pre-eminence of becoming and development over having come into existence and preservation. How does this pre-eminence apply? In a way, it is equivalent to the pre-eminence of the subject over the object, in the sense that a subject is always living and in the process of becoming and development, whereas an object is always something that has already come into existence and is preserved as such. However, development and preservation converge, and subjectivity and objectivity coincide in the sphere of what has come into existence. Within this sphere, creativity gives way to rationality. The principle of unity of creativity and rationality is of the utmost importance for a philosophical theory of feeling.

This principle not only brings to light the inadequacy both of an abbreviated rationality as well as that of a diffused irrationality, but it also allows to study the life of feeling in a way that can do justice to its particular intrinsic value. Feeling and sensation do not only exist in the form of an irrational and generally confusing chaos, nor as a pre-rational and unformed manifoldness, which lacks every form of unity. To characterize them as providing the substance and matter for the formation of unities, which are then considered as valuable, is not sufficient.

Feeling and sensation are not only in the service of higher theoretical and practical knowledge, but are also valuable and meaningful in themselves. They are capable, individually and between themselves, of forming original and meaningful unities. They have the ability to grow and to develop, to concresce and to differentiate themselves, thus creating new unities of feeling and sensation, which have new qualities and intensities. They contribute to the creation of other unities, unities of perception and of other behavior patterns, not as meaningless, isolated elements, but as living moments with an individual and particular value. Creativity to them is not only a principle of becoming, but also a principle of differentiation and further development. Rationality is not only a principle of mere preservation, but also of retention under altered circumstances and of progressive adaptation to them. With regard to its most universal principle of unity, the speculative cosmology of Whitehead is radically pluralistic. This principle is valid for the ever different and innumerable growing and existing unities. As a result, the assumption of a permanently fixed, absolute order is excluded. The problem of order arises anew with each growing unity, which brings forth its own particular order. One of the particularities of this order is the way in which it deals with the risks and dangers that threaten its structured order. Each growing and existing unity contains traces and remains of uncontrolled chaos. The larger the scope of the unity and the wider the world, the greater is the risk that the creation of order may fail, and the larger is the room for ambiguity between precision and vagueness, between meaning and triviality.

The principle of unity of creativity and rationality leads to the consequence that feeling stands in a context that is both creative and rational. As irrational, even destructive elements, feelings can destroy and threaten a growing order. Equally well and rather more so, they contribute to each growing unity. Inasmuch as they form growing and existing, developed and preserved unities, they always partake in the tension between subjectivity and objectivity. In the sphere of feeling, subjectivity and objectivity converge and also move apart. They form the bordering points between development and preservation, and they are peculiar transitions from one to the other. With regard to its universal principle of creative reason, Whitehead's cosmology contains a number of different, yet closely related criteria of reason, among which the criterium of coherence is of special importance. Coherence is here understood in the sense that, ultimately, everything is uniformly connected with everything. As a consequence, each element by itself, each individual part loses its significance as soon as it is separated through abstraction from its concrete, universal context and considered in its isolation and as an abstract entity. A single feeling, for example, taken by itself and separated from the life of feeling and from the concrete general behavior of a living subject is nothing but an abstract feeling. As an abstract entity of this kind, it is without concrete significance. If, on the other hand, a single feeling by itself has a certain significance for life, it can only seemingly be isolated from the life of feeling and from the other contexts of life. Or, to take another example, if a living subject completely distances itself in its behavior from the context that associates it with other living subjects, if it becomes isolated or isolates itself from the living world, then it also loses the meaning of life within itself and for itself. If, however, as a particular subject it has a meaning, then it must again only seemingly have been isolated from its concrete living context. The rational criterion of coherence does not imply that there is only the one and the whole and that this is the whole concrete reality. This criterion does not so much relate to the concrete, as to the abstract, in asserting that the abstract is inseparable from the concrete and as such can have its meaning and significance only in connection with the concrete. As a condition of potential meaning, an abstract entity therefore requires a manifold description, that is, a definition of the respective type of category of the abstract object. It also requires the deepest possible knowledge of the causes of the formation of abstraction and, finally, an as adequate identification as possible of the modes of abstraction and of the function of the abstract within its concrete context. It is obvious that, as a consequence of a potential identification of the conditions of an attribution of meaning to abstract objects, also the conditions of a potential loss of meaning and significance can be pinpointed.

The rational criterion of coherence can thus be applied to the relations of the abstract and the concrete. Not by chance did Whitehead call his philosophy a 'philosophy of the concrete'. In applying the criterion of coherence, one must distinguish between a theoretical and a metatheoretical aspect. The metatheoretical use serves the criticism of traditional metaphysics, whereas the theoretical use comes into bearing in outlining a system of categories and principles, which basically determine the various possible connections between the concrete and the abstract. The criticism of traditional metaphysics is based on the assumption that this metaphysics failed to pay due consideration to the criterion of coherence. Modern metaphysics in particular, with its fundamental Descartian dualism, represents from Whitehead's point of view a paradigmatic violation of this criterion of rationality. The philosophy of feeling and sensation was confronted with a whole range of problems raised by the metaphysical dualism. This becomes obvious from a mere enumeration of all those dualistic traits, which are so hard to reconcile with the phenomena of sensuous-emotional being. First and foremost, there is the *ontological* dualism in the form of the absolute difference between the infinite and the finite, between the infinite and the finite substantiality. This leads directly to the dualism of the principles of creativity and rationality. For the unitary power of being, which creates and preserves all things, should be confined to the one infinite substance (God) in relation to the finite substances, whereas the latter were accorded for themselves and in the relations among themselves a merely imitative finite reason. The ontological dualism and its companion, the dualism of principles, was joined within the sphere of finite things by an *ontic* dualism. As a result, an absolute difference emerged, in the sphere of the existing, created and preserved finite being, between the physical and the spiritual essence, between the somatic and the mental existence. Correspondingly, there emerged the absolute difference between physical and mental behavior. A further dualism appeared, which though bordering on those just mentioned and overlapping with them to a certain extent, has to be clearly distinguished: the *gnoseological* or *alethiological* dualism. It denotes the absolute difference between two essentially different kinds of knowledge, or between two truths and their essentially different authorities; it denotes the absolute difference between *apriori* cognitions and *aposteriori* cognitions, between truths of reason and truths of fact, or between rational grounds and empirical causes.

The problem of dualism in modern metaphysics has always primarily been a problem of inconsistencies and contradictions. The fundamental dualistic features just mentioned entailed, in varying combinations, ever new antinomies for the sphere of the finite. As opposed to divine reason, human reason was thus supposed to be finite reason and yet, at the same time, to have the unlimited capacity to comprehend truths of reason and of fact. As compared to the infinite reason of God, this finite reason was supposed to be a merely duplicate reason, and yet altogether incapable of a representation of the original reason in its creativity. The behavior of finite things, conforming to laws and accessible to reason, was thus expected to correspond to the one and indivisible truth of reason. On the other hand, this behavior was taken to be by no means accessible by one single idea of truth, because of the absolute difference of essence in the behavior of corporeal and mental substances. And the causal behavior of these substances was regarded as corresponding to the general conditions of truths of fact, although due to the absolute difference of essence it was thought of as not being able to correspond to these conditions in general; it is rather considered as exemplifying a corporeal and a mental form of causality. Nor was this essentially different corporeal and mental causality deemed explicable in terms of the difference between reasons and causes. For, ultimately, truths of reason and of fact ought to unite into one uniform truth also with regard to finite things, even if from the viewpoint of the finite, the existence of this unity was impossible to be demonstrated. Whatever the possibilities to solve all these antinomies of the metaphysical dualism, Whitehead's speculative cosmology is more than just a criticism of the inconsistencies of traditional metaphysics, it is more than just a criticism of the 'bifurcation of nature' that originates in the largely institutionalized division of science depending on whether its object are material or mental things. Whitehead's major concern was not the elimination of these antinomies. As theoretical characteristics, he ranked adequacy and applicability higher than consistency. His speculative conceptual system yields a whole range of new thoughts and relations of order that apply not only to metaphysics as such, but also to its connection with a philosophy of the life-world and a philosophy of science; it is not only of importance for the relations between the various positive sciences, but also for the internal relations within any individual discipline of science, such as psychology, which is at the same time concerned with problems of physical and of mental existence.

What exactly does Whitehead's philosophical surmounting of the metaphysical dualism consist of? What relevance does this speculative surmounting have for a philosophical theory of feeling and sensation? An adequate answer to these questions can only be achieved if we consider a further dualistic principle, fundamental of all the dualistic principles mentioned, namely the relativization and equalizing of which is at the core of Whitehead's thought. It is this, the dualism between basic philosophical attitudes and methodological conscience in philosophy; it is a dualism of philosophical belief and philosophical knowledge. This dualism appeared in the history of modern philosophy as the absolute opposition between dogmatism and criticism. It centered around the supposedly incompatible alternative whether something that cannot and need not be proved can be conceded by philosophy the status of being, or whether something so unreasonable and beyond reason ought to be excluded as nonexistent, and the status of existence only be conceded to what can be and has been proved. This opposition has, in particular, appeared in the shape of an absolute difference between the unlimitedness and the limitation of the capacity of human understanding: a difference between the unlimited possibilities of thought and the limited possibilities of experience. It is characteristic for modern philosophy that the discussion of the fundamental question of indetermination and determination, of determination and freedom in the sphere of finite things was set within the framework of metaphysical dualism. That question, which touches the depth of human existence in its essence, is the question of whether the possibility of freedom is and has to remain a matter of philosophical belief, or whether this possibility can become an object of philosophical knowledge. If one assumes Whitehead's speculative viewpoint, then dogmatism appears less dogmatic and criticism less critical than one would have expected them to appear from the viewpoint of philosophical dualism. For in order to achieve a general distinction between a proper and an improper use of reason, criticism must (in this respect uncritically) presuppose a specific notion of the capacity of human understanding as a whole along with its various functions of understanding, as well as a universal concept of philosophical proof. Dogmatism, on the other hand, (in this respect only superficially dogmatic) wants to go beyond the limitations of given experience through thought and its imaginations, in order to discover new and more fundamental possibilities of experience. More than just coincidence, Whitehead draws with ease equally on Spinoza and on Kant in support for his speculative cosmology, the former of which was considered as one of the great exponents of an uncritical metaphysics, whereas the latter was regarded as *the* founder of criticism.

Whitehead borrowed from Spinoza the basic metaphysical concept of *causa sui* and made it the key concept of his cosmology of feeling. He interpreted this concept of an absolute being whose essence necessarily includes its existence in the sense of his principle of unity of creativity and rationality, and then extended this concept of an absolute, or rather of *the* absolute, to all actual and true being as such. He took this concept of *causa sui* in the sense of a *causa libera*, that is in the sense of a being that not only exists *causa sui*, but also as its own cause defines itself in its essence by means of its essence. Kant, on the other hand, provided Whitehead with the idea of a philosophical criticism of reason, which he intended to develop further, by means of a criticism of feeling, to a criticism of concrete reason. As far as a philosophy, a cosmology of feeling and sensation is concerned, everything seems at first to speak against a metaphysical dualism and in favor of its philosophical surmounting. In view of the way in which the phenomena of the simple life of feeling and sensation present themselves to conscious experience, the antithesis to dogmatism appears much more convincing than the fundamental dogmatist thesis of the incompatibility of metaphysical opposites. The basic feelings and sensations do not allow for a straightforward distinction between their coming into being and their existence, between their origination and their retention, and between their becoming and their development; the reason for this is not only their lack of permanent conscience, but also their origin in one way or the other from the essence of the living whose life they accompany since indeterminable time. Concerning the ontic dualism, it is obvious that the phenomena of the life of feeling are contradicting its fundamental tenets, since these phenomena demonstrate to conscience and experience the primordial unity of feeling and the inseparable coherence of its various, physical and mental, corporeal and spiritual components. Experience furthermore teaches us that this primordial psychophysical unity, that the bond between corporeal and mental existence achieved through feeling is preserved even when the two different components differentiate in view of each other, thus increasingly gaining distance from each other until, finally, one predominates over the other. It should be added that, in traditional metaphysics, be it dogmatic or critical, the awareness of the contradiction between their own inherent dualism and the phenomena of the sensuous-emotional existence was acute enough to lead either to a complete renunciation to a theory of this type of being, or to assigning to this theory a particular and exceptional epistemological status, e.g. as a theory of ethics or a theory of aesthetics. Similarly, the gnoseological dualism, the absolute distinction between truths of reason and truths of fact, or between reasons and efficient causes, does not appear to be easily applicable to feelings and sensations. Let us only mention here the elementary feelings of joy of life and fear of death, where it is impossible to say with certainty to what extent they originate from the essence of living or from external causes and reasons. The good reasons we put forward for joy and sadness often conceal the real causes. Reversely, the factual causes we recognize are often insufficient as an explanation for a particular feeling, considering the other source of origin in the essence of the living. This uniform activity of reasons and causes in feelings and sensations remains uniformly active even when the feelings themselves or any other mental instances develop a need to perceive and distinguish causes and reasons, which they succeed in satisfying in one way or the other.

The Dual Principle of Concrete and Abstract and the Possibility of Surmounting the Metaphysical Dualism

Feelings and sensations are basic sensuous-emotional perceptions. Sometimes, under certain circumstances, they can see sharper and hear better than many a conscious realization and observation. In other cases and under other circumstances, however, the traditional prejudice retains its validity, which attributes blindness and deafness to them, thus denying them a real capacity of perception. Provided that feeling and sensation have such a capacity of perception, they take up a peculiar perspective, a point of view on this side, respectively on the other side of the positive difference between belief and knowledge. With regard to their cognition, they are neither capable of nor in need of proof. Yet, they are as self-assured as any other knowledge that can be and has been proved from given premises. In this respect, they seem to offer few, if any reference points for the dualism of philosophical belief and philosophical knowledge or for the opposition of dogmatism and criticism. Especially this sphere of phenomena of sensuous-emotional existence renders so difficult, if not impossible, the task of making universally valid distinctions between determination and indetermination as well as between determination and freedom. The reason is that feeling and sensation quite frequently lack the clear awareness of these differences; quite frequently, it is they who deprive conscience of its clarity, and the living subject of its conscience. The case may also occur that no other but they provide us with a feeling of freedom, such as the feeling of happy relief. At the same time, it is not an infrequent occurrence that these feelings, and often the very same ones, put us in a state of mind of slavery and determination. Yet, the fact that the phenomena of the life of feelings are obviously and in various ways contradictory to the one-sided tenets of metaphysical dualism, cannot amount to renouncing to all those theoretical distinctions that have been declared absolute and incompatible with each other by modern metaphysical dualism. The theoretical application of these distinctions is rather rendered obligatory by the phenomena of the life of feeling themselves. This is the case when the question is about the general description of the differentiated and the higher developed forms of feelings and sensations, as opposed to the more simple and less developed forms. In no way does Whitehead renounce these basic differentiations. His speculative cosmology is not a philosophy of the nondifferentiation of what cannot be differentiated. To speak of a speculative surmounting of the modern metaphysical dualism can mean quite different things: relativization and funtionalization of all important metaphysical differences and oppositions, reduction of the manifoldness of metaphysical oppositions to a minimum or to one single fundamental opposition, and, finally, it can imply the installation of one or more new metaphysical oppositions, which take over the function of cognition from the older ones, thus substituting a traditional metaphysical dualism with a new dualism.

Beyond doubt, Whitehead's surmounting of the Cartesian dualism displays some such elements as have just been mentioned. The dualistic principles of creativity and rationality are put in their perspective. The ontic and the gnoseological dualism are replaced by respectively different functions of living subjects, the difference of which is only of relational validity. Above all, one gains the impression that all important metaphysical oppositions are here reduced to the absolute opposition between the *concrete* and the *abstract*, and that, furthermore, the most important metaphysical oppositions of modern philosophy are replaced by another opposition with a much older tradition, which is here brought to new honors, namely the opposition between reality and possibility, between an actual and a potential form of being. The basic opposition of the concrete and the abstract seems largely to coincide with this fundamental differentiation, which goes back to the Aristotelian tradition and is here renewed.

This differentiation is doubtless the central core in Whitehead's cosmology of feeling, a core that is in itself highly significant for a philosophical theory of feeling and sensation, however one would interpret with its help the surmounting of modern metaphysical dualism. To presuppose the differentiation between an actual and a potential form of being as a fundamental ontological difference, means to bring out this difference also and especially in the realm of feeling and sensation as a cosmo-psychological difference. Above all, a distinction has thus to be made between the feeling of an actual being and the feeling of a potential being, between the feeling of something that is real and something that is possible, but also between the sensation of harmony or of contrast with regard to the realities and possibilities that were respectively the object of such sensation. Furthermore, a distinction has to be made between the manifold ways and means of feeling, which ought to be distinguishable depending on the various forms of connection between what is real and what is possible. As a rule and quite appropriately, a distinction is made between perceptions and fantasies with regard to this ontological difference between the real and the possible, insofar as the perception seems to be directed in the first instance toward the real and existing, whereas the fantasy is primarily orientated toward the irreal and possible. It is therefore possible, by connecting this differentiation with that difference of feelings, to make the following statement: It is necessary to distinguish between perceptive and fantasizing feelings as well as between feelings and sensations within which a perceptive and an imaginative component are joined in one way or the other, be it in a harmonizing, be it in a contrasting manner. Likewise, it is necessary to distinguish between emotional perceptions and emotional fantasies, as well as between various junctions among them. In contrast to the previous distinctions, perception and fantasy here take the leading role and determine the emotional components that are also playing a part, while previously, in a reversed way, feeling had been dominant in perception and imagination. Finally, to make reality and possibility the key principles of a cosmology of feelings also implies to examine the manifold functions that feelings and sensations exert not only in the real and potential development, but also in the potential and real preservation of living subjects.

All the oppositions of the modern metaphysical dualism mentioned above, seem to be reduced in Whitehead's speculative cosmology to the one metaphysically fundamental distinction between the real and the possible. This reduction seems to amount to the functioning of this fundamental distinction as an ontological as well as an ontic, as a gnoseological as well as a methodological fundamental difference. Wherever something real is sensed, something factual is felt, it is through the cosmological principle of reason. Wherever possibilities are sensed or felt, it is through the cosmological principle of creativity. The ontic difference, however, insofar as it is a fundamental metaphysical difference between physical and mental entities, between bodies and minds, appears here as primordial ontic difference between the sensation of the real and the sensation of the possible, as fundamental difference between a perceiving and an imagining feeling. The same holds true for the other metaphysical oppositions, for the absolute differences between truths of fact and truths of reason, between philosophical knowledge and philosophical belief. In one way or the other, they can all be traced back to the fundamental opposition of the real and the possible. This also applies to the fundamental opposition of modern philosophy, the opposition of determination and freedom, which appears in the form of sensation of one or the other. The sensation of the real, the actual, and the factual is each time a sensation of its own causal determination in the same way as traces of the feeling of freedom are present in the sensation of the possible. As elementary feelings of self, these feelings of determination and freedom are much more primordial than the respective ways of conscious knowledge and belief, and are much more deeply connected with the essence of the living than it would appear from the viewpoint of human self-consciousness. The question that remains is: How could this reduction of the traditional metaphysical oppositions to another fundamental opposition bring about the surmounting of the metaphysical dualism? How is it possible that the antinomies created by the dualism can be dissolved in this way? Does this reduction not rather aggravate the dualism and confirm its antinomies? What does the peculiar distinction between the ontological and the cosmo-psychological difference of the actual and the possible really mean? How does this last difference relate to the analogous anthropological difference of human behavior? In which way is one difference connected with the other? Before all: How can this be the foundation of an adequate general description of the life of feelings, insofar as its phenomena stand in a sharp contrast to each of the forms of dualism mentioned?

In Whitehead's speculative philosophy, the possibility to surmount metaphysical dualism depends mainly on a postulate, which he des-

cribed as 'cosmological ideal'. This elementary principle of order in principle enables a regulation of the connection between the concrete and
the abstract, and thus creates the conditions for a respective system of
rules or regulations, namely the system of categories. This postulate or
'ideal' insists on a minimum of different types of entities all of which
share full concretion in an equal and unlimited way. This minimum of
typically different entities consists of (1) the concrete entities in the
proper sense, i.e. the actual entities, (2) the concrete connections formed
by the concrete entities, i.e. the nexus, and (3) the concrete modes of
behavior viz. relations, i.e. the prehensions, which given actual entities
display toward other concrete entities. Between these three types of concrete actual being, there is basically no distinction with regard to their
concretion and actuality because they refer to different categorial aspects.
The three forms of actual concrete being appear together wherever there
is an actual concrete being: a concrete actual entity relates in a concrete
way to those other actual entities with which it forms a concrete connection of behavior; a concrete actual entity stands in a concrete connection
of behavior with other actual entities, a connection that is determined by
the concrete actual behavior between it and other actual entities. It would
be useless to attempt a distinction between these three forms of concrete and actual being according to their level or degree of concretion or
actuality. Aristotle's observation about the relation between actuality
and potentiality also applies generally to these concretions and actualities, be they entities, nexus or prehensions: Actuality has priority over
potentiality with regard to being, knowledge, and time. This three-fold
priority applies in the first place to actual entities, insofar as their actual
being is the basis of every concrete actual behavior and the necessary
condition for the formation of concrete connections of behavior. This
specific priority of actual entities—a direct result of the cosmological
ideal—has been described by Whitehead as 'the ontological principle'.
It prescribes that however many actual entities may actually exist and
however distinct they may be among themselves, these distinctions are
not of the same kind as those that regard the degree of actuality and
concreteness. For this reason, each actual entity is a potential ultimately
valid foundation and reason of being and knowledge, and the search
for such a foundation and reason in the end always refers back to
some concrete actual entity, which is constituted in such and such a way.

   Apparently, the cosmological ideal in its ontological implications
can facilitate the first step in the direction of a surmounting of metaphysical dualism. For it appears as a consequence of this ideal that the
traditional ontic-ontological opposition between the infinite and the
finite, as well as the metaphysical opposition between the infinite substance (God) and the many finite substances or things, do not have the

status of concrete actual being. It thus appears that the relation between the infinite and the finite is merely a relation of thought (*distinctio rationis*). Alternatively, it could appear that the distinction between one infinite and many finite actual entities has to be defined differently (if this is to be a case of a concrete actual difference in behavior) than by reference to the distinctions in a hierarchy of actual entities with regard to their actuality. Even if in this way the old metaphysical opposition between the infinite and the finite being seems to vanish, this does not affect metaphysical dualism as such. To the contrary, its appearance becomes much more dominant as *the* relevant metaphysical opposition of the concrete and the abstract in the form of the fundamental opposition of actuality and potentiality, of reality and possibility. Yet, Whitehead's cosmological ideal and the ontological principle connected with it seem to open up a possibility for the surmounting of the metaphysical dualism. For both the ideal and the principle operate together here and at the same time as principles of coherence. As far as the abolition of the dualism is concerned, this means that metaphysical oppositions, whatever their content, are in their universality abstract definitions. As *abstracta*, they are devoid of meaning and significance, unless they are referred back to concrete actual entities and are connected within the actual behavior of these entities. Only in direct connection with such concrete actual behavior do they have a respective definite significance. Accordingly, each concrete actual entity unites always and necessarily in a specific way these universal oppositions in itself, in the unity of its concrete actual behavior. The result for the fundamental metaphysical opposition of the concrete and the abstract in the form of the actual and the potential is that a concrete actual entity unites, encompasses in itself concretion and abstraction. In its concrete actual behavior it combines something real in its actuality with something possible in its potentiality. Each individual actual entity actualizes in its concrete behavior to other given actual entities a vital connection between the real and the possible. In its actual behavior it relates to the real and the possible and accordingly forms a particular relation to reality and possibility. In this actualization, it represents the unity of an actual double behavior, that is, it relates to the other given actual entities under the double aspect of the real and the possible. Reality and possibility are therefore the two most elementary and primordial perspectives of the actual behavior of an actual entity toward other actual entities. In this way, the double behavior toward the real and the possible transforms itself into the unity of a behavior with a unified double perspective. But does this transformation solve the problem of metaphysical dualism?

The actual entities, toward which a particular actual entity relates in the concrete manner we have just described, constitute the actual world of this actual entity, and the actual entities, with which it has such an actual relation, are for this particular actual entity all actual entities at large. With regard to all these, the actual world is relatively complete. Every concrete actual entity, however simple and undeveloped it may be, has its own specific actual world, which appears to it in the perspective of reality and possibility. It prehends all given actual entities of its actual world under this perspective of the world. The result for the cosmological theory of feelings and sensations is the following: Not only are feelings of the real and the possible different types of entities, which Whitehead calls 'physical feelings' and 'conceptual feelings', but also, and even the more so, these two elementary ways of behavior, which belong to different types, are always dependent on the necessary conditions of a respective concrete actual entity and of a fundamentally unified actual behavior of this entity. These ways of behavior pertaining to different types can be said ultimately to constitute a unified complex actual behavior of a concrete actual entity. In contrast to the previous different ways of behavior, this unified behavior has a unified complex perspective. In this perspective, there is a peculiar contrast between reality and possibility with regard to the given actual entities, which are felt by a particular actual entity. In this respect, all feelings and sensations have an individual perspective that is more or less rich in contrast. In this perspective of their own feeling and sensing, the first access is opened up in an elementary form for the concrete actual entities to their actual world and to the possibilities of their own being and becoming. Even the most elementary and simple feelings and sensations can thus indeed be regarded as cognitions of a concrete actual being. Insofar as it should be possible to trace the other metaphysical oppositions mentioned back to the one metaphysical fundamental opposition of actual and potential being, they will have to be found again as aspects of that fundamental perspective of concrete behavior of feelings: as creative and rational, as physical and mental, as factual and true aspects in the perspective of the real and of the possible. Of course, the question arises: Does the cosmological ideal and the corresponding ontological principle, does this assumption of a unified foundation or reason of unity in the form of the unity of a respective actual entity solve the problem of surmounting metaphysical dualism? Is it not the case that whenever an opposition is applied to something identical and to the unity of this identical entity, a contradiction will necessarily arise rather than the opposition be dissolved? Does one not jeopardize the unity, originally assumed, of a uniform ground and reason if one attempts to solve the contradiction by distinguishing different respects and perspectives of what is opposed? How is it possible, then, for the transformation of the ontic-ontological opposition of reality and possibility into a perspectivist and gnoseological contrast to avoid the contradiction without endangering the unity of the subject, in this case of the subject with its feelings and sensations?

Before all, the question remains: What is the general connection between the ontic-ontological difference on the one hand and the epistemological-methodological difference between actual and potential being on the other? What is the relation of reality and possibility to the sensation of reality and possibility? Could it be that the first difference only exists in the form of the second distinction? In order to do justice to Whitehead's speculative surmounting of metaphysical dualism, we cannot contend ourselves merely with elaborating the antinomic consequences of this dualism. Further than that, we have to search for the reasons of the origin of this modern dualism, which proved to be largely inadequate for generally describing the phenomena of the life of feelings; this not only for the sake of consistency, but also for the sake of adequacy and applicability of the metaphysical theory. In view of the history of European philosophy, Whitehead was convinced to have found on the whole a very simple reason, namely the largely uncontested domination of the fundamental concepts 'thing' and 'substance', which have guided metaphysical thought from time immemorial, and were inevitably bound to come into conflict with the modern concept of 'subject'. These concepts were in his eyes nothing but hypostazations of a rather simple grammatical way of speech, misleading ontologizations of the form of the vernacular clause of statement whose combination of an expression of the subject and the predicate had been elevated and glorified into a universally valid category. To Whitehead, the grammatical form of the clause of statement was incapable generally of expressing complex metaphysical connections. In this respect, his metaphysics of subjectivity emphatically excludes a metaphysics of substance. His critique of the traditional ontology of things and substances has taken up and further developed a central theme in modern philosophy. In contrast to many an idealistic philosophy of science of the last and the present century, Whitehead did not limit his attention to the so-called 'functional concepts', which replaced the concepts of things and substances in modern science, especially in the mathematical natural sciences. Although this aspect was very important to Whitehead, who was after all one of the great scientists of this century, his criticism is more penetrating. It is a metaphysical criticism in the most extensive sense of the word, and it embraces not only the experiences in the sciences, but also those in the pre-scientific life worlds of the living. In this respect, Whitehead's criticism comes close to the deepest and most far-reaching criticism of substance metaphysics in modern philosophy, namely Hegel's speculative criticism.

Priority of Truth or Priority of Life: The Alternative between Hegel's and Whitehead's Metaphyics of Subjectivity

Abstract and Concrete Causality of Life. The speculative criticisms of traditional substance metaphysics by Hegel and Whitehead have many essential points in common. Despite the difference in their conceptual language, they share the same point of departure. Both direct their criticism to the metaphysical fundamental difference between the concrete and the abstract. They agree that the philosophical enterprise inevitably ends up in a dead end when the concepts 'thing' and 'substance' are taken as the most original and fundamental forms of thought and are hence applied as categories for the universal description of being as being in full concretion and actuality. They both anticipate that such a use of these concepts cannot but lead to the most serious of all errors in metaphysics, confusion of the abstract with the concrete. This is the fundamental error Whitehead repeatedly denounced as the 'fallacy of misplaced concreteness'. Both great modern metaphysicians found similar expressions to denote the absence of concretion or concrete actuality, and the lack of living force and effectiveness that attaches to things and substances with regard to their conceptual form.

Hegel, for example, criticized the abstract and formal reflection typically applied to things and substances that only permits that existence be ascribed to them in an abstract and detached sense. His philosophical criticism is in this regard generally directed against all 'reflective philosophy', which develops by depending solely on the guide offered by concepts of substance and thing and which is incapable of understanding the concrete connection between what things and substances *are* in and for themselves and what they are for us. Whitehead spoke in similar terms of the void actuality that cannot be a principle for a philosophy of the concrete, and yet inevitably becomes just such a principle when metaphysical knowledge relies on the categories of thing and substance as its ultimate and fundamental concepts. This invariably results in a confusion of the abstract with the concrete and of the real with the possible. Like Hegel, Whitehead regarded simple declarative sentences of the subject-predicate form as inadequate for a general description of metaphysical relations, even though he would have seen Hegel's dialectic form of expression by means of the 'speculative phrase' as an extrapolation rather than an elimination of this inadequacy. This characteristic of an essence of a particular abstraction that appears as concretion, namely the formal reflection and void actuality of the things and substances, results in a lack of concretion with regard to the content, although in fact such a concretion exists; it also results in the fact that relations remain unclear and inexplicable, although in fact they can be explained and recognized. This lack of concretion and actuality affects the things and substances in three ways: first, in the relation to themselves, that is to their attributes and qualities; second, in their relation to all the other things and substances with which they stand in connections that are particularly defined; and third and most important, in their relation to their behavior towards the external and towards the internal. All these fundamental connections appear only as external relations. The essence as well as the essential relations of the things and substances are concealed behind this exteriority. This form of exteriority confines the access to the essence-ness and to the essential to the realm of mere appearances.

The exteriority of relations in fact applies to all categorial definitions insofar as they apply to things and substances. The most prominent examples are: (1) the relation of unity and manifoldness, be it as relation between the unity of a thing or a substance and the manifoldness of their attributes and qualities, be it as relation between the unity of a thing or a substance and the unity of many things or substances that are connected in a particular way, be it finally as relation between unity and manifoldness of something complex, provided it has the form of a thing or a substance. Similarly undefined is (2) the behavior of things and substances with regard to the difference between position and negation. The lack of definition of content and of actuality applies also in this case to all the three fundamental relations we have mentioned: the behavior towards itself and its own determinations, the behavior towards the other things and substances, and finally the uniform behavior towards the two connected modes of behavior, that towards the internal and that towards the external. Before all, the lack of concretion and actuality in the things and substances affects (3) their causality and their causal behavior. This lack of a void and abstract causality summarizes all the instances of a categorial lack in concretion and abstraction that attach to the things and substances. This is the systematic origin of the ultimate confusion in metaphysics, that of the abstract and the concrete. The abstract character of the causality of things and substances also means that the causal relations of the things and substances towards themselves as well as among each other are purely external relations, which only exist in forms of extension. In their external extension, they are separated from and do not come into contact with the essence and the self-being proper of the things and substances. Reversely, the essence and the self-being are something external and quite unessential for the causal relations of the things and substances. Abstract external causality is defined as lawfulness of change under certain conditions. The essence and the self-being of the being have no concrete relation to neither the conditions of the validity of this lawfulness, nor the lawfulness itself, nor the changes for which the lawfulness is valid. Self-being and essence are here equally unimportant. Seen from the point of view of a particular essence and self-being, this abstract causality is merely phenomenal; it is a causality from and for an external point of view, which may be that of an external observer or thinker. Seen from the point of view of external causality, the assumption of an essence and a genuine self-being of the things and substances becomes superfluous.

The assumption of such an abstract and void causality also renders redundant the fundamental distinction that is attached to every self-being, namely the distinction of a behavior towards oneself and a behavior towards the other. For both of these cases under the provision of external causality, the lawfulness of change only exists if the specific conditions of exteriority as well as of internality are disregarded. The exteriority and abstraction of such a causality is not even affected by the possible distinction between the exteriority of change and the interiority of development. In general, causality with regard to becoming and development of some being is regarded as teleological. Yet, even this teleological causality remains external and, as it were, mechanical if the development in question is merely regarded as something that happens *to* the things and substances or *to* their external relations, but not as a development in concrete relation to the essence and the self-being, that is to say, not as a development of the essence and the self-being proper. The causality of things and substances remains void and abstract also in this case of a purely external, phenomenal becoming and development, or change of something. It is therefore also only a conditional lawfulness of change, even though in this case with a view to certain developments. It retains this character of conditional lawfulness if the relation concerns successively realized means with respect to a particular aim to be realized. One of the most severe confusions of the abstract with the concrete is to misjudge the 'mechanic' or technical character of this external teleological causality and its confusion with the causality that genuinely pertains to the essence, the causality of a development that originates in the essence itself.

The ontological coincidence between Hegel and Whitehead we have just outlined is by no means restricted to important features their critiques of the traditional metaphysics of things and substances have in common. Beyond that, it extends to elementary and fundamental principles of a metaphysics of subjectivity. For Hegel as well as for Whitehead, the being of the subjectivity is the concrete *par excellence*, and it is therefore also the actual being *par excellence* compared with which all other being is abstraction. In contrast to the empty and abstract causality of the things and substances, the causality of the subjects is concrete and actual. Unlike the former, it is also not detached from, but rather directly and concretely related to the essence and self-being of the subjects and indeed defined by it. The causal behavior of the subjects originates in its concreteness and actuality from their essence and self-being. Reversely, through such a concrete causal behavior, the essence and the self-being of the subject achieve a concreteness and actuality that is lacking in the essence and self-being of the things and substances. Far from being merely an actualization of some possibilities in general, the causality of the subjects is an actualization and realization of self with regard to respective and specifically individual possibilities.

The concretion and actuality of subjectivity therefore means: A concrete subject actualizes its internal and external possibilities in its internal and external behavior, by making given possibilities its own. It actualizes itself by joining its external to its internal possibilities in the defined unity of its self-actualization. In this regard, the concrete and actual causality of the subjects does not consist in an abstract lawfulness, but it is the causality of a self-activity, the concrete law of a unique being that realizes itself in the becoming and developing of self. This causality is that of the life that is lived, of the process of life of living subjects. Up to this point, where the metaphysics of subjectivity reveals its character as a metaphysics of life and of the process of life, Hegel and Whitehead are in agreement. Despite these extensive ontological similarities, the differences in their metaphysical systems are not less extensive. They deserve particular attention because they bring about crucial differences in their respective philosophical treatment of the life of feelings and of sensations in general. The ontological differences take their beginning in the identification of subjectivity and the process of life, and they are mainly centered around the definition of the relation between substantiality and subjectivity, and between truth and reality. In the same way as Whitehead, already Hegel had put the blame for the contradictions and antinomies in modern metaphysics on the entanglement of the categories of substance and subject; and both made it their concern to deliver metaphysics from this entanglement of categories and the resulting confusion of the abstract and the concrete. But both great metaphysicians had a different answer to the question of *how* this should be achieved. Hegel considered the two categories of 'substance' and 'subject' as indispensable for metaphysical knowledge and its presentation. He made it the main task of his speculative philosophy to harmonize and reconcile the old dogmatic metaphysics of substance with the new critical metaphysics of subjectivity. In this undertaking, Hegel was led not so much by the idea of the unity of the history of metaphysics, but by the conviction that this task of reconciliation was required by the demand for the cognition and proof of metaphysical truth. In order to achieve this reconciliation between old and new metaphysics, it was necessary to go beyond the categories of life and the process of life toward the categories of 'knowledge' and 'process of knowledge', and to accord priority to the latter. Thus, the meaning of concrete, actual subjectivity could not anymore apply only to the concrete, actual life; it rather had to be extended to theoretical and practical understanding through reason. Life was still considered the foundation of knowledge, but the knowledge now was considered the truth of life.

The Philosophy of the Life of Feeling between the Concepts of Substance and of Subject. Hegel's metaphysics of subjectivity required of itself a proof of its truth, a truth that ran as follows: The being of perceiving subjectivity is the concrete, actual being *par excellence*. There only seemed to be one way to prove this truth: by analyzing this concrete being into its various abstractions and through a synthesis of these abstractions, in such a way that by their combination into a unity the original, concrete subjectivity in its development could be described. Within this proof of truth, the category of 'substance' occupied a key function as one of the decisive abstractions. It was thus possible to explain the defects of its abstraction, which have been described in detail, as defects in the development of concrete subjectivity, as defects in the development of the truth of its knowledge and of the proof of this truth. Contrary to Hegel's metaphysics, Whitehead's speculative philosophy excludes a metaphysics of substance on the basis of principal considerations. To him, the category of substance, even as abstraction, is once and for all misleading. To insist on employing it in metaphysical cognition would entail the inevitable consequence of repeatedly confusing the abstract with the concrete. The concept of 'substance' is a confusion of the potential and the actual being. The desire to find a conclusive proof for metaphysical knowledge does not make any sense for Whitehead, since to him such knowledge is not finished and can in principle never be finished. Through its own change, this knowledge has to make allowance for the change of things, the perpetual coming-to-be and perishing. Because this knowledge cannot be finished, it is not only the criteria of consistence and coherence as demanded by reason, but also the other two criteria of applicability and adequateness that count, more so than any conceivable proof of truth. The fulfillment of these criteria is the only meaningful truth in metaphysics. Through its relation with rationality and creativity, metaphysics unmistakably attains a pragmatical feature that, united with a speculative component of knowledge, makes up a unique combination. Whitehead's speculative cosmology is an ontological hermeneutics and a metaphysical heuristics. Its priorities in the relation of reality and truth are arranged in the opposite way from the speculative philosophy of absolute knowledge of Hegel. Truth does not have priority over reality, but reality over truth. There may be reality without truth, but certainly no truth without reality. The reality of life and of the individual processes of life is more original than the truth of knowledge and the process of its proof of truth. Truth is only one of many functions of life, as incidentally also error and deception, although a very important one: It encourages the development of higher life. But not only that, truth also jeopardizes the continuous existence of life. Assigning the priority of reality over truth does not only include an element of realism, but also an element of criticism, and furthermore prevents a false overestimation of the power of truth.

The priority of reality over truth is only one more essential aspect of the ontological principle. According to this principle, actual being has priority over potential being with respect to being and to time, but as far as knowledge is concerned this priority only applies in certain respects and under certain conditions. With regard to the claim that a metaphysical reconciliation of substantiality and subjectivity in a process of absolute truth is impossible, the ontological principle maintains that there is no actual development of the concrete from the abstract at all. Each real development, be it a development of the higher from the lower, or of the complex from the simple, is always and necessarily the development of something concrete from something concrete. Otherwise, it would only be an abstract, external and phenomenal development. Actual entities as such and in concrete nexus of behavior must be given as precondition in order to enable new processes of the living development of concrete actual entities. The place of the traditional category of substance, whose definition already implies a confusion of the abstract and the concrete, is taken up by a series of 'categories of existence', each of which expresses a basic type of category of a certain relation between actual and potential being. If applied in a uniform and coherent manner, these categories of existence are intended to enable general and adequate descriptions of the different types of process of development of living subjects, while at the same time avoiding that fatal metaphysical confusion. As we have seen, there is a significant difference between the speculative philosophy of Hegel, who adheres to the category of 'substance' within his conceptual framework, and that of Whitehead, who replaces this category by a number of coordinated categories of existence. This necessarily has immediate consequences for their respective general theories of feelings and sensations: It is a crucial point of disagreement, if one founds the philosophical description of the life of feelings and its psychophysical interrelations with Hegel on a 'dialectical logic of substance', or if one founds it with Whitehead on an 'analytical logic of the subject'. The consequences of this difference in application of essentially different categories extend far beyond different descriptions of a seemingly identical range of phenomena, for it also becomes apparent that these seemingly identical problematics can be interpreted in very different metaphysical terms and that, in the respective metaphysical systems, the life of feelings, which can be described in general terms along with its psychophysical relations, is attributed an entirely different significance. In Hegel's "Philosophy of the Absolute Mind," feelings and sensations are the first and elementary self-revelations of *the* absolute mind. In this way, the fact that a physical, somatic element is attached to them and that the nexus in which they appear are always of a psychophysical character is taken to demonstrate that they have a certain defect. This defect is the lack of an absolute spirituality. In Whitehead's speculative cosmology, by contrast, the concrete feelings of the concrete subjects are also elementary factors of being and behavior, but inasmuch as a defect is to be ascribed to them, for example the lack of differentiation or complexity, this defect never has the character of a lack of pure spirituality. According to the principles of this cosmology, feelings and sensations never detach themselves from the foundations of their psychophysical double life.

A comparison of the philosophical theories of the life of feeling in Hegel and Whitehead seems to lead directly to a paradox: Each of these theories claims to surmount the dualism of modern metaphysics, and each of them seems—seen from the opposite side—to get only more deeply entangled in this dualism. From Whitehead's point of view, Hegel's speculative philosophy is an absolute spiritualism, the radical one-sidedness of which confirms—against its own intentions—the immanent continuity of the reign of the dualist metaphysics of substance and thus dooms to failure this modern metaphysics of subjectivity. Seen from the point of view of Hegel's absolute spiritualism, on the other hand, Whitehead's bipolar cosmology appears as nothing more than a new variation of precritical, dualist metaphysics, and a new theoretical guise of naturalism and panpsychism. Do these descriptions by the respective adversaries really correspond to the issues? Must not each of the two metaphysics be rejected when judged in terms of the claim to have surmounted the antinomies of dualism? Could it really be that the metaphysics of subjectivity is the dead end street of modern philosophy? Or is it possible that the philosophical theory of feelings can open up a new perspective here?

Hegel's description in his 'anthropology' of the general life of feelings in nature, as embedded in the psychophysical nexus as the first self-revelation of the absolute mind, is based on a certain categorial scheme, namely that of the dialectical relation between the categories of 'substance' and of 'subject'. This scheme can be described as follows: On the one hand, a substance is in its essence fundamentally different from a subject. This difference in essence is a particular form of the difference in essence between the abstract and the concrete. A substance in its essence, self-being and specific causality lacks precisely the concretion and actuality that is characteristic of the self-actualization of the subject. This fundamental deficiency is the reason why the substance as such, and in its relation to itself as well as to other substances, lacks the specific liveliness of the mind and the actuality of the self-knowledge of a subject endowed with mind. Due to this difference in essence between the substance and the subject, it seems impossible that a substance becomes a subject, a subject develops from a substance. On the other hand, a substance is 'in itself', i.e. potentially a subject. Hence, there are conditions according to which a substance can become a subject; a subject can develop from a substance. Under these conditions, the concrete, living subject in its self-activity and self-realization is the concretization of the abstract essence, self-being and actualization of the void and formal causality of a substance. This self-realization of a concrete subject occurs by means of a revival and spiritualization of the external causal relations of what exists.

Now this schematized dialectical relation between substance and subject, which underlies Hegel's description of a natural life of feelings of the absolute mind, seems to contain a certain contradiction. For the possibility that a concrete subject can develop from substance is affirmed on the one hand, and denied on the other. With Hegel, this contradiction is only solved by overcoming the impossibility in favor of the possibility of such a development. As he has it, the overcoming of this impossibility is not yet possible in the process of the life of nature, but only in the process of the life of the absolute mind. Contrary to the former, the latter process is a process of absolute self-knowledge, which is perfected in the complete transparency of self, in the pure spirituality of an absolute knowledge. The impossibility of the own self-becoming of the absolute self-knowledge is surmounted here, in that the knowing subject in the process of knowing itself recognizes that the presumed difference in essence between it and the substance, or between the own concretion and the abstraction found, is nothing but a superficial and outward appearance. The knowing subject recognizes the abstraction of the substantial being as its own abstracting activity of abstraction; it recognizes the abstraction in question as a particular phase in its self-actualization. This abstraction is its own; it is the abstraction of its own abstract moment of development from the development of the whole for the sake of the latter's actual perfection. This impossibility of the own development from the abstraction of the substance to the concretion of the knowing subject is dissolved; this concrete subject recognizes the reason for this impossibility and recognizes on the ground of this reason its own actual knowledge in its momentary abstract self-actualization. The concrete subject is thus able to oppose the reason for the impossibility with another reason that annihilates the impossibility by annihilating the opposed reason. The process of knowledge in which the knowing subject realizes its self-becoming occurs through the actualization of opposed abstractions, which are at the same time recognized as correlative abstract moments of the process of development. The concrete knowing subject becomes from itself and through itself, by means of the respective specific actualizations of abstract moments of development in the totality of the own self-actualization. In this perspective, it appears that Hegel has in his philosophy of the absolute mind in a certain way anticipated Whitehead's ontological principle. Contrary to what it first may seem, the concrete does here not arise from the abstract. It rather originates, as required by the ontological principle, from the concrete by means of certain abstractions within the concrete itself.

Concretion as a Process of Life or Truth. Seen from Whitehead's cosmology, however, Hegel's specific application of the ontological principle results in an absolute paradox. For it is nothing else than an absolute paradox, if with the perfection of the absolute self-knowledge that amounts to absolute knowledge, not only the development of the subject is ended, but also all becoming and perishing, all continuity, all change, even the process of self-knowledge and with it the distinction between potential and actual being prove to be empty appearance. During the process of self-knowledge, this appearance prevailed, but once the process is brought to perfection, the eternal immortal truth emerges as the truth of the living mind. For Whitehead, this paradox is the price absolute spiritualism has to pay for its effort to reconcile the metaphysics of substance with the metaphysics of the subject. The paradox lies in the incongruity between our common picture of the world that surrounds us, and the conception of this world as devised by the philosophical knowledge of truth. As we have seen, Whitehead placed the priorities in the relation of truth and life in the opposite way as Hegel: For him, the process of life of the living has priority with respect to being, time, and to some extent also to knowledge, over truth and its methical philosophical proof. Not absolute truth, not absolute knowledge are here the yardstick of life, but life in its reality is the yardstick for the respective significance of truth as well as of error. The levels of life that appear in its development, are for Whitehead not levels of truth, neither are they individual steps on the path to prove truth; they are levels in the development of the living itself that attributes to truth and error their respective function of life. The living in its concrete reality is here not the tool of a truth that proves itself; truth and error are rather at the service of life. Life itself is the ground for every possible truth; and truth is a condition of higher life. The notion of finiteness, so fundamental in contemporary philosophy, means from the point of view of a philosophy of the absolute mind: Finite things are not adequate to the absolute mind in its infinity, unless it renders them adequate to itself and to its infinity. From a point of view of a cosmology of life lived, finiteness means: Every development, every coming-to-be and every advance has its price. In the same way as the things that have come into being have to pay by perishing for their coming-to-be, the higher life has to pay for its higher development with the fact that its higher existence is constantly in danger. Truth and error are the conditions for a possible higher life, and at the same time are the risk factors of its higher form of existence. From this angle of the opposite place assigned to the priority of life and truth, the question of possibility has to be approached. Where life has priority over truth, possibility also has priority over the particular negation of impossibility. In this case, the contrast between simple possibilities is regarded as more elementary and original in comparison with the contrast between a possibility and a negation of impossibility in view of a particular definite reality. Here, finally, the simple feeling of the living for its actuality and possibility has priority over the theoretical and practical knowledge of reason about the relation of possibility and impossibility. This reversal of the priorities of life and truth in opposition to speculative idealism lends a particular significance to Whitehead's cosmology of feelings and makes it a worthy object of discussion. Only through this reversal can the symbiosis of creativity and rationality, as we have initially claimed it, be understood.

9.

Which Experiences Teach Us to Understand the World? Observations on the Paradigm of Whitehead's Cosmology*

Robert Spaemann

Still today, Whitehead occupies a unique position in contemporary philosophy. In defiance of dominant contemporary philosophic trends, he undertook to treat nature itself, *peri tes physeos*, whereas in prevalent view the philosophy of nature can only be a philosophy of the natural sciences or an investigation of the spiritual, linguistic, or logical preconditions and implications of scientific theories, or observations and experiments. In retrospect, even Aristotle is regarded as having been an analyst of our talk about nature, and he is rehabilitated as a theoretician of our life-world experience and of our interpretation of nature. Accordingly, this non-scientific philosophy of nature is really a philosophy of human practice inasmuch as the concept of nature fills an indispensable role within this practice. It is not the study of what is as it is independently of us, and the enterprise is thus in either case entirely anthropocentric.

In contrast to this dominant trend, there are some attempts in contemporary philosophy to formulate a philosophy of the living. The endeavors attempt to show from quite different starting points that organic life cannot adequately be understood by reconstructing the organism from its physical elements. These theories, insisting that life cannot be derived from something else are, so to speak, hermeneutic theories of the living. They can be found, among other sources, in the

*For Philipp Kreuzer

work of Thure von Uexküll and Hans Jonas. These theories can be further subdivided into those content with diagnosing a fundamental dualism, and those that will count only living organisms as fundamental actualities, while according to the realm of the inorganic merely the status of 'pre-actuality' (Uexküll). This status can, of course, only be defined as a function of the actuality of the living. With regard to these philosophies, one could even speak of biocentrism instead of anthropocentrism. What distinguishes Whitehead from these biocentric theories is that, in principle, he maintains that nature is a unity. In this respect his thought is analogous to physicalism. So he works out the fundamental categories of nature in close affinity to modern physics. Curiously, as is also true for physicalism, in Whitehead's organic philosophy, inorganic processes assume an ontological priority over organic ones. Unlike the physicalists, however, Whitehead interprets these processes, too, with the help of paradigms taken from the experience of organic life. This means that Whitehead's philosophy is not biocentric, but biomorphic. What distinguishes him from all contemporary philosophers of nature, and connects him closely with Aristotle, is his endeavor to *understand* also — and especially — inorganic nature.

What does 'understanding' mean here? To comprehend a philosopher one must know: What it is that he seeks to understand, and: What does it mean for him to have understood something?

We owe to Aristotle the peculiar distinction between what is better known to us and what is better known 'in itself', between the *gnorimoteron pros hemas* and the *gnorimoteron physei*. According to Aristotle, it is the aim of philosophy to advance beyond what is better known to us and to grasp what is better known in itself, and thus to resolve the initial difference between the two. If we translate the *gnorimoteron* of Aristotle's formula with "what is better known," the formula appears rather paradoxical, for 'knowledge' seems to presuppose somebody who knows something. What could it possibly mean to claim that something is "better known in itself" if it is less well-known to *us*? What could *knowing* mean in this context? Perhaps we can get closer to the sense of this distinction by translating *gnorimoteron* as "more comprehensible" and thus adopt the medieval translation of "intelligibile." After all, it is a familiar occurrence that the reasons that enable us to understand a phenomenon often initially appear less intelligible than the phenomenon itself. That water freezes at zero degrees Celsius becomes more intelligible to us when we know the theory of molecular motion. Initially, however, this theory is less intelligible to us than the fact that water turns into ice. When do we say that we understand something? The answer leads in two opposite directions. Whitehead once illustrated them by reference to Odysseus and Plato. In a very general sense, to understand something is to acquaint oneself with it, *oikeiosis*, and transforming it into the obvious, to that about which there are no questions. Wittgenstein wanted to confine philosophy to this form of understanding. It is no accident that grammatically the perfect form of the verb 'understand' is synonymous with the present. 'I understand something' means 'I have understood something'. There is no "operation called *Verstehen*," but only the disappearance of our lack of understanding (*des Nichtverstehens*). This can be accomplished in a variety of ways.

The variety of the ways in which we understand follows from the variety of the ways in which we fail to understand. We can fail to understand a sentence, for example, because it is spoken too softly, or too indistinctly, or because it is spoken in a language we do not understand. We can also fail to understand it because we do not understand the context to which it belongs, or the intention of the speaker. In each case we would say: 'I don't understand what you are saying'. Our lack of comprehension, however, would have to be overcome in a different way in each case: either by speaking more loudly or more clearly, by translation, or by addition of some sentences. No matter which alternative is chosen, the result is always the same: 'I now understand what was said'. What previously was incomprehensible has now become a part of the world in which I am at home (*in der ich mich auskenne*). This sort of understanding is not relevant only to symbols. If I see a stone flying straight up from the earth's surface, I may investigate further and try to explain the phenomenon, which is incomprehensible because it is unusual. When I realize that somebody is sitting in a dugout throwing stones up in the air, my feeling of uneasiness is almost overcome. At most, there is now something else that I do not understand, and failure to understand this has to be overcome in an entirely different way. The new question is why this person is occupying himself with that strange activity. The clarification of this question can take two different directions: either the affair turns out to be a case of acting in ways with which we are already acquainted, or else we are constrained to expand our feeling for what is normal and to accept a new way of acting, a new form of work, a new pleasure or a new ritual.

Incidentally, this ability of understanding the world by moving from an initial understanding, to its failure and back again to comprehension is also found in higher animals. They can also wonder, and, through clarification, recapture their normal condition and are at home again in the world. If understanding is defined as the disappearance of the failure to understand, it might well be said that the failure to understand begins where symbolism begins, where reference to one event by another event begins, that is, it begins with living organisms. Inorganic entities will always understand the world completely. For them, however, the scholastic adage that *omne quod percipitur per modum percipientis percipitur* (everything which is perceived is perceived by the mode of perceiving) is unreservedly valid. Since there is nothing they fail to understand, inorganic entities cannot extend the limitations of their ability to understand, or their modes of perception. Animals' failure to understand is already a function of the adaptation of delicate organisms whose existence is threatened to the changing conditions of the environment. Their failure to understand is directed to their return to their normal condition of being at home in the world.

Only with human beings does the failure to understand begin to make itself independent so that we have the feeling that our knowledge is only an island in an ocean of ignorance and failure to understand. Kant summed this up by saying that the questions that reason is by its very nature compelled to pose, in principle, transcend any possibility of being answered by reason. Modern anthropology summed it up differently by insisting that human beings have no environment and no fixed *modus percipientis* (mode of perceiving), but are immediately confronted with the 'world'. Unlike the environment, however, it is the world that is initially not understood. For such a being, failure to understand does not mean merely that a phenomenon falls outside of the normality of feeling at home, and requires to be reintegrated. Rather, each normality itself is contingent, and it can always assume the characteristics of a phenomenon that is not understood and so cease to be normality. Even what is most self-evident to us, the *gnorimotaton pros hemas* of Aristotle's distinction, may cease to be self-evident. There emerges a gap between what is better known in itself and what is better known to us. The ideal of an absolute self-evidence, the *noesis noeseos* appears on the horizon. In comparison to this ideal of perfection, all actual understanding seems only 'fragmentary'. Each time a failure to understand is overcome, an even deeper failure to understand results, and this finally leads to apparently hopeless questions such as: "Why is there something rather than nothing?" Here understanding is no longer a function of the process of life, but rather, life is in service of understanding. That makes a maxim such as Rousseau's *vitam impendere vero* (to devote life to truth) possible. This leads us to Plato and away from Odysseus.

What makes this new ideal possible? Whitehead says, reason. We should perhaps rather employ the term *logos*, which implies language. A characteristic of language is that it is not simply an expression of the speaker's condition, but also entails the intention of being understood by the person addressed. The speaker anticipates being heard by an auditor. He undertakes to see himself from the outside, with the eyes of the other or to hear himself through the other's ears. Even before a child learns to say 'I', he learns to refer to himself in the third person, by the name other people have given him. Only as a second step does he learn, to return into himself and to say 'I', knowing that for others he is not an 'I' but rather a 'you' or even an 'he'. What is it for such a being to 'understand'? Or rather: what is it for such a being 'not to understand'? A failure to understand means: to be unable actually to realize the universality, which is always anticipated in speech; it also means: to know that I do not really know what I am as long as I do not know what everything else is and what I am for everything else. Everything is self-evident for the atom inasmuch as there is nothing it does not understand. Again, the concept of God is the concept of a being for which everything is comprehensible because it understands everything as itself, and because it understands everything in connection with everything else as its very self. From its very beginning, philosophy has had no other ideal but the one of divine understanding. Understanding for philosophy has not meant a return to the self-evidence of our normal situation, but the extension and the universalization of this situation, which provides us with the yardstick for normality. In the modern era, Spinoza understood perhaps better than anyone else that philosophy is primarily a redefinition of our life's situation. Philosophy is a mode of life, a *bios*. Platonism too, is an Odyssey; only it does not end with Penelope. Philosophy is a departure into the unforeseeable.

Mankind stumbles on, as Whitehead wrote at the close of *The Function of Reason*, in its task of understanding the world. In my view, Whitehead's importance lies in his having made the ship in which to embark for this journey into the unknown seaworthy again in the twentieth century, after philosophy has for the past two hundred years tried to break off the journey and at last to drop anchor altogether. The metaphor is not so far removed from those used by Kant. It is now time, he insisted, that philosophy must relinquish the exploration of the ocean and instead survey the solid earth that is our own. His program undertakes to establish a definitive normality prescribed by the nature of reason as the ultimate horizon of understanding possible for human beings. Kant, however, recognized the contingency also of this normality, on the one hand, through the reflection on its transcendental constitution, and, on the other hand, by the overpowering remembrance brought to us by the starry heavens and the moral law. The ocean is still there, but we are not to attempt to sail beyond the pillars of Hercules, for the simple reason that we are unable to. Positivism attempted to abolish also this remembrance of openness (*das Offene*) and to place all talk about it on the side of the inhabitants of the Platonic cave under the edict of cognitive ostracism. Once accustomed to regard the world only as the cave cinema, one can finally reinstall the talk about being, and reestablish ontology *within* the cave. Being is then reduced to the appearance on the screen of this cinema. To be, means "to be the value of a bound variable." The lion's existence on the screen consists in my seeing him. I even see him as a creature looking at me. The question, 'Does he also see that I am looking at him?' is alien to the system and ought not be asked. Being is to be an object. Then, of course, the use of the word 'being' in the first and the third person becomes equivocal. In the third person it means something like presence in a place of space-time in the universe. The truth of the claim that I am in pain, by contrast, is totally independent of my location. I am always 'here' without having to know whether this 'here' is located in any given system of coordinates. Here is where I am, and only because I am, there is a 'here'.

The transcendental turn in philosophy was prepared long before it occurred by the objectivism of modern philosophy, by the reduction of actuality to its objective aspect and by modern physicalism. "In physics, there is an abstraction. The science ignores what anything is in itself."[1] Elsewhere, Whitehead writes, "So far as physics is concerned, they—the ultimate entities, R. S.—are wholly occupied in moving each other about, and they have no reality outside this function. In particular for physics, there is no intrinsic reality."[2] Kant discovered that the subject that undertakes this observation of things cannot understand itself in this same way. Of course, Descartes had discovered this before him. However, Kant's new discovery was that the physical view of things is fundamentally anthropocentric or, equivalently, that Newtonian physics presupposes precisely that subjectivity which it cannot understand. The ancient and medieval concept of nature was now banned as anthropomorphism; anthropomorphism is expelled by anthropocentrism. Not anymore is everything similar to us, but it is all the more dissimilar, the more it is reduced to the status of a mere object for us. This anthropocentric perspective is characteristic of transcendental philosophy until Heidegger's *Sein und Zeit*. There, the being of nonhuman things consists in their being-at-hand (*Zuhandenheit*), and being present or being-on-hand (*Vorhandensein*) does not denote a fundamental communion of human existence with non-human being, but is only an abstract form of reduction of being-at-hand. Communal being only exists in the form of being-with (*Mitsein*), that is as the being of other human creatures.

I have mentioned that the anthropocentrism of transcendental philosophy was prepared by the physicalist world view of the Newtonian epoch. Transcendental philosophy did nothing to correct this world view. In all its variations it only affirms and confirms given '*Weltbilder*', just as theories of science affirm and confirm the given science. Transcendental philosophy merely precedes this 'Weltbild' with a reflection that is supposed to allow humans to understand themselves in terms other than those of this deterministic and materialistic world view— a view that results in no longer understanding anything. Objectivism soon caught up with this position of retreat of transcendental philosophy. The conditions for this possibility of experience, which are rooted in the nature of human reason, are now interpreted in terms of the theory of evolution as the 'reverse of the mirror'. The interior is interpreted as the function of objective processes, and man is interpreted as a anthropomorphism. To be sure, transcendental philosophy inquires back into the conditions of the science that accomplishes this kind of explanation. For if science itself is only a product of adaptation, what is there left for it to explain?

Radical naturalists like Quine are not at all intimidated by this argument. Along with the notion of a subjectivity, which constitutes the world, they also give up the concept of a 'true' reality independent of all theory. All that remains is the self-generating universe of the sciences that divide their labor so that physics explains the psychical world and psychology then explains the undertaking of physics. Biology, which is inserted between the two, now becomes increasingly important. This importance, however, does not arise from the fact that it is concerned with a unique actuality in itself, but because it has undertaken to reconstruct the internal as the function of the external and the psychological as a function of complex physical structures. Any question about the status of the totality of this system of divided labor is transformed into a question to be answered within the system itself, and then it is referred from one of the divisions within the system to another so as to answer it.

The key position now occupied by biology in this process of science's self-understanding is indeed thought-provoking. For it points to a feature that biology itself has not yet understood, but which already fifty years ago was the basis for Whitehead's claim that a new cosmology would have to be centered around the concept of organism. The biologist can achieve the conceptual reconstruction of organism only because, as a living being, he is always a unity of the internal and external, a unity of experience and the content that is experienced. His reconstruction of experience from the exteriority of what is objective is merely the attempt to overcome the abstractions that he himself has introduced into actuality. Of course we can try to understand teleological structures by referring to the teleonomy of ultimately mechanical cybernetic systems; but we are only able to do so because we have actually already understood them. To understand an organism by analogy with such systems means to have forgotten that previously we had understood systems as systems, by analogy with whatever is alive. After all, the reduction of actuality to the aspect of mechanical exteriority is nothing more than its anthropocentric reduction to whatever enables us to employ it for our purposes. Moreover, Thure von Uexküll, and later interventionalistic causal theory of scholars like von Wright, made it plausible that causality can be conceived of only in a teleological context. As Reinhard Löw has shown, in the *opus posthumum* Kant went to the extent of replacing the transcendental subjectivity with a bodily *a priori* and therewith took the first step toward surmounting the anthropocentric destruction of anthropomorphism. For a long time no one followed in the direction marked out by this first step of the late Kant. Schelling doubtless could have done so had he known of it.

Biology as the fundamental science of cosmology: this is a notion much more foreign to contemporary biologists than it is to physicists. In general, physicists are far less committed physicalists than are biologists and they have long been engaged in much more subtle reflections about the anticipatory character of time and the synergetic tendencies of matter. The main ambition of biologists is still to avoid taking the living as the paradigm of what is 'actual', but conversely to reconstruct the living as a function of the inorganic. They seek to reconstruct the concrete as a function of the abstract, or to reconstruct what pertains to the subject as a function of what pertains to the object. Whitehead's fundamental contribution consists in emphasizing that the fully concrete can be conceived only as a unity of subject and object. This is an insight he has in common with the German idealistic tradition. Whitehead, however, developed this thought, so to speak, by circumventing idealism, from a speculation that stems from modern physics and whose main proponents are Leibniz and Locke, the latter as interpreted in a Platonic sense. On the assumption that only subject-object unities are concrete and actual, a thesis that claims that the secondary sense qualities are "only subjective" turns out to be empty triviality. In this case, it would merely claim that these qualities are actual only *as experienced*. If the concept of a nonexperienced actuality is a nonconcept, and if all content as experienced content attains actuality, then all content that is experienced is an actual event in Whitehead's sense of the term, and the world consists of such actual events.

It may well be asked what Whitehead really means with the concepts 'experience', or 'feeling', and indeed ' satisfaction' and 'joy' when they are applied as predicates to beings without central nervous systems. At one point, Whitehead himself mentions "belief in the world of men and the higher animals" and contrasts this belief as a *Weltanschauung* with that of 'mechanism'. It is peculiar, however, that in the following, he accords the type of being of the higher animals to everything that exists, only finally to deny it not only to the higher animals, but even to all organisms. Whitehead says about the real actual things that endure (such as stones and animal organisms) that they are all societies, but not actual occasions. Furthermore, there is the question of the extension of the meaning of terms that originally related to the psyche by depsychologizing them, a procedure that was also applied by Leibniz in his concept of perception. This can be answered in the following way: the notion of a concrete actuality cannot even be conceived without attributing to the concrete something like being-in-itself (*Selbstsein*), and being-for-itself (*Für-sich-sein*). Such being-for-itself entails the teleological constitution of condition, disposition and concern. Heidegger defined the being of *Dasein* by these predicates. By denying that nonhuman things are constituted this way, and by defining their being as being-at-hand (*Zuhandenheit*), i.e. by their occurrence in the consummation of human life, he implicitly decided altogether to deny concretion to any nonhuman being. For Heidegger, only the totality of the concerned human consummation of life is concrete. The existence of things is only an abstraction from their being-at-hand (*Zuhandensein*), i.e. a distancing from their concreteness. Thure von Uexküll maintains a similar position in his philosophy of the living when he describes everything that is not alive as a 'pre-actuality' and insists that it only becomes what it is, that is concrete, in the context of an organic environment. It only makes sense to speak of time and causality under the assumption of living beings. Only a living organism can structure the processes of the world into distinct elements. Then, of course, the following questions arise: Why do we experience the environment we encounter as already structured, and as one that certainly does not simply give in to the being-at-hand, but puts up resistance against it? Why is the world by no means only an environment for the living organism but also an overpowering force that can, and does, destroy the relevant environment? With existential ontology and the philosophy of life, Whitehead shares the view that only that is concrete which is not only for other things but rather for which everything else is, i.e. which shapes the world into an environment for itself. "The final real entity is an organizing activity, fusing ingredients into a unity, so that this unity is the reality."[3]

The selective function of negative and positive prehension in Whitehead's sense can be paraphrased as transformation of the world into an environment. Faced with the alternative of either denying actuality to what is not alive or else attributing to it the status of being-for-itself, Whitehead opts for the second. Everything that is, has the characteristic that anything other than it itself is something for it, and that it transforms this other into environment. Everything that is, is a specific and unique teleological design within which anything else gains an ever new and unique significance. A being is defined by the totality of relations in which it stands with all other beings; and our only choice is to understand these relations as purely logical, the ontological realization of which is not different from being thought by a subject external to what is thought; or, alternatively, we could choose to understand what is thought in this way as a 'supraject' in Whitehead's sense. The latter implies that the world is concrete, even without human beings, and that the categories that define the concrete must always be thought as already being instantiated. The further removed a being is from us, the more abstract and devoid of content its instantiation is for us. What 'prehension', 'feeling', 'satisfaction', and ' striving' really mean for an actual event very remote from us must always remain rather abstract. Only if we experience the world ourselves, it becomes concrete for us. This is precisely the point of Whitehead's system: that the world consists only of actual modes of experiencing it and therewith of actual modes of becoming concrete. Whitehead provides a theoretical tool for overcoming both the Heideggerian contrast between existential modalities and categories and the phenomenological contrast of universal ontology and social ontology.

Whitehead's ontology is a universal social ontology, or an ontology of togetherness. Accordingly, in his philosophy, intersubjectivity does not appear as a particular problem, as would necessarily result from an understanding of actuality as mere distinctness in space and time. For Whitehead, intersubjectivity is only one case, which is paradigmatic for us, of the relation in which at any rate everything stands to everything else. This relation in which everything stands with everything else can also be interpreted in terms of the paradigms of intersubjectivity. Only to a certain modern approach would this seem to be an unusual paradox. In reality, this paradigm corresponds more closely to a life-world approach to things than any form of objective reductionism does. Whitehead, who knew this perfectly well, once wrote that he deliberately quoted Wordsworth in order to indicate: "how strained and paradoxical is the view of nature which modern science imposes on our thoughts."[4] This observation echoes Aristotle's when he described Anaxagoras because of his teleological speech as the one sober thinker among all those who are in error.

However, Whitehead distances himself from the life-world interpretation of the world when he denies that organisms, higher animals and human beings, are actual entities and ultimate ontological units. What is the reason for this view? First, obviously the determination, characteristic also of phenomenology, to refrain from all interpretation and to allow only what immediately manifests itself as a self, to count as what is ultimate and concrete. The enduring identity of a perceiving subject, which encompasses a succession of experiences and perceptions, seems never to be immediately given or accessible to experience. In this regard, Whitehead obviously was influenced by Hume's skeptical arguments against identity. It seems that as something immediately experienced, identity can only be the specific act of being itself experienced. But, since these acts are different as events, identity is thus dissolved. Otherwise, identity would have to be conceived of as a substantiality that precedes the acts of its being experienced, and it would then seem to contradict Whitehead's definition of concreteness. Substantiality can become concrete only in the successive events of being prehended. This actualism, however, presents Whitehead with two further difficulties. The first is the problem of singling out the teleologically structured totality of an actual event from the continuous stream of experience and of grasping it as a distinct totality. The second problem is the impossibility of categorizing the specifically human phenomena of reflection, volition and moral responsibility, i.e. those phenomena of self-realization by which identity constitutes itself. It is no accident that Whitehead speaks only of 'feeling', 'prehension' and 'striving', but not of 'thinking', 'volition' and 'responsibility'. If he considers these mediated events as derivative, his ontology, too, remains a form of reductionism. If we follow Whitehead's intention of creating an antidualistic system, we would be required to conceive the categorial system in such a way that it attains its paradigmatic and concrete fulfillment in the highest form of our experiences of value and of self.

As a matter of fact, it seems to me that the Aristotelian concept of substance comes closer to achieving this goal than Whitehead thought. In Whitehead's understanding, Aristotle regarded substance only as *hypokeimenon*, as matter whose identity is defined by a particular location in space and in which all the properties inhere which are predicated of it by our concepts. But in fact, Aristotle makes a distinction between the usual predicates and those we tend to call 'sortal expressions' today. These define a substance already as a *prote energeia*, an *actus primus*, or, in Whitehead's terms, as a fundamental event structured by one and only one "eternal object." This event combines a series of *actus secundi*, that is a series of secondary actual events that are compatible with this event into an ultimate, ontological unit; it then constitutes something of which everything is said but which is said of nothing else. The fundamental event conceived as substance not only integrates other events of the same kind into the unity of one act of prehension as Whitehead's actual entity does, moreover, it integrates once more the very acts of prehension into a comprehensive unity. This unity cannot be identical with Whiteheadian 'society' because this unity brings forth those actual events that prehend the world and are the foundation that makes such societies possible.

The paradigm for this concept of substance is the unity of the subject as a series of acts and states, a unity that experiences itself as a teleologically structured event, which embraces these particular events. In Aristotle's understanding, this subject is a substance because his conception of the substance has always been shaped in analogy to the subject. Once the paradigmatic origin is clear — and Kant was the first to demonstrate it — then it also becomes clear why Whitehead did not go beyond the actuality of his actual event as the ultimate entity. He came to a halt at this point because he did not advance beyond cosmology. In the *Concept of Nature* he speaks of "provisional realism" and suggests that a "complete metaphysics" might perhaps arrive at Berkeley. "An Essay in Cosmology" is the subtitle of *Process and Reality*, a work that deals with the "present epoch of the universe," although in its philosophical theology it advances as far as the conditions of existence for any possible epoch. Even this theology is still tied to the nonpersonal, organic paradigm. In order to advance beyond cosmology towards a fundamental ontology, one would probably have to turn to those modes of experience that are not characterized by "presentational immediacy," but by the reflective realization of the other as other and by self-identification in the mediated return from otherness. Whitehead's concept of 'prehension' rather originates in a sensitive relation to the world. It denotes the simple integration of other events into the own unity that is novel each time. Hence his criticism of the fallacy of 'simple location', i.e. of the notion that each thing can only be where it initially is, and not also elsewhere, where it is prehended. Only judgement renders the 'knowledge' specific by which the other is apprehended as that which is not where the prehending subject is. Whitehead might reply: In order to be apprehended as such an other, it must first be in the prehending subject. That is true enough. Sensible apprehension can indeed not be explained by the notion of simple location. It is only that free act of recognition which is adequately expressed in the word 'being', and hence it is only the 'absolute positing' carried out by a judgement, which locates what has been prehended and is now known where it had initially been. Only in this act of acknowledgement does the subject take back its sensible apprehension of the other and realize that, for its part, it is apprehended by the other in a similar way, so that it is, or is part of, the other's environment. Only by this act of letting-be (*Seinlassen*), the subject constitutes itself as properly being. Such thoughts, however, cannot be conceived within Whiteheadian concepts.

The limitation of Whitehead's cosmology consists in the fact that it does not permit the conditions that constitute the possibility of its own endeavor to be categorically interpreted in their turn. How is it possible to think concretion as concretion *in abstracto*? Despite the firmest intention, Whitehead's philosophy cannot retain its own paradigm of organism in its fundamental identity because it understands reason only as a function of organic creativity, and not as the free coming-to-itself of creativity. His philosophy attempts to read in organism what we are, instead of reading what organism is in those actual events in which we explicitly understand ourselves as free self-being (*Selbstsein*). Whitehead has succeeded in surmounting scientism. His cosmology is still awaiting an ontology to ground it and to understand its possibility.

Notes

1. SMW 190.
2. SMW 193.
3. Ibid.
4. SMW 104.

Part IV

Creativity and Creation

10.

Atom, Duration, Form: Difficulties with Process Philosophy

Wolfhart Pannenberg

Whoever comes in contact with process philosophy today encounters it more often than not in the form of Whitehead's philosophy. This was the way it was for me when I was guest professor in 1963 at the University of Chicago and ran into an entire school of Whitehead adherents in the theological faculty (not, I must say, in the philosophical faculty). Consequently, for the sake of my own intellectual survival I had to come to grips quickly and intensively with the writings of this philosopher, who was at that time hardly known on the continent of Europe.

The experience was enriching. It supplemented the great tradition of German idealism in the latter's serious lack of a philosophy of nature or metaphysics adequate to the demands of our century, one that, from the outset, integrates the horizon of consciousness as mediated by contemporary knowledge of nature with experience as disclosed by the humanities and social sciences. The more time I spent with Whitehead the more I was shocked, however, by the very dogmatic way in which he is read in the U.S.A., in the school of process theology—which has in the meantime become quite influential. In that school Whitehead is taken to be an entirely self-sufficient systematic thinker and, as such, authoritative, like Aristotle in the high scholasticism of the thirteenth century. Many people fail to see Whitehead as an exponent of a wide stream of process thinking, in the context of which his philosophical approach represents only one of the possible and, to some extent, actually explored options.

If one sees Whitehead's philosophy in the neighborhood of thinkers such as Henri Bergson and Samuel Alexander, to name only these two, then one becomes aware of different versions of the process philosophical perspective. It becomes clear that a process philosophical

approach, which dismisses the thought of a timeless, identical substance, must not necessarily be bound to specific hypotheses of Whitehead, such as his doctrine of discrete emergent 'occasions' or elementary
events,[1] as the ultimate realities, and his doctrine of eternal objects as
potentials for the self-realization of these 'occasions'.

Let us turn to the first hypothesis: namely, that actual 'occasions' or
'actual entities' form the final real things which constitute the world
(PR 18/27). This thesis implies an atomistic ontology; Whitehead himself says: "Thus the ultimate metaphysical truth is atomism" (PR35/53).
He calls his philosophy "an atomic theory of actuality" (PR 27/40).
The continuum he takes to be derived from the discreetly emergent
actual entities. Taken by itself, the continuum is only possibility, "potentiality for division" (PR 67/104), and it is by the actual entities divided.
Whitehead thereby enters into conflict not only with Newton's theory
of absolute space and absolute time but also with Bergson. For in the
type of process philosophy developed by Bergson, 'duration' and with it
a form of continuum is fundamental. Bergson's 'duration' is the continuum of becoming itself, while for Whitehead becoming is not continuous; in line with the paradoxes of Zeno, he asserts: "there can be no
continuity of becoming" (PR 35/53).

On this question, Samuel Alexander sides with Bergson, although
Alexander, anticipating Whitehead's somewhat later remarks (PR
321/489f.), criticizes Bergson's opposing space to time. The "spatiali-
zation" of time, which Bergson judges to be the result of the intelligence and which he goes so far as to blame for the errors of traditional
substance metaphysics, Alexander takes to be the essence of time itself
(STD I 143; cf. 149). It is only space that makes continuity possible,
because an instant can be common to different places; above all
because, inversely, many consecutive events can occur at the same place
(STD I 48f.). A succession of instants in themselves would lack continuity; it would consist of perishing instants (STD I 45.) Continuity,
which later Whitehead secured by his subtle theory of 'eternal objects'
and their ingression into the world of actual occasions, is still guaran-
teed in Alexander by a space which had not yet been relativized. To
this extent we can understand Alexander as Whitehead's precursor.

However, Alexander's conception of the infinity of space-time, as
the condition for the determination of finitude, is opposed to Whitehead. Following Samuel Clarke and also Kant's transcendental aesthetic, Alexander thinks of finitude and, above all, individual points/
instants as limitations of infinity. "The infinite is not what is not finite,
but the finite is what is not infinite" (STD I 42).

Like Levinas today, Alexander appeals to Descartes for the constitutive meaning of the infinite with regard to the thinkability of the

finite as such. But then, naturally, atomism cannot be the final metaphysical truth. Alexander shares Bergson's conception of the primordiality of movement as always holistic and continuous (STD I 149). "Motion is not a succession of point-instants, but rather a point-instant is the limiting case of a motion" (STD I 321). The discrimination of point-instants is the product of intellectual abstraction. "They are in fact . . . inseparable from the universe of motion; they are elements in a continuum" (STD I 325). Alexander consequently moves close to Spinoza; space-time is the whole of existing, the infinite, which precedes all finite actuality (STD I 339ff.).

In view of Bergson and Alexander, on the one side, and Whitehead's event-atomism, on the other, therefore, one has to do with two fundamental and alternative approaches for process thinking. To be sure, Alexander attempted to distinguish infinite space-time both from the category of substance and also from a whole of parts (STD I 338ff.), the latter because such a whole in his view is always to be thought of as composed of parts. However, with regard to motion, at least, he spoke indeed of the whole of motion as prior to its individual space-time instants (STD I 321). Conversely, Whitehead proceeds from the ontological priority of discrete events or their components. Does he not thereby fall into the logical *aporiae* of every atomistic metaphysic? They have already been formulated in the concluding parts of Plato's *Parmenides* (*Parm.* 165ef.): without the One the others can be neither one nor many and there would be absolutely nothing.

Many ones are many of the *same* (in the sense of the abstract One), but also *many* in relationship and so parts of a whole; if they do not form a totality, then they cannot be thought of as exemplifying the same One. In any case, an enveloping unity must already be presupposed, if atoms are to be thought of as unities at all.

If I am not mistaken, Whitehead nowhere discusses the logical difficulties attending the systematic concept of atomism: although he discusses in *Adventures of Ideas* 1933 different forms of atomism (AI 159ff.), and in so doing opposes the types of atomism that can be traced back to Democritus, Epicurus, and Lucretius, and from which the positivist interpretation of modern natural science is derived: here the atoms are only externally related, i.e., according to the principle of randomness. These relations are no less external in Newton's mechanics as expressions of laws imposed from without by the will of God. In contrast, Whitehead sees Plato as the originator of a way of looking at things which understands laws (AI 162) and therefore the relationships between things as regulated through them as immanent in the things (AI 156ff.). Whitehead himself is inclined to this conception.

Correspondingly, Whitehead already in *Science and the Modern World* 1925 opposes the description of relations between events solely in terms of external relations, which he finds in the usual accounts of space-time relations (SMW 180). Insofar as the individual events are constituted by the relationships in which they stand, these are internal to the events: ". . . the relationships of an event are internal, so far as . . . they are constitutive of what the event is in itself" (SMW 152). The acceptance of such inner relationships demands, according to Whitehead, the acceptance of a subjectivity of the individual event, as integrative of the manifold relations which constitute it (SMW 180). To that extent, these internal relations represent themselves as acts of the event itself and as such are called 'prehensions.' In Whitehead's main work, *Process and Reality*, this concept stands in the center of his analyses, while the discussions of external and internal relations recede to the background.[2] (Yet the concept of prehensions is even here still defined as "concrete facts of relatedness" [PR 22/32].)

Now each individual event prehends all other events of the world, which it encounters and which it must appropriate as its own: "each actual entity includes the universe, by reason of its determinate attitude towards every element in the universe" (PR 45/71f.).[3]

It may appear that the one-sidedness of atomism is thereby counterbalanced. Indeed, with the thesis that every individual event is conditioned by the totality of all the others, justice is apparently done to the constitutive meaning of the whole for the individual. Still it should be observed that Whitehead does not speak directly of a meaning of the universe for the individual, but only indirectly, on account of the relationship of every event to every other "element" of the universe. Only in this sense does he say: ". . . every actual entity springs from *that* universe which there is for it" (PR 80/124). Since the universe or the space-time continuum is not given as a real whole to the individual event, it is always only this individual event which must integrate into a whole the manifold relationships into which it enters. Consequently, as many perspectives of the universe arise as there are events that emerge. It is no accident that one thinks of Leibniz here. Whitehead explicitly appeals to Leibniz's doctrine of the monads: "I am using the same notion, only I am toning down his monads into the unified events in space and time" (SMW 102). Leibniz, however, with his thesis of the "windowlessness" of monads, would have denied the concrete reality of internal relations. The monads, for Leibniz, do not stand in real relationships to each other but only mirror the primary monad and the universe created by it in refraction of their own respective finite positions.

In consequence, according to Leibniz, natural laws are as much externally imposed on the world as they were in Descartes (AI 170f.).

Whitehead, on the contrary, wants to understand the laws of nature as emerging out of the reciprocal relationships of the things themselves, as expressing these reciprocal relations. Hence, individuals appear to him not only as reflections of the universe but also as subjects of the creative integration of the manifold relations which constitute them, while the spatiotemporal continuum is taken to be the result of an abstraction from the concrete eventness, out of which the relationships among the 'actual entities' emerge (cf. already CN 78).

We must therefore hold that in the end Whitehead's theory of prehension does not really counterbalance the one-sidedness of atomism, because the whole of the universe or of the spatiotemporal continuum, on his account, has no ontological independence over against the monad-like events. Leibniz felt otherwise, because the universe is pre-given to each individual creature as grounded in the thinking of God and is only mirrored by the creature. In Whitehead, however, God is not the creator but only the co-creator of the actual occasion; consequently the elemental events, as self-constitutive, are at the same time the ground of the continuum expressing their nexus, and this continuum is 'derived' from these events.

Through the concept of the subjectivity of individual events, seen as the integrating centers of the manifold of the relationships which constitute them, Whitehead wanted to oppose a more profound vision to the materialistic description of the natural processes, which settles for mere external relationships (SMW 151f.). But the concept of a self-constituting subjectivity of actual occasions leads into new difficulties. On the one hand, the actual occasion or entity ought to be the ultimate constituent of the physical universe. On the other hand, these final constituents of the universe are taken to be still further analyzable into the relations or 'prehensions' which constitute them. Now, Whitehead says, the analysis of an 'actual entity' is only feasible in thought. "The actual entity is divisible; but it is in fact undivided" (PR 227/347). If, however, the analysis of the actual occasion into the prehensions (or internal relations) which constitute it is only feasible by virtue of mental abstraction, then we are faced with a problem. How is it possible to continue to interpret the actual occasion itself as a process with different phases, in which it generates itself (PR 26/39), while asserting that the end phase of this process, on the other hand, ought to be identical with the complete duration of the event (PR 283/434)?

When Whitehead, in *Process and Reality*, presents a genetic analysis with its differentiation of various phases in the self-constitution of the event (cf.,e.g., PR 26 f./40, 248 f./380 f.), he becomes liable to the suspicion of confusing the abstract and concrete, thereby committing the "fallacy of misplaced concreteness," which he has often astutely criticized in other thinkers. If we cannot, in fact, really divide the actual occasion further but can only abstractly differentiate the relationships which constitute its identity, then we cannot, by the same token, characterize the actual occasion as being the result of a process in which these aspects, which can only be distinguished in the abstract, are actually integrated. This is even more difficult since these relations themselves are said to be constituted only by the actual occasion.

Whitehead assuredly needs this way of looking at things, if he wants to be able to affirm the subjectivity of actual occasions as *causae sui* (PR 86/131, 88/135, cf. 25f./38). If one conceives of the actual occasion as merely determined by the happenstance of the relations which constitute it, then it is only thought as an object, which as such cannot be separated from its field but is nothing other than the systematically adjusted set of modifications of the field (CN 190).[4] It seems, however, that Whitehead must assume the subjectivity of the event in order to be able at all to assert its autonomy. It is therefore the condition of Whitehead's atomistic interpretation of reality. If, however, the independence of actual occasions is thought of as self-constitution, then it seems to follow that the actual occasion itself must be reconceived as a process which integrates that which precedes it, thus constituting its own identity. This conception remains self-contradictory because the actual occasions are claimed to be the ultimate components of reality, not integration of more primitive components. This basic thesis cannot be reconciled with the assumptions of the actual occasions' self-constitution.

Now Whitehead's "genetic analysis" of the actual occasion, doubtless, amounts to an extrapolation which forces onto the interpretation of actual occasions the experiential structure of more highly organized forms of life. Whitehead himself described this procedure of his speculative philosophy as the method of imaginative generalization (PR 5/8, cf. 4ff./7ff.); it is precisely the principle of self-constitution as creativity which forms, in his own philosophy, the central instance of applying this method (PR 7/11). Whitehead's doctrine of the subjectivity of actual occasions shares many individual features with the philosophical psychology of William James. More specifically, Whitehead's doctrine deals, on the one hand, with the momentary character of the I and, on the other hand, with the description of each I-instant as being a momentary integration of experience and especially of the past of such I-instants. Presumably, Whitehead's theory of the subjectivity of actual occasions can be interpreted, to a very large extent, as a generalization of this idea of the I in William Jame's psychology, a generalization achieved by applying this idea to the (interpretation of the) foundations of physics.

It was not for nothing that Whitehead considered William James alongside Bergson and Dewey among the thinkers to whom his chief work is especially indebted. In *Science and the Modern World* he even compared James to Descartes as a founder of a new era of philosophy (SMW 205f.).

The demonstration of such connections is certainly not enough to substantiate our objection to Whitehead's claims. The procedure of imaginative generalization obviously plays a considerable role in any formation of philosophical concepts. Whitehead himself says, however, that such procedure has the character of tentative formulations (PR 8/12) and that it requires, along with inner consistency and coherence, confrontation with facts: "Speculative boldness must be balanced by complete humility before logic and before fact" (PR 17/25).

Measured by this yardstick, it would seem illegitimate to extrapolate the structures of subjectivity in order to interpret actual occasions, because in contrast to James's psychology of subjectivity, which has to do with a real succession of moments of experience, Whitehead's thought cannot claim such real succession in the genesis of the individual actual occasion. James's psychology of the self can conceive each individual moment of experience as a new integration of previous experience, because the successive moments are really distinct and because the relation of the later to the earlier, as their integration, constitutes the special quality of human, subjective relations in the medium of experience, reflection, and memory. Whitehead, for his part, can only use the factual universal relationship of all events as a basis for applying the Jamesian model of subjectivity to the relationship that obtains between newly emerging events and all the other events and so also their predecessors. It is very questionable whether there exists here a sufficient measure of analogy. The I, which according to James always emerges momentarily, relates itself in no way to all preceding events but only to the earlier experiences made present to it by memory. The human faculty of memory, however, is a highly specialized function which cannot, without further ado, be attributed to all natural processes.

Moreover, the integrating performance of the momentarily emerging I is, in James, conditioned by the fact that neither the human body, on the one hand, nor the 'social self', the sum of social expectations concerning the individual's performance, on the other hand, emerge instantaneously; they both, rather, represent *continua*, in relation to which each momentary synthesis of the I (*die punktuelle Ichsynthese*) can function as the principle of novelty and creativity.

Whitehead's speculative extrapolation of the principle of subjective integration, momentarily achieved, may overestimate the measure of uniformity encountered in the real world. (The generalization of the structure of the human I, as understood by James [but disengaged from the problematic of the self as distinguished from the I], leads paradoxically to the reduction to the place of elementary processes). These more complex forms of natural evolution are merely described as diversely ordered series, 'societies', of actual occasions, which, because of the abstract structural moments reproduced in their sequence and systematically modified, appear as stable unities without finally being such. In *Process and Reality*, the comparatively brief treatment of this topic already suggests that the ontological dignity of stable and per-during forms is considered secondary in contrast to the structure of actual occasions. If we were to suppose, however, that the formation of higher forms were already deciphered, in principle, with the correct description of actual occasions, of which all higher forms consist, then we would repeat the style of thinking characteristic of materialism, the very thing to which Whitehead wanted to offer an alternative.

The fact that the emergence of form cannot be derived from the actual occasions of which they might consist shows once again that the unity of the field cannot be reduced to elementary momentary events which appear in it. In view of the metaphysical relevance of the form as actuality, not merely as structure in the sense of Whitehead's 'eternal objects', we see once more how one-sided the atomistic inter-pretation of reality is; it cannot do justice to wholeness as a metaphysi-cal principle of equal dignity with that of individual discreteness.

Curiously, however, it is precisely Whitehead's genetic analysis of actual occasions with all its paradoxes which offers new points of view that could help at this impasse. According to Whitehead, the phases of concrescence are not to be thought of as temporally successive, since the event is what it is as an undivided unity. Therefore, the represen-tation describing a process of genesis appeared to us as paradoxical. But Whitehead's analyses illuminate the understanding of processes whose phases certainly must be thought of as temporally successive, in which, however, the final aim (*das Werdeziel*) of the form is already present.

In any event, all life processes seem to be of this nature. In the process of its growth the plant or animal is always this plant or this animal, although its specific nature indeed comes fully to light only in the result of its genesis. By way of anticipation it is in each instant already that which it only becomes in the process of its growth. The identity of its being is assuredly not that of a momentary event but resides in the identity of its nature, of its essential form, which per-dures throughout the course of some particular time. By anticipating its essential form in the process of its growth, a being's substantial iden-tity is linked together with the notion of process.

In Whitehead's genetic analysis of elementary processes, the con-cepts of 'subjective aim' and 'superject' play a similar role. Already in *Process and Reality* Whitehead himself spoke occasionally of anticipatory feelings with respect to subjective aim (PR 278/424f.; cf. 214f./ 327f.). He did so above all in *Adventures of Ideas* (AI 250f.). To be sure, Whitehead does not go so far as to describe the significance of antici-pation for the formation of the subject, as constituting its subjectivity out of a future which already determines the present by way of antici-pation. Rather in Whitehead, anticipation means that the subject, con-stituting itself in the present, includes also its future relevance for others (its 'objective immortality') in the act of its self-constitution.

Whitehead did not exhaust the theoretical potential of the ele-ment of anticipation implied in the concept of 'subjective aim'. Aris-totle's analysis of motion, which forms the background to all teleological descriptions of processes, went much further in that direction. Aris-totle interpreted the very anticipation of the final state of natural move-ment in the moved as entelechy. Although this resulted in turning the action of the future end upon the present becoming into the effective-ness of a living organism's seed with respect to its future end, he never-theless spoke of an effect of the end upon the process of becoming. This does not happen in Whitehead, because he sees becoming in each of its stages as self-constitutive. This is why, despite his use of teleological language, the element of anticipation cannot really become constitutive in his interpretation of subjectivity.

The idea of the radical self-creation of each actual occasion is the reason why Whitehead's metaphysics cannot be reconciled with the biblical idea of creation nor, therefore, with the biblical idea of God. To be sure, American process theology has attempted to interpret Whitehead's concept of creativity in terms of the divine activity of creation.[5] In Whitehead himself, however, the constitution of each actual entity's subjectivity remains always a self-constitution, and this despite the dependence of each actual entity upon God, who provides it with the conditions of its self-realization through its 'initial aim'. This short-coming follows from the fact that Whitehead relates the teleological structure of becoming to the elementary level of actual occasions, which are called processes but do not allow for temporal extension in the sense of a succession of phases in time, since actual occasions, of which everything else is supposed to consist, are indeed said to be momen-tary and undivided.

The matter would be otherwise if we limit the applicability of Whitehead's genetic analysis to processes that take place in time, instead of using that analysis to explain the constitution of actual occasions. Then the 'subjective aim' of the process would have to do with the future of one's own essential completion in the future, a future which would still be to come. This completion could not simply be in the power of the present decision but would eventually be reached or not reached by such a decision. Correspondingly the anticipation of one's own essential completion in the future would gain greater significance for the constitution of subjectivity; the latter could not be identified with the self-creation of present decisions but would be dependent on the manifestation of the whole of one's own essential completion in each present.

Certainly such a conception would no longer be that of an atomistic metaphysic. It would no longer attribute subjectivity to the simplest actual occasions. Rather from the impossibility of such attribution (because it implies the paradoxical assumption of a nontemporal process), there would arise an argument to the effect that the autonomy of finite being and subjectivity can increase with the complexity of forms rather than being fully pronounced as early as in the elementary occasions. The unity of the field from which actual occasions proceed would no longer be traceable to a network of relations which is itself constituted only by these occasions. Rather the unity of the field would have to be seen along with the unity of the forms which appear in increasing differentiation on higher levels of natural processes, keeping in mind that such unity of the forms cannot be derived from actual occasions although it consists of such occasions.

Such a view of the matter would be, as I said, no longer atomistic, because it does not limit reality (in the sense of what is actual) to the undivided elementary actual occasions.

For that reason alone, however, it would not step outside the circle of process philosophies, although it would hold to the idea of an essential identity of the being which becomes in the process of its genesis, as an idea encompassing this whole process; thus it would link the fundamental intention of the concept of substance with the process perspective. It is precisely in that direction that Whitehead's analysis of genetic processes, with his concept of the subject as 'superject' of one's own process of formation, has developed important impulses, even if these impulses bear fruit only after they have been liberated from the limitation to momentary actual occasions and its attendant atomism. They are thereby also liberated from the *aporiae* which burden them in the theoretical context of such assumptions.

Notes

STD—Samuel Alexander. *Space, Time and Deity.* 1920; New York: Macmillan, 1966.

1. More precisely 'actual occasion' designates the primary constituents of events: "an actual occasion is the limiting type of an event with only one member" (PR 73/113).

2. This may be connected with the fact that now relations may be characterized as reciprocal (the complex of mutual prehensions, PR 194/295), while SMW still distinguishes, in an Aristotelian sense, between internal and external relations (analogous to the difference between *relatio realis* and *relatio rationis* in scholastic philosophy). Cf. also PR 222f./340 and 50/79.

3. Cf. 123: "each actual entity is a locus for the universe," as early as *The Concept of Nature* (1920), 152. Later Whitehead relates this idea to the concept of a physical field (PR 80/123f.).

4. In *The Concept of Nature* Whitehead still did not view, one must remember, the point-flash or event-particle as the ultimate real component of the natural world: "You must not think of the world as ultimately built up of event particles," he expressly says there (CN 172, cf. 59). The world is rather "a continuous stream of occurrences which we can discriminate into finite events forming by their overlappings and containings of each other and separations a spatio-temporal structure" (CN 172f.; cf. also AI 161).

5. So, especially, John Cobb, *God and the World* (Philadelphia: Westminster, 1965).

11.

Creativity as Universal Activity

Jan Van der Veken

If one decides on the European philosophical scene to develop an interest in process philosophy and consider it with a basically positive attitude, one will be obliged to face up to a number of persistent difficulties. I will assess several of these difficulties that emerge constantly, in order to inquire whether there might be some common connection between them. Then I will propose a reinterpretation of Whitehead's category of creativity as general or universal activity, in an effort to dispense with many of these problems.

I.

An objection frequently voiced is that Whitehead was a typical practitioner of 'onto-theology', as defined and criticized by Heidegger. Even though Whitehead and Heidegger were mutually ignorant of one another's work, Heidegger's overall critique of western metaphysics is still especially significant for Whiteheadians. Heidegger reproached traditional metaphysics since the time of Plato for its onto-theological character, in which Being (*Sein*) had time and again come to mean merely "entities-which-exist" (*Seiendes*), substance, first cause, or God. Heidegger's critique of traditional metaphysics also appears to apply to Whitehead.

Whitehead apparently concerns himself entirely with 'existents' [i.e., *Seiendes*, or "entities-which-exist"]. Although 'actual entities' are conceived dynamically, they are nonetheless always 'realities' and never 'reality' or 'Being itself'. Likewise, at least from the period of *Religion in the Making* 1926 and *Process and Reality* 1929 on, Whitehead holds that God is *an* actual entity, although the only *everlasting* entity. It turns out that the proper analogue to Heidegger's conception of Being in the

178

Whiteheadian scheme cannot be a determinate actual entity, nor can the analogue be seen as God. Rather, the analogue for 'Being' as Heidegger uses this term, can only be creativity. Creativity for Whitehead, as Being for Heidegger, is all inclusive, all-overpowering process that never itself appears and yet reveals itself in everything that really happens.

The analogy between Whitehead's interpretation of creativity and Heidegger's understanding of Being as *Ereignis* ("event") surely points in this direction. However, since Whitehead later, i.e., after *Science and the Modern World* 1925 understood creativity as "without a specific character," the two philosophical systems are also alienated from one another. Accordingly our proposal: If one ascribes to creativity a richer, not merely a formal meaning—in particular, if creativity is really *active*— then the dialogue with the later Heidegger becomes much easier. In addition, it will also no longer be necessary to interpret God as the highest existent, as still *a* being or *Seiendes*—nor as *an* actual entity, over against others. God will rather be seen, on this reinterpretation, as a dimension of creativity and not creativity itself, somewhat as the holy (*das Heilige*) is for Heidegger.

Creative neo-Thomists such as Norris Clarke,[1] who have entered into a dialogue with Whitehead, raise another objection. Likewise here the main theme is the relationship between God and creativity. Clarke, to be sure, wants to ascribe a determinate role to the concept of creativity. In his view, however, creativity is not something ultimate: the 'creative advance' of all that is finite is itself produced by God. Clarke is himself well aware that Whitehead has a good reason for rejecting the traditional concept of creation. If God had produced *everything* without another ground or reason than a particular, unconditioned and freely willed decision, then God would in the end be finally "the supreme author of the play"[2] and, as a result, as much responsible for evil as for good. So Clarke is also forced to acknowledge that God does not decide everything unilaterally and unconditionally. Thus the difference between *universal* creativity, and specifically *divine* creativity (or alternatively, between creativity and God) is also in this respect very important.

Finally there remains the dialogue with German idealism, which could be very stimulating for a creative Whitehead interpretation. As a result of such a dialogue, it might be possible to demonstrate that the analogy drawn by Whitehead between his system and "philosophies of the Hegelian school" is in no way gratuitous or superfluous. Moreover, directly in reference to our central thesis, it would appear that a consideration of the relationship between the absolute and God might prove very illuminating. In particular, we might verify in all cases that more than a merely formal role ought to be ascribed to the absolute or to the ultimate. The ultimate creativity may be more than a 'category'.

II.

All of the foregoing problems have a common background and an inner connectedness. The real problem, phrased in non-Whiteheadian language, seems to be that each of these relationships can be portrayed as occurring between the finite and the infinite, between existents and Being, or between determinate realities and reality *per se*. Whitehead himself suggests: "The finite essentially refers to an unbounded background,"[3] "to the background which is the unbounded Universe."[4]

How should we understand the relation of "the finite" to this "unbounded background?" And what sort of ontological status does this 'unbounded universe' have? Here our specific Whiteheadian concern converges with one of the great problems of classical philosophy: as Whitehead himself puts it, "in all philosophic theory there is an ultimate which is actual in virtue of its accidents."[5]

Whitehead undoubtedly is thinking at this point of Spinoza, who offered him in *Science and the Modern World*, to a certain extent at least, a central philosophical paradigm, as Whitehead's phrase, 'substantial activity', suggests.[6] However according to Spinoza, substance and God coincide with one another, which Whitehead cannot envision. As a result, from Whitehead's perspective, the following question haunts our inquiry in the background: what relation obtains between the ultimate metaphysical principle and God? In other words, do the philosophical and religous ultimates coincide with one another or not?

Now Whitehead is of the opinion that there is a good reason why God and philosophical ultimate (creativity) do *not* coincide. First, he conceives of freedom as a universal category, which applies to everything that is self-constituting. If there was an instance that decided everything, then no more place would remain for the self-determination of actual entities. Secondly, there stands the problem of evil. If God is the sole determining instance, then he is also responsible for everything. Whitehead stands quite clearly on the side of David Hume in the latter's critique of traditional theism, of God as the "all-powerful Creator" (suggesting at the same time the identity of the philosophical and religous ultimates).[7] In reaction to traditional creation doctrine, the specific activity of actual entities, according to Whitehead, is moved into the foreground: these must not only exist in themselves, they must also be the 'creator' of themselves: they are *causa sui*.

The firm emphasis on the ontological principle makes Whitehead's system into an ontological pluralism, which perhaps is pressed too far. The principle: "No actual entity, then no reason"[8] is in fact never rigorously upheld within his own system, for he likewise apportions to creativity functions that also amount to a genuine *explanation*.[9] Creativity itself is finally the reason *why* there are actual entities, *why* again and again new actual entities arise, and *why* they are also connected with one another. Whitehead's creativity must come to be understood as general or *universal activity*, and that means also that creativity really has to have *done* something in the sense of being active, of really accomplishing something.

If creativity within the system really comes to be understood as universal activity which is necessarily limited ("some particular *how* is necessary"),[10] then it is not necessary to conceive of this limitation of creativity as a distinct actual entity, in the form of the Whiteheadian God. Rather, the limitation of creativity is as ultimate as creativity itself; no single actual entity would ever be able to have the selfsame philosophically ultimate meaning.

Whether the first limitation of creativity can rightly be understood as 'God', however, is another question. The word *God* is definitely a religious category. The question amounts to the following: Does the sustaining and driving power which is at work in the universe reveal the characteristics that the *religious* person ascribes to "God?" In other words, is creativity internally directed towards truth, goodness, and harmony—or must we understand it instead as fate, as an anonymous power? This question can only be answered on the basis of one's own individual experience, which one either is able or is not able to do. For this reason the issue of the variant meanings of "the particular how"[11] of the limitation of creativity is a religious, and not purely a philosophical matter.

This issue is transformed into a philosophical problem, however, because, as philosophers, we are also required to be able to express what the religious person says about the final limitation of the ultimate within the universal connections of a philosophical system. In *this* sense, God cannot be portrayed as an exception to the general metaphysical principles. It is not necessary, however, that God simply be understood as an actual entity like all the others. This extraordinary claim by Whitehead is, by the way, not consistently maintained by Whitehead himself until the very end of his systematic project. By then it is definitely the case for Whitehead that God is an exceptional and *everlasting* actual entity, in which primordial (conceptual) and consequent (dative) phases are related in precisely the opposite way than is the case for all other actual entities.

III.

In what follows we will attempt to show how Creativity as universal activity, interpreted in a fuller sense, is on this representation able to be qualified in such a manner that the religious person is permitted to recognize it as divine.

In order to elicit what Whitehead really wants to say, it is necessary to see what creativity is *not*: "The creativity is *not* an external agency with its own ulterior purposes."[12] Creativity is not exterior to or outside of actual entities. However, it does not follow from this text that creativity is not some legitimate form of agency or active principle. The text suggests, in point of face, that creativity is an '*internal* agency'; it is *immanent*. Creativity is identical with the one and the many, with the category of the ultimate; however it is also "a creative advance into novelty,"[13] hence it is the principle that explains the existence of a unified, dynamic universe. To conceive of creativity as something abstract, not real—or even to account for it as an "eternal object" as R.J. Connelly has attempted[14]—is in our opinion entirely unacceptable.

Current thought about creativity has perhaps been too strongly influenced by the idea that Whitehead saw creativity as the same as the Aristotelian principle of matter:

> 'Creativity' is another rendering of the Aristotelian 'matter', and of the modern 'neutral stuff'. But it is divested of the notion of passive receptivity, either of 'form', or of external relation; it is the pure notion of the activity conditioned by the objective immortality of the actual world.[15]

The second sentence here is at least as important as the first: Creativity only *resembles* the Aristotelian matter principle, and that only insofar as it has no specific character. Creativity should otherwise only be compared with first substance (*substantia prima*).

Another model for the interpretaion of creativity is the 'receptacle'. Walter Stokes has offered this analogy.[16] And it is true that creativity can be viewed as similar to the receptacle in its unifying function, although in *Adventures of Ideas* the Platonic *hypodoche* is more to be compared to the 'extensive continuum'.

Here also, however, the analogy should not be pressed too far. In order to fulfill its basic underlying function (the category of the ultimate encompasses not only creativity, but also the one and the many), creativity must be more than merely a passive receptacle. Accordingly I want to propose that creativity not be interpreted in analogy to Aristotelian *hyle* or *materia prima*, but instead that it be conceived more adequately as substantial or all-encompassing activity. *Substantial activity*[17] is not by accident the word which Whitehead has chosen in *Science and the Modern World*.

Spinozistic substance is quite unequivocally *causa sui*. It is also necessary: it simply cannot fail to exist. There is overall nothing other than substance; because there is also nothing (nor can there be anything) outside of creativity, not actual entities but their reciprocal relatedness (i.e., creativity , the one, the many) should be interpreted as *causa sui*. That creativity should have a cause besides creativity itself is absurd. If one interprets creativity more closely along the lines of Spinozistic substance than along the lines of a nonexisting *hyle*, then creativity is better able to fulfill the function that Whitehead—albeit implicitly—has alloted to it.

This function of creativity is first of all to be *general* activity.[18] This means, in standard philosophical terminology, to be all-encompassing reality, though in a dynamic sense. It is also meaningful that 'the real' for Whitehead cannot exist without the 'realities' (the existents, or *Seiendes*), or outside of these realities.

The second function of creativity consists in its being also an *explanatory principle*. Creativity is the reason or ground for the source of unending actual entities ("the reason for the origin of that occasion of experience").[19] Only creativity itself and its first limitation are 'without why'—i.e., devoid of antecedent explanation.

IV.

There are different texts of Whitehead that underscore these several points concerning the *activity of creativity*. I would like to quote just a few of these.

Creativity is *active*: it is termed 'substantial activity' or 'general activity';[20] it is "the pure notion of the activity conditioned by the objective immortality of the actual world";[21] "It is that ultimate notion of the highest generality at the basis of actuality".[22]

Creativity is something *real*:—Walter Stokes, in his well-known dissertation on the function of creativity has given an interpretation in this sense: "[Creativity is] totally ordered to the actualization of new occasions. [It] is the ultimate subject to which the process of actualization is ascribed. Though not actual, creativity is *as real as actual occasions*."[23] "The efficient cause of the novel actual entity is Creativity conditioned by the actual entities of the actual world."[24]

Creativity has *explanatory* value: "Creativity explains also why there are new occasions: 'The creative advance is the application of this ultimate principle of creativity to each novel occasion which it *originates*.' "[25]

Creativity is a *ground* or *reason*: (It would be better to read this as 'modes' or instances of creativity.) In *Science and the Modern World*, God is not a real entity or *Seiendes*, but rather the first qualification of being, or the firm and foremost limitation of substantial activity. All themes converge in the text of *Adventures of Ideas*, where creativity is explicitly termed 'reason': "The initial situation includes a factor of activity which is the reason for the origin of that occasion of experience. This factor of activity is what I have called 'Creativity'."[26]

Our proposal thus amounts to this: that creativity first and foremost be conceived as substantial or universal activity—in a real and proper sense, and not merely in a formal sense. This interpretation can itself be shown to follow from Whiteheadian texts. One should also note that Process and Reality is not the whole of Whitehead. Perhaps his earlier perspectives are the most intelligible, whether or not these are fully formulated.[27] It could be after all that Process and Reality is not at all as final a statement as has frequently been claimed. There are texts prior to Process and Reality as well as afterwards that cannot entirely be brought into accordance with that opus magnum. So in Science and the Modern World 'substantial activity' connotes process; and the concrete realities (later portrayed as 'actual entities') are 'attributes' of [this] substance.[28] (It would be better to read this as 'modes' or 'instances' of creativity.) In Science and the Modern World, God is not a real entity or Seiendes, but rather the first qualification of being, or the firm and foremost limitation of substantial activity.

In a highly original but also controversial interpretation, Laurence F. Wilmot[29] has emphasized the meaning of the theme of the immanence of God in each actual entity. He advances the thesis that in Adventures of Ideas the implicit Platonic scheme of Process and Reality is basically abandoned. Subsequently Whitehead claims in Adventures of Ideas that one must give special attention to the immanence of God in the world, as this, he remarks, was examined by the Alexandrian theologians of the fourth century.[30] Although Wilmot appears, in my opinion, to prove too much of a good thing, one is still able to establish from him that Whitehead abandoned the Platonic solution of the relationship between God and the world as insufficient. The canonical Whiteheadian texts establish mainly that one should go further than Plato, and—if a bit less firmly—further than Process and Reality.

V.

The immanence of God in the world must now be given consideration. It appears that the earlier positions on this problem are unsatisfactory. It is not in fact sufficient to say that God is present (or is prehended) only through the 'initial aim'[31] in a new actual entity. Only as the limitation or qualification of creativity, and not as an actual entity, can God be "in unison of becoming with every other creative act."[32] Were God exclusively consequent with regard to the genesis of particular actual entities, then all the more would we be able to talk of "the objectification of the world in God,"[33] although *not* of God's being *with* all creation, or even more to the point, *in* all creation.

The teleological influence of God on the process of becoming is in any case of such significance that Whitehead — precisely in this sense — has spoken of 'creation'.[34] However, most of the representatives of the classical creation doctrine find that quite unconvincing. If God is not truly active *in* each new occasion, then these must be *causa sui*, which seems a sharp contradiction to that classical doctrine.

Let us try to conceive the relationship between God and creativity differently, namely thus: that creativity is viewed as a universal activity, which is efficacious in all events, and that God as the primordial limitation of this process coordinates all events from within. Then it becomes much simpler to accept the immanence of creativity *and* the immanence of God in all events.[35] This does not need to be un-Whiteheadian. This interpretation follows only the arguments of *Science and the Modern World* closely, where Whitehead does not yet view God as a distinct actual entity, and conceives creativity explicitly as 'substantial activity'.

I am entirely in agreement with this: that the distinction between creativity ("creative advance into novelty")[36] or reality on the one hand, and God on the other, is very important. Yet one should recognize further the distinction between God and all 'modes' or actual entities. It does not suffice to say that God represents no exception to the metaphysical categories. Creativity *is* the exception, for it is the final or all-encompassing metaphysical category, and God is its first limitation. God is in *Science and the Modern World* not a determinate reality over against other realities. God is rather the religious qualification of reality, a definite manner in which to interpret or to impart a specific (i.e., religious) meaning to the 'principle of concretion'. In other words, God is a religious name, that believers give intuitively to the all-encompassing process on the basis of particular experiences of a certain manner, which allows them to see and interpret that all-encompassing process (reality; 'substantial activity') in a specific, i.e. religious way. In this sense God is a 'category of meaning' and not just a category of being.

It would naturally be wonderful if one could clear several objections against the Whiteheadian system of thought out of the way in a *single* stroke, or through a *single* revision. That would of course constitute too far-reaching a goal. What I have attempted here is only a 'research project'. It should therefore incite and creatively nurture a dialogue with the great philosophical traditions, including Spinoza, Hegel, and Heidegger, which Whitehead and Whiteheadians have begun — and in a certain respect, *only* have begun.

Notes

1. W. Norris Clarke, S.J.: *The Philosophical Approach to God. A Neo-Thomist Perspective* (Winston-Salem, NC: Wake Forest University Press, 1979).

2. SMW 223.

3. "Mathematics and the Good," in P. Schilpp, ed.: *The Philosophy of Alfred North Whitehead* (LaSalle, IL: Open Court Press, 1951), 670.

4. Ibid., 674.

5. PR 7.

6. SMW 220.

7. PR 342-343: "God in the image of an imperial ruler, God in the image of a personification of moral energy, God in the image of an ultimate philosophical principle. Hume's *Dialogues* criticize unanswerably these modes of explaining the system of the world."

8. PR 19. That is "the Ontological Principle." Whitehead writes: "It could also be termed the 'principle of efficient, and final, causation'. This ontological principle means that actual entities are the only *reasons*; so that to search for a *reason* is to search for one or more actual entities." (PR 24) "The ontological principle can be summarized as: no actual entity, then no reason." (PR 29)

9. AI 230. "Explanation" is my rendering or understanding of the meaning of Whitehead's term "reason." André Cloots has written a doctoral dissertation on the topic *Van Creativiteit naar Allesomvattendheid. De vraag naar het ultieme in de proces-filosofie van Alfred North Whitehead en Charles Hartshorne* (Leuven, 1978). In an article titled "Creativity and God in Whitehead and Hartshorne," which he read during the "European Weekend on Process Philosophy" in Leuven in 1978, Cloots proposed his important interpretation of the ontological principle, in the presence of Ch. Hartshorne himself.

   On account of his adherence to the strict proscription of the ontological principle, Cloots does not call creativity a *ground* or reason in the literal sense of these words. Nonetheless he does see creativity as the ultimate clarifying and descriptive principle: "By being the ultimate descriptive notion, describing the nature of things, it is also the ultimate explanatory principle" [in *Whitehead's Legacy*, eds. P. Jonkers and J. Van der Veken (Leuven: Institute of Philosophy, 1981), p. 51]. The term "explain" appears on several occasions, e.g.: "But what Whitehead wants to explain by creativity are especially two things: namely the ongoingness of the world and the solidarity of it, or in one word, 'the ongoing history of the one Universe' (AI 192)" (Ibid., 51).

   "To explain" and "to provide a ground" are so closely linked in my view that creativity can and must still be understood as *'ground'*. This interpretation is, by the way, also suggested by the text of AI 230, which Cloots cites and to which he correctly attaches such great significance.

10. SMW 221.

11. Ibid.

12. PR 222.

13. Ibid.

14. Cf. R.J. Connelly: *Whitehead vs. Hartshorne: Basic Metaphysical Issues* (Lanham, MD: University Press of America, 1981). See also the critical comments on this point in a review of Connelly's book by Gary Bollinger: *Process Studies*, 12, no. 1 (1982).

15. PR 31.

16. Cf. Walter E. Stokes, S.J.: *The Function of Creativity in the Metaphysics of Whitehead*, Diss. (St. Louis University), 1960.

17. SMW 220.

18. Ibid.

19. AI 230.

20. SMW 220.

21. PR 31.

22. Ibid.

23. Walter Stokes, op. cit., p. 104. Emphasis added.

24. Ibid., 153.

25. PR 21. Emphasis added.

26. AI 230. Emphasis added.

27. Arthur E. Murphy poses the question of *which* "Whitehead" will become objectively immortal, in an essay entitled: "Whitehead's 'Objective Immortality'," in *Reason and the Common Good. Selected Essays of Arthur E. Murphy*, eds. W. H. Hay, M. G. Sinder, and A. E. Murphy (Englewood Cliffs, NJ: Prentice-Hall, 1963), 163-172. Will it be, he asks, the systematic Whitehead of *Process and Reality*, or "the explanatory Whitehead, insisting on the endless resourcefulness and many-sidedness of thought, confronting all intellectual systems (including that of *Process and Reality*) with the importance of their omissions, and providing in his own thinking some fine examples of ways in which this can in fact be done, in which the as-yet-unsayable can be said, if we have the wit and wisdom to fit our language to the structure of the concrete facts and not merely to the 'rationality' of our system. One or the other of these Whiteheads can follow, but not both" (p. 172).

Murphy bases much of this critique on the ontological principle and on the drastic conclusions which Whitehead seems to draw from it ("The rest is silence"): "But even here his teaching remains equivocal and a choice must be made. Philosophers look for reasons, but what kind of reasons?" (Ibid.) Murphy shows a preference for the early Whitehead, prior to PR. He takes the consequent nature of God as an artificial, ad-hoc concept: "But it left me profoundly dissatisfied. I could see it then, and I can see it now, only as an unhappy expression of that hardening of the categories in which ideas that have ceased to function *as* ideas are set up as the necessary structure of existence to which, in the name of rationality, all our thinking must finally conform" (Ibid., 166).

To our great joy, Dorothy Emmet, in her contribution to this volume, expresses her preference even more strongly for this "first Whitehead" through SMW, where his fundamental insights approach more nearly the truth than in the system of PR.

28. SMW 221.

29. Laurence F. Wilmot: *Whitehead and God. Prolegomena to Theological Reconstruction* (Waterloo, Ontario: Wilfred Laurier University Press, 1979).

30. The key texts upon which Wilmot relies are found in AI 213-216: "These Christians have the distinction of being the only thinkers who in a fundamental metaphysical doctrine have improved upon Plato. . . . What metaphysics requires is a . . . solution which exhibits the World as requiring its union with God, and God requiring his union with the World. . . . The problem came before the Christian theologians in highly special forms. . . . I am not making any judgment about the details of the theology. . . . My point is that in the place of Plato's solution of secondary images and imitations, they demanded a direct doctrine of immanence."

31. PR 108, 224, 244.

32. PR 345.

33. PR 521.

34. PR 225: "In this sense, God can be termed the creator of each temporal actual entity."

35. "This permanent actuality passes into and is immanent in the transient side." Cf. "Process and Reality," in *Essays in Science and Philosophy* (New York: The Philosophical Library, 1948), 126.

36. PR 222, 128.

12.

Creativity: A New Transcendental?

Reto Luzius Fetz

The term 'transcendental' as used by the pre-Kantians or scholastics denotes those concepts that transcend the universality of the Aristotelian generic terms or categories. In scholasticism, the transcendentals are the properties or characteristics that pertain to any and all existents and explain what every existent is. The proposal I intend to develop in this discussion is that Whitehead's concept of creativity can best be understood as such a transcendental, and that the concept of creativity understood in this way appears as a new transcendental in contrast to the classical tradition. In order to locate this thesis, we shall begin by explaining the conception of creativity as it was understood by Whitehead. This explanation can be achieved with the help of three distinctions.

The first distinction is that Whitehead's concept of creativity cannot adequately be understood as a concept of physics or of the philosophy of nature, but must rather be regarded as an eminently metaphysical notion. True enough, Whitehead's concept of creativity is strongly influenced by an understanding of actuality based on physics, biology and the theory of evolution. Yet, inasmuch as for Whitehead creativity is the unique and autonomous self-determination of actuality, the concept of creativity must fall outside the domain of the natural sciences as they were understood by Whitehead.[1]

The second distinction is that Whitehead's concept of creativity cannot adequately be interpreted by reference to Greek metaphysics, as is also true of so many key notions of his metaphysics. This becomes apparent already on a superficial level, because *creare*, 'to create', is not a term in Greek metaphysics, and no Greek equivalent can be found either in Plato or in Aristotle, both of which Whitehead otherwise frequently relies upon. Expressions such as ' immanence', and 'transcendence', or 'creator', and 'creature', which are used in connection

with Whitehead's concept of creativity, demonstrate clearly that medieval Christian metaphysics of creation is the indispensable background
for Whitehead's notion of creativity.

The third distinction is that Whitehead's concept of creativity presents a novelty also in comparison to the doctrine of medieval metaphysics of creation. Two important abstract nouns, 'creativity' and
'creatureliness', are derived from the Latin verb '*creare*'. Only the concept of creatureliness, which is an important theological notion, is normally related to medieval metaphysics of creation. 'Creativity', by
contrast, is a modern concept with important anthropological connotations. These two concepts stand for opposite historical tendencies.
Both notions, creatureliness and creativity, are found in Whitehead,
but with a significant shift in emphasis: creativity is transformed from
a primarily anthropological concept into a universal metaphysical
one—in a similar way as in Bergson's *Creative Evolution*.[2] Also in this
regard Whitehead appears as a metaphysician of actuality, combining
Greek and medieval thought with a contemporary problem.

I.

The first section of this discussion will provide the foundation for
the main thesis to be defended here, which is really a double thesis:
Whitehead's conception of creativity can best be understood as a transcendental in the scholastic sense; if this is true, it is also the case that
Whitehead introduced a new transcendental. We will begin with the
first element of this double thesis.

Comparison of Whitehead's 'category of the ultimate',[3] which
encompasses creativity, and the medieval doctrine of the transcendentals, represented here by Thomas Aquinas,[4] shows in the first place
that the category of the ultimate and the transcendentals have the
same formal status in their respective systems of thought. More precisely, the category of the ultimate occupies in Whitehead's categorial
scheme the same position vis-à-vis the rest of the categorial groups as
the transcendentals do with respect to the ten Aristotelian categories.
Both Thomas and Whitehead explicitly maintain that these are not
additional categories, but rather the categorization of what is generally
presupposed by all the other categories. It is a categorization of what
we imply in our thought even if we do not necessarily express it when
bringing to mind a being as such. In the famous first article of his
Quaestio prima de veritate, Thomas distinguishes between two forms of
propositions that involve being. The first expresses a special mode of
being, a "*specialis modus entis*," similar to the Aristotelian categories.
The second form of proposition expresses those characteristics that

generally pertain to any being as a being, that is a "*modus generalis consequens omne ens*," a "general mode consequent on all being," denoting of course, the transcendentals. In a similar way, Whitehead removes the category of the ultimate from the other three groups of categories he has delineated with the help of the two concepts of the special and the general. "The Category of the Ultimate expresses the general principle presupposed in the three more special categories."[5]

Second, comparison of Thomas's transcendentals and the basic concepts that form the category of the ultimate, points to some surprising parallels in their content. Thomas cites as transcendental concepts: *ens* (being), *res* (thing), *unum* (one), *aliquid* (something), *verum* (true), *bonum* (good).[6] Whitehead says, "'Creativity', 'many', 'one', are the ultimate notions involved in the meaning of the synonymous terms 'thing', 'being', 'entity'."[7] Three Whiteheadian terms coincide with Thomistic ones. 'Being' or 'entity' coincides with the Thomistic *ens*, 'thing' with *res*, and 'one' with *unum*. Thomas's interpretation of the term *aliquid*, namely as *aliud quid* ('something else'), as being as it is distinct from others, *esse ab aliis divisum*,[8] is clearly related to Whitehead's term 'many', which he associates with disjunctive diversity. Finally, we may suspect that the transcendentals *bonum* ('good') and *verum* ('true'), as relational determinations of being that pertain to the spiritual human soul, reappear in a generalized form in Whitehead's principle of relativity, according to which every being is a potential datum for another being.[9]

Several additional reasons can be adduced in support of these suggestions of both formal and substantial agreements between the Whiteheadian and the scholastic employment of the transcendentals. In fact, to interpret Whitehead's concept of creativity as a transcendental determination of being can help to reconcile the divergent interpretations of Whitehead that have hitherto been proposed, and in particular it can eliminate the difficulties of these interpretations.[10] In backing up this argument, I shall focus on a few points.

A first point in support of our thesis are those passages in Whitehead that make it clear that creativity is not to be sought beyond its concrete appearance in actual entities.[11] Charles Hartshorne noticed that such passages are best interpreted if Whitehead's notion of creativity is understood as an analogous concept that has the same function as the concept of being in the Aristotelian tradition.[12] For my part, I believe that Whitehead's notion of creativity is nothing but an intensified formulation of the Aristotelian conception of being as *energeia*, as the act of being, or of the scholastic conception of *actus essendi*.[13]

Whitehead's well-known comparison of creativity with Aristotelian 'prime matter' can be cited as a second point.[14] It has often been said that this comparison is only valid from Whitehead's perspective, namely with regard to the formal indeterminateness of creativity, his conception of which was equally radical as that of prime matter. On the other hand, this comparison is not valid inasmuch as Aristotelian prime matter means pure potency, whereas Whiteheadian creativity, by contrast, means pure actuality. This inconsistency can be overcome if we see in creativity the act of being of formal determinations of forms. In this case, it is still true that creativity is not a form in itself, but at the same time it becomes apparent why creativity is to be conceived as the actuality of reality and not as its potentiality. Moreover, we also avoid the danger of interpreting Whiteheadian creativity as an irrational moment, only because it is in itself the unformed element in his system. Being as the act of being, the *esse* as compared to the *essentia*, is precisely not an additional determination of forms; according to Kant's famous example, there is no difference between one-hundred actual Thalers and one-hundred imaginary ones as far as the definition of their contents is concerned, without there being any need to declare the act-of-being-actual to be an irrational element.[15]

Finally, for the direct proof that Whitehead transforms the concept of creativity into a transcendental concept, we can call upon those texts in which he makes it plain that, as genuine creation, creativity pertains both to God *and* to the temporal creatures, and not to God alone as was the understanding of medieval metaphysics of creation.[16] This leads to the second part of my double thesis, that is to the claim that *if* creativity is a transcendental in Whitehead, it is a *new* transcendental when viewed against the background of scholastic, especially Thomistic metaphysics, and that it marks a consequential departure from traditional doctrines of creation.

Thomas formally says that *creatio* (creation) is the very own work of God, the *propria Dei actio*, that *creare* (to create) pertains to God alone, and that it is impossible for any creature actually to create something, neither on its own initiative, nor as one of God's tools.[17] Thomas thus adopts John of Damascus's statement that the creatures are not *creatores* (creators).[18] We are dealing here with a strict disjunction: only God is *creator*, all other beings are creatures. In other words, creativity in the strict sense pertains to God alone, and only creatureliness to all the other beings. By contrast, Whitehead makes it perfectly clear that creativity is characteristic of all beings, and not only of God, although he does not deny that God's creativity is very special and unique.[19] He thus attributes to creativity the status of a transcendental. In scholastic thought a transcendental was, of course, characterized by the fact that it can be said of God in an eminent way—*summum ens, summum bonum* (the supreme being, the supreme good)—but of all other creatures by analogy. Whitehead stretches his attribution of creativity to the creatures so that he ultimately does not hesitate to admit, alongside the traditional relation of creation, also the complete inversion of this relation. "It is as true to say that God creates the World, as that the World creates God."[20]

A statement like the one just cited seems important for the clarification of the meaning Whitehead accords the term 'create'. Against our claim that Whitehead transforms creation, which had earlier been attributed exclusively to God, into a universal determination of being, one could object that it is not the same thing that is being spoken of in the two cases. This objection is justified by the fact that in contemporary linguistic use, 'creativity' is primarily, indeed almost exclusively, an anthropological category. As such, it mainly means the faculty of 'innovation', whereas the traditional, theological use of *creare* denotes the *creatio ex nihilo* (creation out of nothing).

In view of this divergence in meaning, statements such as the one above make it clear that Whiteheadian creativity is indeed conceived as successor of the theological notion of *creatio*, even if Whitehead was primarily concerned with creativity on the part of the subject and of natural subjectivity, and thus altogether with creativity of the events in nature. The question about the connection between his notion of creativity and the traditional one is certainly not resolved by reference to the fact that, despite its clearly modern connotations, Whiteheadian creativity also aspires to be a theological concept of creation. At this point in the argument, Whitehead scholarship tends to move on to the question of how far the creativity Whitehead attributes to God coincides with the traditional notion of the *creatio ex nihilo*. However, I shall not approach this question directly, but rather indirectly by a detour. The preliminary question that leads us to the center of the traditional, as well as of the Whiteheadian doctrine of creation and permits a genuine comparison of the two doctrines is, in my view, the question of the metaphysics of relation that stands behind the relevant concept of creation. Accordingly, we will embark on a discussion of these problems by a comparative analysis of creation as a relation.

II.

Traditional metaphysics of creation is essentially a metaphysics of relation since God can only be a creator because of his relation to his creatures. Conversely, creatures only exist as creatures because of their relation to their divine creator. Thomas of Aquino's formal answer to the question of what *creatio* is, runs as follows: For the creatures, creation can only be understood as a relation to the creator as the principle of the creature's being. "*Relinquitur quod creatio in creaturis non sit nisi relatio quaedam ad Creatorem, ut ad principium sui esse.*" ("It remains that creation in the creatures is nothing else but a certain relation to the Creator, as to the principle of its being.")[21] It is doubtless with this conception in view that Whitehead asserts in *Adventures of Ideas* that there are 'two doctrines' available to explain the process of a being's formation, the first of which he characterized as follows: "One is that of the external Creator, eliciting his final togetherness out of nothing."[22] It is correct to speak of an 'external Creator' inasmuch as for traditional metaphysics the creator is 'external' to his creatures in the sense that he does not coincide with them; he is a being that is genuinely distinct from the creatures. By no means is it permissible to interpret this relation to the 'external Creator' as an 'external' relation itself. Quite to the contrary, for classical metaphysics it is *the* paradigm of an 'internal' relation that constitutes the essence of the finite being itself.[23] To put it paradoxically, we are faced here with an internal relation to an external being. Clarification of this seeming paradox will assist us in defining more clearly the traditional concept of creation, and in assessing Whitehead's originality in deviation from it.

A two-fold distinction seems necessary to accomplish this: the classical distinction between 'external' and 'internal' relations, and another distinction which is independent of the former, and yet, so to speak, its spitting image. I shall term this 'the distinction between intrinsic and extrinsic relations'. The well-known distinction between internal and external relations goes in its essence back to the scholastics and it gained new prominence in the discussion between Russell and Bradley.[24] An internal relation is one that pertains to the very nature of the thing, and is therefore constitutive of this thing.[25] A relation is external, by contrast, when it is attached to an already constituted being, or, to employ Aristotelian terminology, when it is of accidental nature. In both cases, the relata may pertain to the same thing, or they may actually coincide or else they may constitute different things and beings.

In order to eliminate this confusion, which can lead to fatal misunderstandings in the discussion of creation and creativity, a second distinction, that between extrinsic and intrinsic relations, seems necessary. I term a relation extrinsic when the relata *qua* beings, i.e. regarded as things, substances or real essences, are external to one another. Their relation then connects two things, substances or real essences with one another. By contrast, I term a relation intrinsic when its relata belong to the same thing or to the same real essence.[26] By combining these two distinctions, we obtain four combinations that can be arranged according to their increasing interior nature. There will be external extrinsic, external intrinsic, internal extrinsic and internal intrinsic relations. All four combinations are logically conceivable and seem to manifest themselves in actuality. The relation of a fish to a boat is an everyday example of a relation that is both external and extrinsic. An extrinsic but internal relation would be constituted by the relation of the fish to the water. As an example of an intrinsic but external relation, we could cite the relation between the color of the fish and the characteristics of its motion through water. Finally, the relation between these characteristics of its motion through water and the fish's physical structure are an example of an intrinsic and internal relation.

Having established these tools for attaining distinctions, we can now embark on a comparative analysis of the traditional notion of creation and Whitehead's concept of creativity. As we have said above, Thomas Aquinas understood *creatio* as a *"relatio quaedam ad Creatorem, ut ad principium sui esse"* (a "certain relation to the Creator as to the principle of its being").[27] Insofar as the relation to the principle of being is concerned, this is doubtless an internal relation. However, insofar as Whitehead is correct in describing this principle of being as an 'external Creator',[28] we are obviously dealing with an extrinsic relation. Viewed this way, creation, as it applies to creatures, is in our terminology an internal, yet extrinsic relation. Indeed, the classical tradition of Christian metaphysics, for which Thomas serves here as the prime exponent, understands *creatio in creaturis* (creation in the creatures) as such an internal, extrinsic relation.

This points directly to the originality of Whitehead's thought. He saw creativity as an internal, but simultaneously — and more so — as an intrinsic relation. We can now formulate the distinction between Whitehead and the tradition as follows: For the tradition, *creare* (to create) is only an internal *extrinsic* relation. Whitehead, too, conceives it as such an internal and extrinsic relation, but primarily regards it as an internal and *intrinsic* relation. The most important terms by which Whitehead explicitly treats creativity as an internal and intrinsic relation are: *'causa sui'* ('cause of itself'), 'self-creating creature', 'immanent creativity', and 'self-realization'. Its most significant indirect manifestation is the doctrine that concrescence is a subject-superject relation. On the other hand, creativity is spoken of as an internal and *extrinsic* relation under the rubrics: 'co-creator of the world', 'transcendent creativity', 'transition', and 'objective immortality'.

It is easy enough to find passages where Whitehead underlines the pre-eminence of the creation as an internal *intrinsic* relation. The notion of the *causa sui*, for example, is explained with the sentence: "The creativity is not an external agency."[29] The relation is explicated in texts such as the following: "There are not two actual entities, the creativity and the creature. There is only one entity which is the self-creating creature."[30] Or with reference to the subject-superject relation: "An actual entity is at once the subject of self-realization, and the superject which is self realized."[31]

The second element of the double thesis proposed at the outset, the thesis which maintains that Whitehead interpreted creativity in a new way as a transcendental, can now be given a more adequate foundation. It was precisely because he regarded it as an internal and *intrinsic* relation that Whitehead elevated creativity to the rank of a transcendental. This is attested in the first place by the convertibility of actuality and self-creation: "An actuality is self-realizing, and whatever is self-realizing is an actuality."[32] Second, we need to point out the universality of this relation: "All actual entities share with God this characteristic of self-causation."[33] As an internal and intrinsic relation, creativity applies especially to God, and more precisely (and this is easily overlooked) already with regard to his primordial nature, described by Whitehead as the "primordial created fact," which can thus be regarded as "creature of creativity" and not merely "a condition for creativity."[34] God's primordial nature as a creature, however, is exceptional because it is unconditioned, atemporal and possible only once.

The priority of creativity as an internal intrinsic relation over creativity as an internal extrinsic relation is apparent in the priority of concrescence over transition, which, as objective immortality, is only the transmission of the results of the former. "The actual entity as self-creating creature passes into its immortal function of part-creator of the transcendent world."[35] In Whitehead's view, creativity interpreted as a passing on comes very close to the lexical meaning of the verb *creare* (to create). "'Passing on' becomes 'creativity', in the dictionary sense of the verb *creare*, 'to bring forth, beget, produce'."[36] Particularly in this regard, Whitehead would be perfectly justified to invoke the contemporary concept of creativity since, despite the defects in its precision, "there is relatively complete agreement that products rich in consequences . . . have a claim to the title of 'creative'."[37]

Whitehead expresses the transcendental aspect of creativity as potential internal *extrinsic* relation with the term 'principle of relativity'. This principle insists that no entity can avoid the possibility of being included anew, and with its particularity, in a process that leads beyond itself. Every being is a potential for the becoming of another being.[38] For Whitehead, however, the intrinsic and the extrinsic aspects of creativity are internally connected to one another. The self-creation of an 'actual entity' is guided by the ideal of itself as individual fulfillment *and* as transcended co-creator of other beings.[39] Accordingly, creativity as a whole is the binary rhythm of self-creation and co-creation of the transcending other.[40]

What is the advantage in asserting the superiority of self-creation over cocreation of an other, and of 'immanent' over 'transcendent creativity'? In Whitehead's view, the main advantage is the increase of freedom for each individual being. In other words, freedom is gained from the overwhelming burden of an exclusively efficient causality exercised by the preceding given other, including even God. "The freedom inherent in the universe is constituted by this element of self-causation."[41]

The elevation of freedom to the status of a fundamental characteristic of every being is a clear expression of the fact that in Whitehead the modern shift towards the subject has attained metaphysical validity, as the 'reformed subjectivist principle' insists.[42] The other question, of course, is: what is revealed most clearly by Whitehead's new, transformed understanding of creativity when we look back to traditional metaphysics? The notion of taking part in, or the doctrine of participation,[43] is the core of classical metaphysics of creation, especially in its Thomistic version. The doctrine insists that all created being exists only by participation in the uncreated being of God, in the "*ipsum per se subsistens*" (in that "what subsists by itself").[44] Accordingly, for Thomas, participation in God is essentially participation in being. Whitehead's elevation of creativity to the rank of a transcendental seems to me to be exemplified ultimately in his conception of participation in being, which is implicitly conceived as participation in creativity, and this is a fundamental novelty, at least in relation to Thomistic metaphysics. This thought has been put forward before by Charles Hartshorne, who maintains that for Whitehead 'being' means creative-being (*Schöpferisch-Sein*) and participation in the creative-being of the others.[45]

For Aquinas, the act of creation is the basis for participation, although there is no participation in the act of creation itself. All beings participate in the being of God insofar as, and because, they are created by God, but that is far from creatures' participation in creativeness itself, which remains the exclusive activity of God. Thomas does speak of creatures' participation in God's power, "*participatio divinae virtutis*,"[46] but he never goes so far as to call the activity of the creature *creatio*. The systematic reason seems to me once again that, for Thomas, creation can only be an internal extrinsic relation, so far as the creatures are concerned. It is a property of being (*Seins-Habe*) which internally constitutes the creatureliness of the creature, but this property can only be given to the creature from without, by God. Even by virtue of its participation in God, the creature is never thought capable of any analogous creative-being.

Hartshorne's claim that being in Whitehead's sense signifies creative-being and participation in the creative-being of others, appears in a marked contrast to the traditional view. Yet, Hartshorne's analysis is certainly correct and tallies with our analysis of the concept. This distinction between the own creative-being and participation in the creative-being of the others is consistent with the distinction we have

drawn between creativity as an internal intrinsic relation and creativity as an internal extrinsic one. Hartshorne also accords priority to the
former. Only because an entity can be creative on its own accord, can
one attribute creative-being to it. In this creative-being it remains
dependent on the others; the creativity of the relevant being is participation in the creativity of the others. That is especially true for God.
Self-creation of each temporal creature is possible only through participation in God's primordial nature. For Whitehead, this primordial
nature is the atemporal creature of divine creativity *and* the condition
for the creativity of every temporal creature.[47] In addition, the temporal creatures participate among themselves insofar as each of them
enters into its successors as part-creator.[48] Finally, God also participates
in the creative act of the temporal creatures, which he absorbs in a
transformed form, thus elevating, preserving and annihilating them at
the same time; it is from this process that his 'consequent nature' results.
Whitehead thus acknowledges not only a participation of the world in
God as Thomas had done, but also a participation of God in the world.
The reciprocity of this relation is expressed in his famous statement
that it is as true that God creates the world as that the world creates
God, that it is just as true that God is immanent in the world as that
the world is immanent in God, or that it is just as true that God tran-
scends the world as that the world transcends God.[49]

In this way, the participation of creativity constitutes the unity of
actuality.[50] Creation is no longer to be conceived as the solitary act of
God, but as a social act. "Each task of creation is a social effort, employing the whole universe."[51]

III.

The question we postponed earlier has become all the more imper-
ative by the comparison between the classical and the Whiteheadian
metaphysics of creation. This is the question of whether the same thing,
or at least something similar, is meant when Thomas Aquinas and
Whitehead speak of *creare* and *creatio*, or 'creation' and 'creativity'. Put-
ting the question in these terms already concedes that the same word
need not stand for the same concept or refer to the same thing. The
systematic reasons for this are that the logical status of these concepts
is not identical in the two cases and neither is the thing to which they
are applied.

We can start with their logical status. If the preceding analysis is at
all correct, it follows almost automatically that their logical status cannot be the same in both cases. To put it concisely, the difference is that
for Thomas '*creare*' and '*creatio*' are exclusive concepts, pertaining only

to God. In this exclusiveness, they are *univocal*, and Thomas strives at all cost to sustain the purity of this univocity. By contrast, for Whitehead they are *analogous* terms, and he does everything he can to attribute even the smallest role in the totality of actuality to every being and to turn creation into social occurrence.

Creation as a univocal concept is fully consistent with the classical concept of a *creatio ex nihilo* (creation out of nothing). For Thomas, the *ex nihilo* is a pure negation equivalent to *non ex aliquo* (not out of something else). Creation does not mean that something that already exists is brought forth. Instead, it is a radical calling-into-being, it is the bridging of the absolute gap between nothing and something.[52] However, there is a further traditional concept, which accords that creation can also mean the transformation of something into something better, *in melius reformare*. Thomas explicitly points out that in such cases the term *creatio* is applied equivocally.[53] His tendency to preserve the purity of the univocity of the *creatio ex nihilo* is more than obvious in his refusal to accept any 'addition' of creation in works of nature and of art.[54] Along the same lines, he strongly emphasizes with regard to the distinction between primary and secondary causes that a secondary cause instituted by God as an instrument can never be a genuinely creative medium.[55]

A more precise interpretation of these statements can be achieved if we pay closer attention to the relevant historical situation, considering, in particular, the direction in which the defensive tendency of these negations is aimed. The notion of *creatio ex nihilo* was framed primarily in an attempt to avoid postulating uncreated matter, a matter which would be the real location for the distance from God and the source of evil. The Thomistic insistence that there can be no creative medium, for its part, was directed against the neoplatonic understanding of creation as a cascading emanation in which the supreme releases a second highest from itself and this second highest then releases a third highest and so on. The refutation of such notions is certainly not a pressing issue anymore, and least so for Whitehead. For our comparison of the traditional *ex nihilo* concept of creation with Whitehead's notion of creativity, we can therefore leave aside what the concept was intended to deny; instead, we have to concentrate on its positive implications. Is there any connection between the positive elements of the traditional concept of creation and those in Whitehead's notion of creativity? And if so, what is it?

I believe that this connection is to be found in precisely that which, according to Whitehead, formally constitutes creativity, namely 'the principle of novelty'. [56] It can be shown, both textually and in terms of its content, that there is indeed an internal connection between the classical concept of *creatio ex nihilo* and the Whiteheadian concept of creativity understood as the principle of novelty.

Negatively speaking, creation out of nothing means that God has not created the creatures out of *something*; it means that there was not something pre-existent that was simply transformed. This highlights the understanding that the *ex nihilo* is nothing else but the radical novelty of the created as created. Expressed in a positive way, the *creatio ex nihilo* means the radical beginning of being, the "*inceptio essendi*", as Thomas called it.[57] This beginning must not be misinterpreted as a temporally initial act, for it must continue for so long as the creature exists, which would otherwise sink back into nothing. Decisive for the *creatio ex nihilo* is not the question about the temporal beginning, but rather the essentially metaphysical aspect that, at least for Thomas, being created implies being radically new, that is, it implies the novelty of being altogether, the *novitas essendi*. The most detailed article in which Thomas discusses the question of what the creation in the creatures is, closes with the sentence which insists that *creatio* is a "*relatio quaedam ad Deum cum novitate essendi*" (creation is a "certain relation to God with a newness of being").[58] Viewed from the perspective of the creature, creation is the relation that guarantees the novelty that enters the world through it. In general, creation is that relation as a result of which there exists something with every creature.

Now, the passage from *Adventures of Ideas*[59] that has already partially been cited shows that Whitehead's definition of creativity as the principle of novelty was certainly understood by him as a transformation of the concept of novelty implicit in the notion of *creatio ex nihilo*. This is a question of how to interpret the process, which constitutes a real being. At this point, Whitehead contrasts his theory of creativity with the *creatio ex nihilo* or, as he explicitly says, against the "external Creator, eliciting this final togetherness out of nothing." He continues: "The word Creativity expresses the notion that each event is a process issuing in novelty. Also if guarded in the phrases Immanent Creativity, or Self-Creativity, it avoids the implication of a transcendent Creator. . . . Still, it does convey the origination of novelty."[60] Whitehead says three things very clearly here: First, the traditional doctrine of creation relies on the 'external Creator', or as we have termed it, on an internal *extrinsic* relation. Second, he insists that in his theory, creation is primarily an internal *intrinsic* relation, something he calls 'immanent creativity', or 'Self-Creativity'. Third, he establishes that the origination of novelty is the element that he has taken over from the tradition and transformed in his concept of creativity. "Still it does convey the origination of novelty."

If this "origination of novelty" is an element common to both classical theory and Whitehead's concept of creation, the question becomes pressing of what difference there is between the two concepts particularly with respect to this novelty. It is perfectly obvious that there is a significant difference between them. For, as we have seen, the *creatio ex nihilo* can be explained in a radical way as the creation of novelty. By contrast, Whiteheadian creativity as principle of novelty does obviously not imply a *creatio ex nihilo*, but rests upon what has been before, upon its 'objective immortality'. The question can therefore be formulated as follows: Why is the novelty of creation in the classical tradition conceived so radically as *novitas essendi* (novelty of being), and why is it anchored in the concept of the *creatio ex nihilo*? Why does Whitehead support a creation of novelty, which need not be a *creatio ex nihilo*? The answer, it seems, is that there has been a change in the understanding of nature and of the world. The key term is *evolution*, or in Whitehead's language, 'creative advance'.

Thomas's metaphysics is built on Aristotelian physics. This physics understands natural events in their extension through time as essentially reproductive. They are events in which the natural beings are not *produced* as genuinely new natural beings, but are constantly *reproduced*. This conception is theoretically founded on the affirmation of the priority of actuality over potentiality, which applies, according to Aristotle, explicitly in a temporal sense to the members of a species: There must always be an actual member of a species that precedes its potential successors.[61] Thomas accepted this thesis and incorporated it into his metaphysics of creation. Its most general expression is found in formulae such as *"agens agit sibi simile"* ("that which moves does so in a way similar to itself"), or *"factum opportet esse simile facienti"* ("what is being produced is necessarily similar to what is producing"). Applied to natural events it runs: *"Agens naturale non producit simpliciter ens, sed ens praeexistens et determinatum ad hoc vel ad illud."* ("A natural motion does not simply produce a thing, but a thing that pre-existed and has been predetermined to this or that.")[62]

The consequence of this physics for the metaphysics of creation is that from the very outset the creation of nature (to speak in biblical terms, after the work of the six days) must be considered complete. All the species are present, they are subsequently reproduced, but no new species are produced. "Addition can be made daily to the number of individuals, for the perfection of the universe. But nothing can be added that pertains to the number of species".[63] In order to ensure this reproduction, God created the living beings in their adult forms.[64] This does not mean, of course, that creation was only an initial act, which called the creatures into being so that from then on they could simply continue in existence. Rather, it is a continual act since otherwise the creatures would regress back into nothing. This continual act produces nothing new, at least not in nature.[65] It only conserves what exists. It is no accident that *creatio* as *"creatio continua"* ("continuous creation") is called *"conservatio"* ("conservation").[66] To my mind, this Thomistic view of metaphysics is an exact parallel to Aristotelian physics where natural events are conceived as events of reproduction.

For Thomas, the connection between philosophy of nature and metaphysics of creation was quite intentional. He strove to acquire the correct understanding of nature because, as he said, error with respect to the creatures turns into a false understanding of God.[67] Today, it remains for us to ask how far Aquinas's metaphysics of creation is burdened with a false understanding of nature, conditioned by the historical circumstances. At least, it can be said that nature appeared to Thomas as "a static morphological universe,"[68] to put it in Whitehead's words, which is devoid of the element Whitehead termed the 'creative advance'.[69]

Creative advance is the Whiteheadian term for the totality of natural events, for the current of cosmic happenings, insofar as this is not simply reproduction, but a production of new actual entities of a higher level. This concept of creative advance does not apply to one individual or actual entity, but to the universe as a whole: "The universe is a creative advance into novelty."[70] This creative advance is explained by the fact that each individual actual entity, in comparison to the entities that constitute it, is a new entity.[71] This is especially true when an entity actualizes forms of definiteness that have not previously been actualized in the world of this entity. In view of this process, Whitehead introduced the special category of 'conceptual reversion', which he describes as the means by which "novelty enters the world."[72] This process is one of the more profound reasons why, in contrast to Aristotle, Whitehead interpreted forms primarily as potentialities and why they therefore do not coincide with, but rather transcend, the forms of the actual. Consequently, the act of being of such actual entities must be interpreted as creativity in the strict sense insofar as it involves the actualization of hitherto unrealized forms of definiteness. In Whitehead's system, such creativity is an internal intrinsic relation between the subject and the superject, or between the presence of the possible as an idea and its actualization. Here, too, we are dealing with a genuine *"relatio cum novitate essendi"* ("relation with a newness of being").[73]

This explains why both Thomas and Whitehead conceive of genuine creation as a 'relation with a newness of being.' Whereas Thomas still associates this novelty with the concept of the *creatio ex nihilo*, Whitehead does not. As seen against the background of the nonevolutionary Aristotelian philosophy of nature, which saw the natural events as events of reproduction, the novelty that has to be traced back to

God could only be understood as the novelty of mere being (*esse simpliciter*), i.e. the novelty of being or existing at all. This novelty, which needs to be traced back to God within the events of reproduction, is only the radical novelty of being at large. It is free from any presupposition; instead of 'nothing' now 'something' can *be* there. Within Whitehead's framework of evolutionary philosophy of nature, by contrast, it is possible to maintain the creation of something genuinely novel as process immanent to the world. The immanently created novelty is, however, only a relative, and not a radical novelty that can be described by the vogue term 'innovation'. But innovation is a relational concept whose *terminus a quo* (the term from which to start) is not nothing, but rather something previously existent, and thus distinct from genuine novelty; as a genuinely innovative process, Whiteheadian creativity is therefore not without presuppositions. And it may be for this reason that Whitehead describes creativity as a 'principle of novelty' without connecting it to the *creatio ex nihilo*.

The difference between the traditional univocal concept of creation and Whitehead's analogous notion of creativity as seen from this perspective, which primarily is one of the philosophy of nature,[74] turns out to be a question about the sort and the extent of novelty. The univocal concept of creation in Thomas's metaphysics is aimed at a radical novelty free from any presupposition. But it does so with respect to nature because the Aristotelian philosophy of nature does not recognize genuine novelty, or rather innovation, in the events of nature. Whitehead's analogous concept of creativity, by contrast, takes into account that genuine novelty is possible although not as radical, absolute novelty, but as relative innovation which by its essence is not free from presuppositions. Whitehead's concept of creativity is based on an evolutionary, and at the same time a nonreductionistic interpretation of nature, which also incorporates the implications of the anthropological use of the key term 'creativity'.

Notes

1. SMW 133.

2. Bergson's *L'évolution créatrice* (Paris, 1907) [*Creative Evolution*, tr. Arthur Mitchell, (London, 1911)] was anticipated in France by Théodule Armand Ribot's *Essai sur l'imagination créatrice* (Paris, 1900) [*Essay on the Creative Imagination*, translated by A. H. N. Baron, (London, Chicago 1906)]. A similar psychological application of the adjective 'creative' appears in Eng-

lish and American work at the beginning of the twenties. By contrast, the substantive 'creativity' appears to have been used as a psychological term only from 1931 on (and so after the appearance of the most of Whitehead's major works). The empirical enterprise known as 'creativity research' dates from after 1950. Cf. J. Ritter et al. *Historisches Wörterbuch der Philosophie* [*Historical Dictionary of Philosophy*], vol. 4 (Basel: Schwabe 1976) 1194-1196.

3. PR 21-22.

4. St. Breton provides a brief, but excellent, account in his *"L'idée de transcendental et la genèse des transcendentaux chez saint Thomas d'Aquin,"* in *Saint Thomas d'Aquin aujourd'hui (Recherches de philosophie*, VI, Paris, 1963), 45-74.

5. PR 21.

6. Thomas Aquinas: *Quaestiones disputatae de veritate*, 1, 1.

7. PR 21.

8. Thomas Aquinas: *De Veritate*, 1, 1.

9. PR 22.

10. Cf. the list compiled by W.E. Stokes: "Recent Interpretations of Whitehead's Creativity," in *The Modern Schoolman* 39 (1962): 309-333.

11. PR 7, 18.

12. Cf. Charles Hartshorne: "Whitehead's Metaphysics" in Victor Lowe, Charles Hartshorne and A. H. Johnson: *Whitehead and the Modern World* (Boston: Beacon Press 1950), 40-41 and his "Le principe de la relativité philosophique chez Whitehead" ("Whitehead's Principle of Philosophical Relativity") in *Revue de Métaphysique et de Morale* 55 (1950): 28.

13. Leibniz's equation of substance and force is the principle historical source for this. The observation of A. Parmentier in *La philosophie de Whitehead et le problème de Dieu (The Problem of God in Whitehead's Philosophy)* (Paris: Beauchesne 1968), seems highly apposite. According to Parmentier, Whiteheadian creativity is to be understood as "une transposition leibnizienne de l'être en tant qu'être de l'aristotélisme" ("a Leibnizean transformation of the Aristotelian being *qua* being.") (287-288).

14. PR 31.

15. Comparison with the Thomistic *esse* seems informative in dealing with the complicated situation for Whitehead interpretation that arises because, on the one hand, Whitehead describes creativity as "the universal of universals characterizing ultimate matter of fact." (PR 21) This has led some readers to interpret creativity as an eternal object with A. H. Johnson (cf. Stokes *Recent Interpretations*, 313-316). On the other hand, Whitehead also explains that creativity is, "the ultimate behind all forms, inexplicable by forms."

(Ibid.) This, of course excludes the identification of creativity with eternal objects, described as "forms of definiteness." (PR 22) Thomas describes being as "*maxime formale omnium*" ("the most formal of all things") (*Summa theologiae*, [New York, 1947], I, 7, 1) or again as "*formale respectu omnium, quae in re sunt*" (whatever is "formal in respect of everything found in a thing") (*Summa theologiae*, I, 8, 1) and finally as "*universalissimum*" ("the most universal") of descriptions (*Summa theologiae*, I, 45, 5), although 'esse' is certainly not a form in the sense of a principle of determination whose content can be defined and which can be thought abstractly. Accordingly, it is quite correct for Hartshorne ("*Whitehead's Metaphysics*," 41) to describe creativity with an expression reminiscent of Aristotle (*De anima* III 8, 432a 2) as the "form of the forms," although even this is not free from ambiguity. More precisely, the same thing applies to creativity, which is, "the ultimate notion of the highest generality at the base of actuality" (PR 31) as applied to Thomistic being so far as the actualizing effect, characteristic of both, is concerned. Both may be described as the *actualitas omnium actuum*" ("actuality of every actuality"). "*Hoc quod habet* esse, *efficitur actu existens. Unde patet quod hoc quod dico* esse *est actualitas omnium actuum, et propter hoc est perfectio omnium perfectionum.*" ("That which has *being* is brought about by the act of being. What I call *being* is therefore the actuality of every actuality and accordingly is the fulfillment of all perfection.") (*Quaestiones disputatae de potentia*, in: *Quaestiones disputatae*, II (Turin and Rome, 1953), 7, 2 ad 9). On the '*actualitas absoluta*', that is, the original and profoundest meaning of the Thomistic '*esse*', which seems to me the real analogon to Whitehead's 'creativity' (although for Thomas, this '*actualitas*' is created by God, and cannot be creativity on its own account), cf. particularly the commentary by Thomas on *Peri Hermeneias* I, 3 16b 19 ff. (*In Peri Hermeneias lectio* 5, edited by Spiazzi, [Turin and Rome, 1964], especially 29). Also C. Fabro: "Le retour au fondement de l'être" ["The Return to the Foundation of Being"] in *S. Thomas d'Aquin aujourd'hui*, especially 187.

16. PR 22, 85, 348.

17. Thomas Aquinas: *Summa contra gentiles*, ii, 21.

18. Ibid.

19. PR 7, 31-32.

20. PR 348.

21. Thomas Aquinas: *Summa theologiae*, I, 45, 3.

22. AI 303.

23. "*Non oportet quod (creatura) habet ordinem essentialem nisi ad dantem esse (= Deum).*" ("It ought not to be said that a creature has an essential order unless it is given by God.") Thomas Aquinas: *Scriptum super libros Sententiarum Petri Lombardi* (Paris, 1871), II d. 1, 1, 2 ad 2.

24. Cf. the article "Beziehung, interne/externe" ("Relation: Internal/External") in J. Ritter et.al. *Historisches Wörterbuch der Philosophie*, I: 909-910.

25. Consistent with this, Thomas Aquinas speaks of '*relatio essentialis*' ('essential relation') or '*ordo essentialis*' ('essential order') (see note 23). Cf. A. Horvath: *Metaphysik der Relationen (Metaphysics of Relations)* (Graz, 1914), 29 and A. Krempel: *La Doctrine de la relation chez S. Thomas d'Aquin (The Doctrine of Relation in Thomas of Aquino)* (Paris: Vrin 1952), 526-529.

26. The expressions 'extrinsic' and 'intrinsic' are applied in a similar way to relations by Thomas in *Quaestiones disputatae de potentia*, 7, 9.

27. Thomas Aquinas: *Summa theologiae*, I, 45, 3.

28. AI 303.

29. PR 222.

30. RM 202.

31. PR 222. Ivor Leclerc, *Whitehead's Metaphysics* (Bloomington and London: Allen & Unwin 1975) emphasizes this leading motive of the Whiteheadian rendition of creativity. "It is the basic activity of self-creation generic to all individual actual entities." (84).

32. PR 222.

33. Ibid.

34. PR 31.

35. PR 85.

36. PR 213.

37. J. Ritter et.al., *Historisches Wörterbuch der Philosophie*, 4: 1194-1195.

38. PR 213.

39. PR 85.

40. RM 92.

41. PR 88.

42. PR 160, 166.

43. The discussion of this point still owes much to the fundamental studies of L.-B. Geiger: *La participation dans la philosophie de S. Thomas d'Aquin (Participation in the Philosophy of Thomas of Aquino)* (Paris: Vrin 2nd ed. 1953) and C. Fabro: *Participation et Causalité selon S. Thomas d'Aquin (Participation and Causality according to Thomas of Aquino)* (Louvain and Paris: Publications universitaires de Louvain 1961).

44. Thomas Aquinas: *Summa theologiae*, I, 44, 1.

45. Charles Hartshorne: "La Creatividad participada," in: *Revista de Filosofia de la Universidad de Costa-Rica* 3 (1962): 243. Cited by A. Parmentier *La philosophie de Whitehead*, 276.

46. Thomas Aquinas: *Quaestiones disputatae de potentia*, 3, 1.

47. PR 31.

48. PR 85.

49. PR 348.

50. AI 231.

51. PR 223.

52. Thomas Aquinas: *Summa theologiae*, I, 45, 1 and ad 3.

53. *Summa theologiae*, I, 45, 1 ad 1.

54. *Summa theologiae*, I, 45, 8.

55. Thomas Aquinas: *Summa contra gentiles*, II, 21.

56. PR 21.

57. Thomas Aquinas: *Quaestiones disputatae de potentia*, 3, 3.

58. Ibid.

59. AI 303.

60. Ibid.

61. Aristotle: *Metaphysics* IX.8.1049b 17 ff.

62. Thomas: *Quaestiones disputatae de potentia*, 3, 1.

63. Thomas Aquinas: *Summa theologiae*, I, 118, 3 ad 2.

64. *Summa theologiae* I, 94, 3.

65. Immaterial human souls are the exception. According to Thomas they cannot be merely the effect of a natural reproductive event (*Summa theologiae*, I, 118, 2). In contradistinction to nature, human history is the history of salvation within which the 'return' of the creatures to God occurs according to a progressive, and not a cyclic, order.

66. Thomas Aquinas: *Summa theologiae*, I, 104, 1.

67. Thomas Aquinas: *Summa contra gentiles*, II, 3.

68. PR 222.

69. It must, of course, be admitted that at least the six-day work of creation envisioned by Thomas is interpreted as a successive construction of the order of actuality. The Aristotelian hierarchy of beings is thereby reinter-

preted as a sequential order within which the higher forms presuppose the lower ones, even though they do not originate from them, as they are especially created by God (Cf. *Summa theologiae*, I, 74, 2 ad 4). Taken in its strictest sense, the *'formatio'* of higher beings does not result from nothing since it presupposes a *"rerum substantia quodammodo informis"* ("a substance of things, in a manner of speaking informed") (*Summa theologiae* I, 74, ad 2). Thus, for Thomas, the six days of creation signifies a genuine 'creative advance', which is effected by the creator and not, as is the case for Whitehead, by the creativity of the creatures. It may be asked, as L.-B. Geiger does in *Philosophie et spiritualité* II (Paris: Editions du Cerf 1963), 290 whether the extension and intensification of the meaning of the six-day endeavor of creation in the sense of a genuine evolutionary conception does not accord more fully with the dynamic of an *exitus* and *reditus*, which runs through Thomas's *Summae*. The reproduction of events in the Greek sense of a 'return of the same thing' remains totally foreign to this set of concepts.

70. PR 222.

71. PR 21.

72. PR 249.

73. Thomas Aquinas: *Quaestiones disputatae de potentia*, 3, 3.

74. In the discussion of this paper, Robert Spaemann and Wolfhart Pannenberg argued that the central metaphysical foundation for the *esse* of the creatures — the transmission of their *actus essendi* by God — does not really seem to have been worked over by Whitehead. Like Aristotle, Whitehead was content to accept an analysis of coming-into-being of entities which are assumed to be given, without ever inquiring into what it is that actualizes their being or investigating the grounds for the possibility of this enactment. Now, it cannot be denied that the grounds for the possibility of creativity, which Whitehead ascribed to the creatures understood as *causa sui*, seem to be explained by their *forms of definiteness* ('eternal objects' and God as a 'principle of concretion'). Yet they are not explained so far as their *actualization* or *enactment* of these forms of definiteness is concerned, although this is what constitutes the self-being of the 'actual entities'. The tension between potency and act, which Thomas saw as prevailing between the *essentia* (essence) and the *esse* (being) of finite entities and which requires recourse to God as the *esse subsistens* (self-subsistent being), without a doubt reappears in a radical fashion in Whitehead's distinction between the subject and the superject, and creativity is introduced in order to bridge this gulf. Then the question would have to be investigated whether, and how, creation (as effected by God) can be conceived as the condition for the possibility of the creativity (of the creatures). But this would be a systematic task leading well beyond the comparison of Whitehead and Thomas undertaken here, a task which might very well constitute the central problem of a metaphysics of creation which sets out to reflect the genuine insights of both philosophers.

The Authors

Dorothy Emmet was born in 1904. She studied at Lady Margaret Hall, Oxford, and in 1929 participated in Whitehead's seminars at Harvard. She has been a lecturer and subsequently professor at the University of Manchester and now lives in Cambridge. Her publications include: *Whitehead's Philosophy of Organism* (London, 1932, second edition 1966); *The Nature of Metaphysical Thinking* (London, 1945); *Function, Purpose and Powers* (London, 1958); *Rules, Roles and Relations* (London, 1966); *The Moral Prism* (London, 1979); and *The Effectiveness of Causes* (1984).

Reto Luzius Fetz was born in 1942 and is professor of philosophy at the University of Eichstätt. He studied philosophy in Fribourg, Switzerland, and he completed his Habilitation in 1978. He has been a member of the staff at the Centre International d'Epistémologie Génétique in Geneva and lecturer at the Pädagogische Hochschule in St. Gallen. His publications include: *Ontologie und Innerlichkeit* (*Ontology and Inwardness*) (Fribourg, 1976); *Whitehead: Prozessdenken und Substanzmetaphysik* (*Whitehead: Process Thought and Substance Metaphysics*) (Freiburg and Munich, 1981); and papers on philosophic anthropology, Piaget's genetic epistemology, and the theory of symbols.

Wolfgang Künne was born in 1944 and is professor of philosophy at the University of Hamburg. His publications include: "Hegel als Leser Platons" ("Hegel's Reading of Plato") in *Hegel-Studien* (1979); "Verstehen und Sinn" ("Sense and Understanding") in *Allgemeine Zeitschrift für Philosophie* (1981); "Megarische Aporien für Freges Semantik" ("Megaric Aporea for Frege's Semantics") in *Zeitschrift für Semiotik* (1982); "Indexikalität" ("Indexability") in *Grazer Philosophische Studien* (1983); *Abstrakte Gegenstände: Semantik und Ontologie* (*Abstract Objects: Semantics and Ontology*) (Frankfurt a.M., 1983); "Strawson: Deskriptive Metaphysik" ("Strawson: Descriptive Metaphysics") in *Grundprobleme der grossen Philosophen, Gegenwart III* (*Problems of the Great Philosophers: Contem-*

porary Thought) edited by J. Speck, (Göttingen, 1984); "Wahrheit" ("Truth") in Philosophie: Ein Grundkurs (A Basic Course in Philosophy) edited by F. Martens and H. Schnädelbach (Reinbek, 1984); and "Vom Sinn der Eigennamen" ("The Meaning of Proper Names") in E.M. Alves editor, Namenzauber (The Magic of Names) (Frankfurt a.M. 1986).

Ivor Leclerc was born in 1915 and studied philosophy in Cape Town and London. He is the Fuller E. Callaway Professor (Emeritus) of Metaphysics and Moral Philosophy at Emory University in Atlanta. His publications include: Whitehead's Metaphysics (London and New York, 1958 and Lanham, 1986); The Nature of Physical Existence (London and New York, 1972), The Philosophy of Nature (Washington, D.C., 1986). He has also edited: The Relevance of Whitehead (London and New York, 1961) and The Philosophy of Leibniz and the Modern World (Nashville, 1973).

Wolfhart Pannenberg was born in 1928 and has studied Protestant theology and philosophy. He is professor of systematic theology at the Ludwig Maximilian University of Munich. His publications include: Grundzüge der Christologie (Christology) (Gütersloh, fifth edition 1976); Grundfragen der systematischen Theologie (Basic Issues of Systematic Theology) two volumes (Göttingen, 1967,1980); Gottesgedanke und menschliche Freiheit (Concepts of God and Human Freedom) (Göttingen, 1972); Das Glaubensbekenntnis (The Creed) (Gütersloh, fourth edition 1972); Wissenschaftstheorie und Theologie (Science and Theology) (Frankfurt a.M., 1973); and Anthropologie in theologischer Perspektive (Antropology from the Theological Point of View) (Göttingen, 1983).

Hans Poser was born in 1937, and is now professor of philosophy at the Technische Universität of Berlin. His publications include: Zur Theorie der Modalbegriffe bei G.W. Leibniz (Modal Concepts in Leibniz) (Wiesbaden, 1969); papers on modal theory, rationalism, the German enlightenment, the philosophy of mathematics and the philosophy of science. He has edited the following works: G.H. v. Wright: Handlung, Norm und Intention (Action, Norm and Intention) (Berlin, 1975); Philosophie und Mythos (Philosophy and Myth) (Berlin, 1979); Wandel des Vernunftbegriffs (Conceptual Change) (Freiburg and Munich, 1981); Philosophische Probleme der Handlungstheorie (Philosophical Issues in Action Theory) (Freiburg and Munich, 1982). He was the co-editor of Einstein-Symposion Berlin (Berlin Einstein Symposium) (Berlin, 1979); and Ontologie und Wissenschaft (Ontology and Science) (Berlin, 1984).

Friedrich Rapp was born in 1932. He studied physics and philosophy and is now professor of philosophy at the University of Dortmund.

His publications include: *Analytische Technikphilosophie (Analytical Philosophy of Technology)* (Freiburg and Munich, 1978); with R. Jokisch and H. Linder, *Determinanten der technischen Entwicklung (The Factors in Technical Development)* (Berlin, 1980). He has edited *Naturverständnis und Naturbeherrschung (Comprehending and Conquering Nature)* (Munich, 1981). He was the co-editor of *Technikphilosophie in der Diskussion (The Philosophy of Technology in Discussion)* (Braunschweig and Wiesbaden, 1982); *Philosophie und Wissenschaft in Preussen (Philosophy and Science in Prussia)* (Berlin, 1982); and *Contemporary marxism: Essays in Honour of J.M. Bochenski* (Dordrecht, 1984).

Robert Spaemann was born in 1927. His studies included philosophy, history, theology and Romance languages. He is currently professor of philosophy at the University of Munich. Among his publications are: *Der Ursprung der Soziologie aus dem Geist der Restauration (The Origins of Sociology in the Spirit of the Restoration)* (Munich, 1959); *Reflexion und Spontaneität (Reflection and Spontaneity)* (Stuttgart, 1963); *Zur Kritik der politischen Utopie (A Critique of Utopia)* (Stuttgart, 1977); *Rousseau: Bürger ohne Vaterland ((Rousseau: Citizen without a Country)* (Munich, 1980); *Moralische Grundbegriffe (The Fundamental Concepts of Morality)* (Munich, 1982); and *Philosophische Essays (Philosophical Essays)* (Stuttgart 1983). With R. Löw he is the author of *Die Frage Wozu? Geschichte und Wiederentdeckung des teleologischen Denkens (Why? The History and Rediscovery of Teleological Thought) (Munich 1981).*

Rainer Specht was born in 1930. He has studied philosophy, Catholic theology and Romance languages and is currently professor of philosophy at the University of Mannheim. His publications include: *Commercium mentis et corporis. Über Kausalvorstellungen im Cartesianismus (Commercium mentis et corporis: The Representation of Causality in Cartesianism)* (Stuttgart, 1966); and *Innovation und Folgelast (Innovation and the Burden of Consequences)* (Stuttgart, 1972).

Jan Van der Veken was born in 1932. He studied philosophy, theology and classics in Louvain, Mechelen and Paris. He is currently professor of philosophy at the Catholic University of Louvain. Professor Van der Veken has served as president of the European Society for Process Thought. His publications range over phenomenology, the language of religion and process philosophy. Amongst others they include: "Can the True God be the God of One Book" in *Religious Experience and Process Theology* edited by H.J. Cargas and B. Lee (New York, 1976); "Whitehead's Filosofie van de Creativiteit" in *Tijdschrift voor Filosofie 41.1* (1980); "Whitehead's God is not Whiteheadian Enough" in *White-*

head und der Prozessbegriff (Whitehead and the Concept of Process) edited by H. Holz; and E. Wolf-Gazo (Freiburg and Munich, 1984) and _Procesdenken. Een Orientatie_ (Louvain, third edition 1985).

Reiner Wiehl was born in 1929. He is professor of philosophy at the University of Heidelberg. His philosophic interests include: philosophical psychology, hermeneutics and ontology. Amongst his publications are a translation, introduction and commentary on Plato's _Sophist_ (Hamburg, 1967); an introduction to Whitehead's philosophy in the German translation of _Adventures of Ideas_ (Frankfurt a.M., 1971), _Die Vernunft in der menschlichen Unvernunft. Das Problem der Rationalität in Spinozas Affektenlehre (Reason In Human Irrationality. The Problem of Rationality in Spinoza's Doctrine of Affects)_ (Göttingen, 1983): and moreover papers on philosophical psychology and action theory.

Ernest Wolf-Gazo was born in 1947. He is an assistant professor of philosophy at the University of Münster. His publications include: "Trends in German Philosophy: A Critical View" in _Tijdschrift voor Filosofie 42.2_ (1980); "Whitehead: Prozessdenken in Philosophie und Theologie" ("Whitehead: Process Thought in Philosophy and Theology") in _Theologische Revue 76.5_ (1980); "Einige Bermerkungen zum Evolutionsbegriff als Leitfaden einer neuen Philosophie der Natur" ("Remarks on the Concept of Evolution as a Leading Theme for a New Philosophy of Nature") in _Acts of the XII German Philosophical Congress_ in Innsbruck 1981; "The Concept of Power as a Guiding Principle: On the Linkage between Whitehead, Locke, and Leibniz" in _Acts of the IV International Leibniz Congress_ in Hannover 1983. He has edited _Whitehead: Einführung in seine Kosmologie_ (Introduction to Whitehead's Cosmology) (Freiburg and Munich, 1980); and was the co-editor of _Whitehead und der Prozessbegriff (Whitehead and the Concept of Process)_ (Freiburg and Munich, 1984).

Abbreviations

The following are the abbreviations of the titles and editions of Whitehead's books employed in notes:

AI   *Adventures of Ideas*, New York: Macmillan 1933.

CN   *The Concept of Nature*, Cambridge: Cambridge University Press 1920.

FR   *The Function of Reason* (1929), Boston: Beacon Press 1958.

MT   *Modes of Thought*, New York: Macmillan 1938.

PNK   *An Enquiry Concerning the Principles of Natural Knowledge*, Cambridge: Cambridge University Press 1919, second edition 1925.

PR   *Process and Reality* (1929), corrected edition edited by D.R. Griffin and D. W. Sherburne, New York: The Free Press 1978.

RM   *Religion in the Making*, New York: Macmillan 1926.

SMW   *Science and the Modern World*, New York: Macmillian 1925, second edition 1926.

Index of Names

Index of Subjects

219